I0330971

C-3594 CAREER EXAMINATION SERIES

This is your PASSBOOK for...

911 Operator

Test Preparation Study Guide
Questions & Answers

NLC®

NATIONAL LEARNING CORPORATION®

COPYRIGHT NOTICE

National Learning Corporation

212 Michael Drive, Syosset, NY 11791
(516) 921-8888 • www.passbooks.com
E-mail: info@passbooks.com

PASSBOOK® SERIES

THE *PASSBOOK® SERIES* has been created to prepare applicants and candidates for the ultimate academic battlefield – the examination room.

At some time in our lives, each and every one of us may be required to take an examination – for validation, matriculation, admission, qualification, registration, certification, or licensure.

Based on the assumption that every applicant or candidate has met the basic formal educational standards, has taken the required number of courses, and read the necessary texts, the *PASSBOOK® SERIES* furnishes the one special preparation which may assure passing with confidence, instead of failing with insecurity. Examination questions – together with answers – are furnished as the basic vehicle for study so that the mysteries of the examination and its compounding difficulties may be eliminated or diminished by a sure method.

This book is meant to help you pass your examination provided that you qualify and are serious in your objective.

The entire field is reviewed through the huge store of content information which is succinctly presented through a provocative and challenging approach – the question-and-answer method.

A climate of success is established by furnishing the correct answers at the end of each test.

You soon learn to recognize types of questions, forms of questions, and patterns of questioning. You may even begin to anticipate expected outcomes.

You perceive that many questions are repeated or adapted so that you can gain acute insights, which may enable you to score many sure points.

You learn how to confront new questions, or types of questions, and to attack them confidently and work out the correct answers.

You note objectives and emphases, and recognize pitfalls and dangers, so that you may make positive educational adjustments.

Moreover, you are kept fully informed in relation to new concepts, methods, practices, and directions in the field.

You discover that you are actually taking the examination all the time: you are preparing for the examination by "taking" an examination, not by reading extraneous and/or supererogatory textbooks.

In short, this PASSBOOK®, used directedly, should be an important factor in helping you to pass your test.

911 OPERATOR

DUTIES

Receives, monitors and switches emergency telephone calls, operates communication equipment and computerized inquiry terminals, and dispatches radio messages to police, fire and ambulance personnel. Performs related duties as required.

SCOPE OF THE EXAMINATION

Written test will be designed to test for knowledge, skills, and/or abilities in such areas as:

1. Understanding descriptions of two-way radio procedures, installation, and operation;
2. Record keeping, including fire, ambulance, and police;
3. Clerical aptitude;
4. Coding and decoding information; and
5. Understanding and interpreting written material.

HOW TO TAKE A TEST

I. YOU MUST PASS AN EXAMINATION

A. WHAT EVERY CANDIDATE SHOULD KNOW

Examination applicants often ask us for help in preparing for the written test. What can I study in advance? What kinds of questions will be asked? How will the test be given? How will the papers be graded?

As an applicant for a civil service examination, you may be wondering about some of these things. Our purpose here is to suggest effective methods of advance study and to describe civil service examinations.

Your chances for success on this examination can be increased if you know how to prepare. Those "pre-examination jitters" can be reduced if you know what to expect. You can even experience an adventure in good citizenship if you know why civil service exams are given.

B. WHY ARE CIVIL SERVICE EXAMINATIONS GIVEN?

Civil service examinations are important to you in two ways. As a citizen, you want public jobs filled by employees who know how to do their work. As a job seeker, you want a fair chance to compete for that job on an equal footing with other candidates. The best-known means of accomplishing this two-fold goal is the competitive examination.

Exams are widely publicized throughout the nation. They may be administered for jobs in federal, state, city, municipal, town or village governments or agencies.

Any citizen may apply, with some limitations, such as the age or residence of applicants. Your experience and education may be reviewed to see whether you meet the requirements for the particular examination. When these requirements exist, they are reasonable and applied consistently to all applicants. Thus, a competitive examination may cause you some uneasiness now, but it is your privilege and safeguard.

C. HOW ARE CIVIL SERVICE EXAMS DEVELOPED?

Examinations are carefully written by trained technicians who are specialists in the field known as "psychological measurement," in consultation with recognized authorities in the field of work that the test will cover. These experts recommend the subject matter areas or skills to be tested; only those knowledges or skills important to your success on the job are included. The most reliable books and source materials available are used as references. Together, the experts and technicians judge the difficulty level of the questions.

Test technicians know how to phrase questions so that the problem is clearly stated. Their ethics do not permit "trick" or "catch" questions. Questions may have been tried out on sample groups, or subjected to statistical analysis, to determine their usefulness.

Written tests are often used in combination with performance tests, ratings of training and experience, and oral interviews. All of these measures combine to form the best-known means of finding the right person for the right job.

II. HOW TO PASS THE WRITTEN TEST

A. NATURE OF THE EXAMINATION

To prepare intelligently for civil service examinations, you should know how they differ from school examinations you have taken. In school you were assigned certain definite pages to read or subjects to cover. The examination questions were quite detailed and usually emphasized memory. Civil service exams, on the other hand, try to discover your present ability to perform the duties of a position, plus your potentiality to learn these duties. In other words, a civil service exam attempts to predict how successful you will be. Questions cover such a broad area that they cannot be as minute and detailed as school exam questions.

In the public service similar kinds of work, or positions, are grouped together in one "class." This process is known as *position-classification.* All the positions in a class are paid according to the salary range for that class. One class title covers all of these positions, and they are all tested by the same examination.

B. FOUR BASIC STEPS

1) Study the announcement

How, then, can you know what subjects to study? Our best answer is: "Learn as much as possible about the class of positions for which you've applied." The exam will test the knowledge, skills and abilities needed to do the work.

Your most valuable source of information about the position you want is the official exam announcement. This announcement lists the training and experience qualifications. Check these standards and apply only if you come reasonably close to meeting them.

The brief description of the position in the examination announcement offers some clues to the subjects which will be tested. Think about the job itself. Review the duties in your mind. Can you perform them, or are there some in which you are rusty? Fill in the blank spots in your preparation.

Many jurisdictions preview the written test in the exam announcement by including a section called "Knowledge and Abilities Required," "Scope of the Examination," or some similar heading. Here you will find out specifically what fields will be tested.

2) Review your own background

Once you learn in general what the position is all about, and what you need to know to do the work, ask yourself which subjects you already know fairly well and which need improvement. You may wonder whether to concentrate on improving your strong areas or on building some background in your fields of weakness. When the announcement has specified "some knowledge" or "considerable knowledge," or has used adjectives like "beginning principles of..." or "advanced ... methods," you can get a clue as to the number and difficulty of questions to be asked in any given field. More questions, and hence broader coverage, would be included for those subjects which are more important in the work. Now weigh your strengths and weaknesses against the job requirements and prepare accordingly.

3) Determine the level of the position

Another way to tell how intensively you should prepare is to understand the level of the job for which you are applying. Is it the entering level? In other words, is this the position in which beginners in a field of work are hired? Or is it an intermediate or advanced level? Sometimes this is indicated by such words as "Junior" or "Senior" in the class title. Other jurisdictions use Roman numerals to designate the level – Clerk I, Clerk II, for example. The word "Supervisor" sometimes appears in the title. If the level is not indicated by the title, check the description of duties. Will you be working under very close supervision, or will you have responsibility for independent decisions in this work?

4) Choose appropriate study materials

Now that you know the subjects to be examined and the relative amount of each subject to be covered, you can choose suitable study materials. For beginning level jobs, or even advanced ones, if you have a pronounced weakness in some aspect of your training, read a modern, standard textbook in that field. Be sure it is up to date and has general coverage. Such books are normally available at your library, and the librarian will be glad to help you locate one. For entry-level positions, questions of appropriate difficulty are chosen – neither highly advanced questions, nor those too simple. Such questions require careful thought but not advanced training.

If the position for which you are applying is technical or advanced, you will read more advanced, specialized material. If you are already familiar with the basic principles of your field, elementary textbooks would waste your time. Concentrate on advanced textbooks and technical periodicals. Think through the concepts and review difficult problems in your field.

These are all general sources. You can get more ideas on your own initiative, following these leads. For example, training manuals and publications of the government agency which employs workers in your field can be useful, particularly for technical and professional positions. A letter or visit to the government department involved may result in more specific study suggestions, and certainly will provide you with a more definite idea of the exact nature of the position you are seeking.

III. KINDS OF TESTS

Tests are used for purposes other than measuring knowledge and ability to perform specified duties. For some positions, it is equally important to test ability to make adjustments to new situations or to profit from training. In others, basic mental abilities not dependent on information are essential. Questions which test these things may not appear as pertinent to the duties of the position as those which test for knowledge and information. Yet they are often highly important parts of a fair examination. For very general questions, it is almost impossible to help you direct your study efforts. What we can do is to point out some of the more common of these general abilities needed in public service positions and describe some typical questions.

1) General information

Broad, general information has been found useful for predicting job success in some kinds of work. This is tested in a variety of ways, from vocabulary lists to questions about current events. Basic background in some field of work, such as sociology or economics, may be sampled in a group of questions. Often these are principles which have become familiar to most persons through exposure rather than through formal training. It is difficult to advise you how to study for these questions; being alert to the world around you is our best suggestion.

2) Verbal ability

An example of an ability needed in many positions is verbal or language ability. Verbal ability is, in brief, the ability to use and understand words. Vocabulary and grammar tests are typical measures of this ability. Reading comprehension or paragraph interpretation questions are common in many kinds of civil service tests. You are given a paragraph of written material and asked to find its central meaning.

3) Numerical ability

Number skills can be tested by the familiar arithmetic problem, by checking paired lists of numbers to see which are alike and which are different, or by interpreting charts and graphs. In the latter test, a graph may be printed in the test booklet which you are asked to use as the basis for answering questions.

4) Observation

A popular test for law-enforcement positions is the observation test. A picture is shown to you for several minutes, then taken away. Questions about the picture test your ability to observe both details and larger elements.

5) Following directions

In many positions in the public service, the employee must be able to carry out written instructions dependably and accurately. You may be given a chart with several columns, each column listing a variety of information. The questions require you to carry out directions involving the information given in the chart.

6) Skills and aptitudes

Performance tests effectively measure some manual skills and aptitudes. When the skill is one in which you are trained, such as typing or shorthand, you can practice. These tests are often very much like those given in business school or high school courses. For many of the other skills and aptitudes, however, no short-time preparation can be made. Skills and abilities natural to you or that you have developed throughout your lifetime are being tested.

Many of the general questions just described provide all the data needed to answer the questions and ask you to use your reasoning ability to find the answers. Your best preparation for these tests, as well as for tests of facts and ideas, is to be at your physical and mental best. You, no doubt, have your own methods of getting into an exam-taking mood and keeping "in shape." The next section lists some ideas on this subject.

IV. KINDS OF QUESTIONS

Only rarely is the "essay" question, which you answer in narrative form, used in civil service tests. Civil service tests are usually of the short-answer type. Full instructions for answering these questions will be given to you at the examination. But in case this is your first experience with short-answer questions and separate answer sheets, here is what you need to know:

1) Multiple-choice Questions

Most popular of the short-answer questions is the "multiple choice" or "best answer" question. It can be used, for example, to test for factual knowledge, ability to solve problems or judgment in meeting situations found at work.

A multiple-choice question is normally one of three types—

- It can begin with an incomplete statement followed by several possible endings. You are to find the one ending which *best* completes the statement, although some of the others may not be entirely wrong.
- It can also be a complete statement in the form of a question which is answered by choosing one of the statements listed.

- It can be in the form of a problem – again you select the best answer.

Here is an example of a multiple-choice question with a discussion which should give you some clues as to the method for choosing the right answer:

When an employee has a complaint about his assignment, the action which will *best* help him overcome his difficulty is to

A. discuss his difficulty with his coworkers
B. take the problem to the head of the organization
C. take the problem to the person who gave him the assignment
D. say nothing to anyone about his complaint

In answering this question, you should study each of the choices to find which is best. Consider choice "A" – Certainly an employee may discuss his complaint with fellow employees, but no change or improvement can result, and the complaint remains unresolved. Choice "B" is a poor choice since the head of the organization probably does not know what assignment you have been given, and taking your problem to him is known as "going over the head" of the supervisor. The supervisor, or person who made the assignment, is the person who can clarify it or correct any injustice. Choice "C" is, therefore, correct. To say nothing, as in choice "D," is unwise. Supervisors have and interest in knowing the problems employees are facing, and the employee is seeking a solution to his problem.

2) True/False Questions

The "true/false" or "right/wrong" form of question is sometimes used. Here a complete statement is given. Your job is to decide whether the statement is right or wrong.

SAMPLE: A roaming cell-phone call to a nearby city costs less than a non-roaming call to a distant city.

This statement is wrong, or false, since roaming calls are more expensive.

This is not a complete list of all possible question forms, although most of the others are variations of these common types. You will always get complete directions for answering questions. Be sure you understand *how* to mark your answers – ask questions until you do.

V. RECORDING YOUR ANSWERS

Computer terminals are used more and more today for many different kinds of exams.

For an examination with very few applicants, you may be told to record your answers in the test booklet itself. Separate answer sheets are much more common. If this separate answer sheet is to be scored by machine – and this is often the case – it is highly important that you mark your answers correctly in order to get credit.

An electronic scoring machine is often used in civil service offices because of the speed with which papers can be scored. Machine-scored answer sheets must be marked with a pencil, which will be given to you. This pencil has a high graphite content which responds to the electronic scoring machine. As a matter of fact, stray dots may register as answers, so do not let your pencil rest on the answer sheet while you are pondering the correct answer. Also, if your pencil lead breaks or is otherwise defective, ask for another.

Since the answer sheet will be dropped in a slot in the scoring machine, be careful not to bend the corners or get the paper crumpled.

The answer sheet normally has five vertical columns of numbers, with 30 numbers to a column. These numbers correspond to the question numbers in your test booklet. After each number, going across the page are four or five pairs of dotted lines. These short dotted lines have small letters or numbers above them. The first two pairs may also have a "T" or "F" above the letters. This indicates that the first two pairs only are to be used if the questions are of the true-false type. If the questions are multiple choice, disregard the "T" and "F" and pay attention only to the small letters or numbers.

Answer your questions in the manner of the sample that follows:

32. The largest city in the United States is
    A. Washington, D.C.
    B. New York City
    C. Chicago
    D. Detroit
    E. San Francisco

1) Choose the answer you think is best. (New York City is the largest, so "B" is correct.)
2) Find the row of dotted lines numbered the same as the question you are answering. (Find row number 32)
3) Find the pair of dotted lines corresponding to the answer. (Find the pair of lines under the mark "B.")
4) Make a solid black mark between the dotted lines.

VI. BEFORE THE TEST

Common sense will help you find procedures to follow to get ready for an examination. Too many of us, however, overlook these sensible measures. Indeed, nervousness and fatigue have been found to be the most serious reasons why applicants fail to do their best on civil service tests. Here is a list of reminders:

- Begin your preparation early – Don't wait until the last minute to go scurrying around for books and materials or to find out what the position is all about.
- Prepare continuously – An hour a night for a week is better than an all-night cram session. This has been definitely established. What is more, a night a week for a month will return better dividends than crowding your study into a shorter period of time.
- Locate the place of the exam – You have been sent a notice telling you when and where to report for the examination. If the location is in a different town or otherwise unfamiliar to you, it would be well to inquire the best route and learn something about the building.
- Relax the night before the test – Allow your mind to rest. Do not study at all that night. Plan some mild recreation or diversion; then go to bed early and get a good night's sleep.
- Get up early enough to make a leisurely trip to the place for the test – This way unforeseen events, traffic snarls, unfamiliar buildings, etc. will not upset you.
- Dress comfortably – A written test is not a fashion show. You will be known by number and not by name, so wear something comfortable.

- Leave excess paraphernalia at home – Shopping bags and odd bundles will get in your way. You need bring only the items mentioned in the official notice you received; usually everything you need is provided. Do not bring reference books to the exam. They will only confuse those last minutes and be taken away from you when in the test room.
- Arrive somewhat ahead of time – If because of transportation schedules you must get there very early, bring a newspaper or magazine to take your mind off yourself while waiting.
- Locate the examination room – When you have found the proper room, you will be directed to the seat or part of the room where you will sit. Sometimes you are given a sheet of instructions to read while you are waiting. Do not fill out any forms until you are told to do so; just read them and be prepared.
- Relax and prepare to listen to the instructions
- If you have any physical problem that may keep you from doing your best, be sure to tell the test administrator. If you are sick or in poor health, you really cannot do your best on the exam. You can come back and take the test some other time.

VII. AT THE TEST

The day of the test is here and you have the test booklet in your hand. The temptation to get going is very strong. Caution! There is more to success than knowing the right answers. You must know how to identify your papers and understand variations in the type of short-answer question used in this particular examination. Follow these suggestions for maximum results from your efforts:

1) Cooperate with the monitor

The test administrator has a duty to create a situation in which you can be as much at ease as possible. He will give instructions, tell you when to begin, check to see that you are marking your answer sheet correctly, and so on. He is not there to guard you, although he will see that your competitors do not take unfair advantage. He wants to help you do your best.

2) Listen to all instructions

Don't jump the gun! Wait until you understand all directions. In most civil service tests you get more time than you need to answer the questions. So don't be in a hurry. Read each word of instructions until you clearly understand the meaning. Study the examples, listen to all announcements and follow directions. Ask questions if you do not understand what to do.

3) Identify your papers

Civil service exams are usually identified by number only. You will be assigned a number; you must not put your name on your test papers. Be sure to copy your number correctly. Since more than one exam may be given, copy your exact examination title.

4) Plan your time

Unless you are told that a test is a "speed" or "rate of work" test, speed itself is usually not important. Time enough to answer all the questions will be provided, but this does not mean that you have all day. An overall time limit has been set. Divide the total time (in minutes) by the number of questions to determine the approximate time you have for each question.

5) Do not linger over difficult questions

If you come across a difficult question, mark it with a paper clip (useful to have along) and come back to it when you have been through the booklet. One caution if you do this – be sure to skip a number on your answer sheet as well. Check often to be sure that you have not lost your place and that you are marking in the row numbered the same as the question you are answering.

6) Read the questions

Be sure you know what the question asks! Many capable people are unsuccessful because they failed to *read* the questions correctly.

7) Answer all questions

Unless you have been instructed that a penalty will be deducted for incorrect answers, it is better to guess than to omit a question.

8) Speed tests

It is often better NOT to guess on speed tests. It has been found that on timed tests people are tempted to spend the last few seconds before time is called in marking answers at random – without even reading them – in the hope of picking up a few extra points. To discourage this practice, the instructions may warn you that your score will be "corrected" for guessing. That is, a penalty will be applied. The incorrect answers will be deducted from the correct ones, or some other penalty formula will be used.

9) Review your answers

If you finish before time is called, go back to the questions you guessed or omitted to give them further thought. Review other answers if you have time.

10) Return your test materials

If you are ready to leave before others have finished or time is called, take ALL your materials to the monitor and leave quietly. Never take any test material with you. The monitor can discover whose papers are not complete, and taking a test booklet may be grounds for disqualification.

VIII. EXAMINATION TECHNIQUES

1) Read the general instructions carefully. These are usually printed on the first page of the exam booklet. As a rule, these instructions refer to the timing of the examination; the fact that you should not start work until the signal and must stop work at a signal, etc. If there are any *special* instructions, such as a choice of questions to be answered, make sure that you note this instruction carefully.

2) When you are ready to start work on the examination, that is as soon as the signal has been given, read the instructions to each question booklet, underline any key words or phrases, such as *least*, *best*, *outline*, *describe* and the like. In this way you will tend to answer as requested rather than discover on reviewing your paper that you *listed without describing*, that you selected the *worst* choice rather than the *best* choice, etc.

3) If the examination is of the objective or multiple-choice type – that is, each question will also give a series of possible answers: A, B, C or D, and you are called upon to select the best answer and write the letter next to that answer on your answer paper – it is advisable to start answering each question in turn. There may be anywhere from 50 to 100 such questions in the three or four hours allotted and you can see how much time would be taken if you read through all the questions before beginning to answer any. Furthermore, if you come across a question or group of questions which you know would be difficult to answer, it would undoubtedly affect your handling of all the other questions.

4) If the examination is of the essay type and contains but a few questions, it is a moot point as to whether you should read all the questions before starting to answer any one. Of course, if you are given a choice – say five out of seven and the like – then it is essential to read all the questions so you can eliminate the two that are most difficult. If, however, you are asked to answer all the questions, there may be danger in trying to answer the easiest one first because you may find that you will spend too much time on it. The best technique is to answer the first question, then proceed to the second, etc.

5) Time your answers. Before the exam begins, write down the time it started, then add the time allowed for the examination and write down the time it must be completed, then divide the time available somewhat as follows:
   - If 3-1/2 hours are allowed, that would be 210 minutes. If you have 80 objective-type questions, that would be an average of 2-1/2 minutes per question. Allow yourself no more than 2 minutes per question, or a total of 160 minutes, which will permit about 50 minutes to review.
   - If for the time allotment of 210 minutes there are 7 essay questions to answer, that would average about 30 minutes a question. Give yourself only 25 minutes per question so that you have about 35 minutes to review.

6) The most important instruction is to *read each question* and make sure you know what is wanted. The second most important instruction is to *time yourself properly* so that you answer every question. The third most important instruction is to *answer every question*. Guess if you have to but include something for each question. Remember that you will receive no credit for a blank and will probably receive some credit if you write something in answer to an essay question. If you guess a letter – say "B" for a multiple-choice question – you may have guessed right. If you leave a blank as an answer to a multiple-choice question, the examiners may respect your feelings but it will not add a point to your score. Some exams may penalize you for wrong answers, so in such cases *only*, you may not want to guess unless you have some basis for your answer.

7) Suggestions
   a. Objective-type questions
      1. Examine the question booklet for proper sequence of pages and questions
      2. Read all instructions carefully
      3. Skip any question which seems too difficult; return to it after all other questions have been answered
      4. Apportion your time properly; do not spend too much time on any single question or group of questions

5. Note and underline key words – *all, most, fewest, least, best, worst, same, opposite,* etc.
6. Pay particular attention to negatives
7. Note unusual option, e.g., unduly long, short, complex, different or similar in content to the body of the question
8. Observe the use of "hedging" words – *probably, may, most likely,* etc.
9. Make sure that your answer is put next to the same number as the question
10. Do not second-guess unless you have good reason to believe the second answer is definitely more correct
11. Cross out original answer if you decide another answer is more accurate; do not erase until you are ready to hand your paper in
12. Answer all questions; guess unless instructed otherwise
13. Leave time for review

b. Essay questions
1. Read each question carefully
2. Determine exactly what is wanted. Underline key words or phrases.
3. Decide on outline or paragraph answer
4. Include many different points and elements unless asked to develop any one or two points or elements
5. Show impartiality by giving pros and cons unless directed to select one side only
6. Make and write down any assumptions you find necessary to answer the questions
7. Watch your English, grammar, punctuation and choice of words
8. Time your answers; don't crowd material

8) Answering the essay question

Most essay questions can be answered by framing the specific response around several key words or ideas. Here are a few such key words or ideas:

M's: manpower, materials, methods, money, management
P's: purpose, program, policy, plan, procedure, practice, problems, pitfalls, personnel, public relations

a. Six basic steps in handling problems:
1. Preliminary plan and background development
2. Collect information, data and facts
3. Analyze and interpret information, data and facts
4. Analyze and develop solutions as well as make recommendations
5. Prepare report and sell recommendations
6. Install recommendations and follow up effectiveness

b. Pitfalls to avoid
1. *Taking things for granted* – A statement of the situation does not necessarily imply that each of the elements is necessarily true; for example, a complaint may be invalid and biased so that all that can be taken for granted is that a complaint has been registered

2. *Considering only one side of a situation* – Wherever possible, indicate several alternatives and then point out the reasons you selected the best one
3. *Failing to indicate follow up* – Whenever your answer indicates action on your part, make certain that you will take proper follow-up action to see how successful your recommendations, procedures or actions turn out to be
4. *Taking too long in answering any single question* – Remember to time your answers properly

IX. AFTER THE TEST

Scoring procedures differ in detail among civil service jurisdictions although the general principles are the same. Whether the papers are hand-scored or graded by machine we have described, they are nearly always graded by number. That is, the person who marks the paper knows only the number – never the name – of the applicant. Not until all the papers have been graded will they be matched with names. If other tests, such as training and experience or oral interview ratings have been given, scores will be combined. Different parts of the examination usually have different weights. For example, the written test might count 60 percent of the final grade, and a rating of training and experience 40 percent. In many jurisdictions, veterans will have a certain number of points added to their grades.

After the final grade has been determined, the names are placed in grade order and an eligible list is established. There are various methods for resolving ties between those who get the same final grade – probably the most common is to place first the name of the person whose application was received first. Job offers are made from the eligible list in the order the names appear on it. You will be notified of your grade and your rank as soon as all these computations have been made. This will be done as rapidly as possible.

People who are found to meet the requirements in the announcement are called "eligibles." Their names are put on a list of eligible candidates. An eligible's chances of getting a job depend on how high he stands on this list and how fast agencies are filling jobs from the list.

When a job is to be filled from a list of eligibles, the agency asks for the names of people on the list of eligibles for that job. When the civil service commission receives this request, it sends to the agency the names of the three people highest on this list. Or, if the job to be filled has specialized requirements, the office sends the agency the names of the top three persons who meet these requirements from the general list.

The appointing officer makes a choice from among the three people whose names were sent to him. If the selected person accepts the appointment, the names of the others are put back on the list to be considered for future openings.

That is the rule in hiring from all kinds of eligible lists, whether they are for typist, carpenter, chemist, or something else. For every vacancy, the appointing officer has his choice of any one of the top three eligibles on the list. This explains why the person whose name is on top of the list sometimes does not get an appointment when some of the persons lower on the list do. If the appointing officer chooses the second or third eligible, the No. 1 eligible does not get a job at once, but stays on the list until he is appointed or the list is terminated.

X. HOW TO PASS THE INTERVIEW TEST

The examination for which you applied requires an oral interview test. You have already taken the written test and you are now being called for the interview test – the final part of the formal examination.

You may think that it is not possible to prepare for an interview test and that there are no procedures to follow during an interview. Our purpose is to point out some things you can do in advance that will help you and some good rules to follow and pitfalls to avoid while you are being interviewed.

What is an interview supposed to test?

The written examination is designed to test the technical knowledge and competence of the candidate; the oral is designed to evaluate intangible qualities, not readily measured otherwise, and to establish a list showing the relative fitness of each candidate – as measured against his competitors – for the position sought. Scoring is not on the basis of "right" and "wrong," but on a sliding scale of values ranging from "not passable" to "outstanding." As a matter of fact, it is possible to achieve a relatively low score without a single "incorrect" answer because of evident weakness in the qualities being measured.

Occasionally, an examination may consist entirely of an oral test – either an individual or a group oral. In such cases, information is sought concerning the technical knowledges and abilities of the candidate, since there has been no written examination for this purpose. More commonly, however, an oral test is used to supplement a written examination.

Who conducts interviews?

The composition of oral boards varies among different jurisdictions. In nearly all, a representative of the personnel department serves as chairman. One of the members of the board may be a representative of the department in which the candidate would work. In some cases, "outside experts" are used, and, frequently, a businessman or some other representative of the general public is asked to serve. Labor and management or other special groups may be represented. The aim is to secure the services of experts in the appropriate field.

However the board is composed, it is a good idea (and not at all improper or unethical) to ascertain in advance of the interview who the members are and what groups they represent. When you are introduced to them, you will have some idea of their backgrounds and interests, and at least you will not stutter and stammer over their names.

What should be done before the interview?

While knowledge about the board members is useful and takes some of the surprise element out of the interview, there is other preparation which is more substantive. It *is* possible to prepare for an oral interview – in several ways:

1) Keep a copy of your application and review it carefully before the interview

This may be the only document before the oral board, and the starting point of the interview. Know what education and experience you have listed there, and the sequence and dates of all of it. Sometimes the board will ask you to review the highlights of your experience for them; you should not have to hem and haw doing it.

2) Study the class specification and the examination announcement

Usually, the oral board has one or both of these to guide them. The qualities, characteristics or knowledges required by the position sought are stated in these documents. They offer valuable clues as to the nature of the oral interview. For example, if the job involves supervisory responsibilities, the announcement will usually indicate that knowledge of modern supervisory methods and the qualifications of the candidate as a supervisor will be tested. If so, you can expect such questions, frequently in the form of a hypothetical situation which you are expected to solve. NEVER go into an oral without knowledge of the duties and responsibilities of the job you seek.

3) Think through each qualification required

Try to visualize the kind of questions you would ask if you were a board member. How well could you answer them? Try especially to appraise your own knowledge and background in each area, *measured against the job sought*, and identify any areas in which you are weak. Be critical and realistic – do not flatter yourself.

4) Do some general reading in areas in which you feel you may be weak

For example, if the job involves supervision and your past experience has NOT, some general reading in supervisory methods and practices, particularly in the field of human relations, might be useful. Do NOT study agency procedures or detailed manuals. The oral board will be testing your understanding and capacity, not your memory.

5) Get a good night's sleep and watch your general health and mental attitude

You will want a clear head at the interview. Take care of a cold or any other minor ailment, and of course, no hangovers.

What should be done on the day of the interview?

Now comes the day of the interview itself. Give yourself plenty of time to get there. Plan to arrive somewhat ahead of the scheduled time, particularly if your appointment is in the fore part of the day. If a previous candidate fails to appear, the board might be ready for you a bit early. By early afternoon an oral board is almost invariably behind schedule if there are many candidates, and you may have to wait. Take along a book or magazine to read, or your application to review, but leave any extraneous material in the waiting room when you go in for your interview. In any event, relax and compose yourself.

The matter of dress is important. The board is forming impressions about you – from your experience, your manners, your attitude, and your appearance. Give your personal appearance careful attention. Dress your best, but not your flashiest. Choose conservative, appropriate clothing, and be sure it is immaculate. This is a business interview, and your appearance should indicate that you regard it as such. Besides, being well groomed and properly dressed will help boost your confidence.

Sooner or later, someone will call your name and escort you into the interview room. *This is it.* From here on you are on your own. It is too late for any more preparation. But remember, you asked for this opportunity to prove your fitness, and you are here because your request was granted.

What happens when you go in?

The usual sequence of events will be as follows: The clerk (who is often the board stenographer) will introduce you to the chairman of the oral board, who will introduce you to the other members of the board. Acknowledge the introductions before you sit down. Do not be surprised if you find a microphone facing you or a stenotypist sitting by. Oral interviews are usually recorded in the event of an appeal or other review.

Usually the chairman of the board will open the interview by reviewing the highlights of your education and work experience from your application – primarily for the benefit of the other members of the board, as well as to get the material into the record. Do not interrupt or comment unless there is an error or significant misinterpretation; if that is the case, do not hesitate. But do not quibble about insignificant matters. Also, he will usually ask you some question about your education, experience or your present job – partly to get you to start talking and to establish the interviewing "rapport." He may start the actual questioning, or turn it over to one of the other members. Frequently, each member undertakes the questioning on a particular area, one in which he is perhaps most competent, so you can expect each member to participate in the examination. Because time is limited, you may also expect some rather abrupt switches in the direction the questioning takes, so do not be upset by it. Normally, a board member will not pursue a single line of questioning unless he discovers a particular strength or weakness.

After each member has participated, the chairman will usually ask whether any member has any further questions, then will ask you if you have anything you wish to add. Unless you are expecting this question, it may floor you. Worse, it may start you off on an extended, extemporaneous speech. The board is not usually seeking more information. The question is principally to offer you a last opportunity to present further qualifications or to indicate that you have nothing to add. So, if you feel that a significant qualification or characteristic has been overlooked, it is proper to point it out in a sentence or so. Do not compliment the board on the thoroughness of their examination – they have been sketchy, and you know it. If you wish, merely say, "No thank you, I have nothing further to add." This is a point where you can "talk yourself out" of a good impression or fail to present an important bit of information. Remember, *you close the interview yourself.*

The chairman will then say, "That is all, Mr. ______, thank you." Do not be startled; the interview is over, and quicker than you think. Thank him, gather your belongings and take your leave. Save your sigh of relief for the other side of the door.

How to put your best foot forward

Throughout this entire process, you may feel that the board individually and collectively is trying to pierce your defenses, seek out your hidden weaknesses and embarrass and confuse you. Actually, this is not true. They are obliged to make an appraisal of your qualifications for the job you are seeking, and they want to see you in your best light. Remember, they must interview all candidates and a non-cooperative candidate may become a failure in spite of their best efforts to bring out his qualifications. Here are 15 suggestions that will help you:

1) Be natural – Keep your attitude confident, not cocky

If you are not confident that you can do the job, do not expect the board to be. Do not apologize for your weaknesses, try to bring out your strong points. The board is interested in a positive, not negative, presentation. Cockiness will antagonize any board member and make him wonder if you are covering up a weakness by a false show of strength.

2) Get comfortable, but don't lounge or sprawl

Sit erectly but not stiffly. A careless posture may lead the board to conclude that you are careless in other things, or at least that you are not impressed by the importance of the occasion. Either conclusion is natural, even if incorrect. Do not fuss with your clothing, a pencil or an ashtray. Your hands may occasionally be useful to emphasize a point; do not let them become a point of distraction.

3) Do not wisecrack or make small talk

This is a serious situation, and your attitude should show that you consider it as such. Further, the time of the board is limited – they do not want to waste it, and neither should you.

4) Do not exaggerate your experience or abilities

In the first place, from information in the application or other interviews and sources, the board may know more about you than you think. Secondly, you probably will not get away with it. An experienced board is rather adept at spotting such a situation, so do not take the chance.

5) If you know a board member, do not make a point of it, yet do not hide it

Certainly you are not fooling him, and probably not the other members of the board. Do not try to take advantage of your acquaintanceship – it will probably do you little good.

6) Do not dominate the interview

Let the board do that. They will give you the clues – do not assume that you have to do all the talking. Realize that the board has a number of questions to ask you, and do not try to take up all the interview time by showing off your extensive knowledge of the answer to the first one.

7) Be attentive

You only have 20 minutes or so, and you should keep your attention at its sharpest throughout. When a member is addressing a problem or question to you, give him your undivided attention. Address your reply principally to him, but do not exclude the other board members.

8) Do not interrupt

A board member may be stating a problem for you to analyze. He will ask you a question when the time comes. Let him state the problem, and wait for the question.

9) Make sure you understand the question

Do not try to answer until you are sure what the question is. If it is not clear, restate it in your own words or ask the board member to clarify it for you. However, do not haggle about minor elements.

10) Reply promptly but not hastily

A common entry on oral board rating sheets is "candidate responded readily," or "candidate hesitated in replies." Respond as promptly and quickly as you can, but do not jump to a hasty, ill-considered answer.

11) Do not be peremptory in your answers

A brief answer is proper – but do not fire your answer back. That is a losing game from your point of view. The board member can probably ask questions much faster than you can answer them.

12) Do not try to create the answer you think the board member wants

He is interested in what kind of mind you have and how it works – not in playing games. Furthermore, he can usually spot this practice and will actually grade you down on it.

13) Do not switch sides in your reply merely to agree with a board member

Frequently, a member will take a contrary position merely to draw you out and to see if you are willing and able to defend your point of view. Do not start a debate, yet do not surrender a good position. If a position is worth taking, it is worth defending.

14) Do not be afraid to admit an error in judgment if you are shown to be wrong

The board knows that you are forced to reply without any opportunity for careful consideration. Your answer may be demonstrably wrong. If so, admit it and get on with the interview.

15) Do not dwell at length on your present job

The opening question may relate to your present assignment. Answer the question but do not go into an extended discussion. You are being examined for a *new* job, not your present one. As a matter of fact, try to phrase ALL your answers in terms of the job for which you are being examined.

Basis of Rating

Probably you will forget most of these "do's" and "don'ts" when you walk into the oral interview room. Even remembering them all will not ensure you a passing grade. Perhaps you did not have the qualifications in the first place. But remembering them will help you to put your best foot forward, without treading on the toes of the board members.

Rumor and popular opinion to the contrary notwithstanding, an oral board wants you to make the best appearance possible. They know you are under pressure – but they also want to see how you respond to it as a guide to what your reaction would be under the pressures of the job you seek. They will be influenced by the degree of poise you display, the personal traits you show and the manner in which you respond.

ABOUT THIS BOOK

This book contains tests divided into Examination Sections. Go through each test, answering every question in the margin. We have also attached a sample answer sheet at the back of the book that can be removed and used. At the end of each test look at the answer key and check your answers. On the ones you got wrong, look at the right answer choice and learn. Do not fill in the answers first. Do not memorize the questions and answers, but understand the answer and principles involved. On your test, the questions will likely be different from the samples. Questions are changed and new ones added. If you understand these past questions you should have success with any changes that arise. Tests may consist of several types of questions. We have additional books on each subject should more study be advisable or necessary for you. Finally, the more you study, the better prepared you will be. This book is intended to be the last thing you study before you walk into the examination room. Prior study of relevant texts is also recommended. NLC publishes some of these in our Fundamental Series. Knowledge and good sense are important factors in passing your exam. Good luck also helps. So now study this Passbook, absorb the material contained within and take that knowledge into the examination. Then do your best to pass that exam.

EXAMINATION SECTION

EXAMINATION SECTION
TEST 1

DIRECTIONS: Each question or incomplete statement is followed by several suggested answers or completions. Select the one that BEST answers the question or completes the statement. *PRINT THE LETTER OF THE CORRECT ANSWER IN THE SPACE AT THE RIGHT.*

1. The transmission of signals by electromagnetic waves is referred to as 1.____

   A. biotelemetry B. radio
   C. noise D. all of the above

2. The transmission of physiologic data, such as an ECG, from the patient to a distant point of reception is called 2.____

   A. biotelemetry B. simplex
   C. landline D. none of the above

3. The assembly of a transmitter, receiver, and antenna connection at a fixed location creates a 3.____

   A. transceiver B. radio
   C. biotelemetry D. base station

4. The portion of the radio frequency spectrum between 30 and 150 mhz is called 4.____

   A. very high frequency (VHF) B. ultrahigh frequency (UHF)
   C. very low frequency (VLF) D. all of the above

5. A _______ is a miniature transmitter that picks up a radio signal and rebroadcasts it, thus extending the range of a radiocommunication system. 5.____

   A. transceiver B. repeater C. simplex D. duplex

6. The portion of the radio frequency spectrum falling between 300 and 3,000 mhz is called 6.____

   A. ultrahigh frequency (UHF) B. very high frequency (VHF)
   C. very low frequency (VLF) D. none of the above

7. One cycle per second equals one _______ in units of frequency. 7.____

   A. hertz B. kilohertz C. megahertz D. gigahertz

8. The sources of noise in ECG telemetry include 8.____

   A. loose ECG electrodes
   B. muscle tremors
   C. sources of 60-cycle alternating current such as transformers, power lines, and electric equipment
   D. all of the above

9. The method of radio communications called _______ utilizes a single frequency that enables either transmission or reception of either voice or an ECG signal, but is incapable of simultaneous transmission and reception. 9.____

A. duplex
B. simplex
C. multiplex
D. none of the above

10. A terminal that receives transmissions of telemetry and voice from the field and transmits messages back through the base is referred to as a 10.____

A. transceiver
B. remote control
C. remote console
D. ten-code

11. The role of dispatcher includes 11.____

A. reception of requests for help
B. arrangements for getting the appropriate people and equipment to a situation which requires them
C. deciding upon and dispatching of the appropriate emergency vehicles
D. all of the above

12. A dispatcher should NOT 12.____

A. maintain records
B. scope a problem by requesting additional information from a caller
C. direct public safety personnel
D. receive notification of emergencies and call for assistance from both individual citizens and public safety units

13. The professional society of public safety communicators has developed a standard set of ten codes, the MOST common of which is 10- 13.____

A. 1
B. 4
C. 12
D. 18

14. What is the meaning of 10-33? 14.____

A. Help me quick
B. Arrived at scene
C. Reply to message
D. Disregard

15. One of the MAIN purposes of ten-codes is to 15.____

A. shorten air time
B. complicate the message
C. increase the likelihood of misunderstanding
D. none of the above

Questions 16-20.

DIRECTIONS: In Questions 16 through 20, match each translation of a commonly used ten-code with its appropriate code, listed in Column I.

COLUMN I

A. 10-1
B. 10-9
C. 10-18
D. 10-20
E. 10-23

16. What is your location? 16.____

17. Urgent. 17.____

18. Signal weak. 18.____

19. Arrived at the scene. 19.____

20. Please repeat. 20.____

KEY (CORRECT ANSWERS)

1.	B	11.	D
2.	A	12.	C
3.	D	13.	B
4.	A	14.	A
5.	B	15.	A
6.	D	16.	D
7.	A	17.	C
8.	D	18.	A
9.	B	19.	E
10.	C	20.	B

TEST 2

DIRECTIONS: Each question or incomplete statement is followed by several suggested answers or completions. Select the one that BEST answers the question or completes the statement. *PRINT THE LETTER OF THE CORRECT ANSWER IN THE SPACE AT THE RIGHT.*

1. FCC rules prohibit 1.____

   A. deceptive or unnecessary messages
   B. profanity
   C. dissemination or use of confidential information transmitted over the radio
   D. all of the above

2. Penalties for violations of FCC rules and regulations range from 2.____

   A. prison to death
   B. $20,000 to $100,000
   C. $100 to $10,000 and up to one year in prison
   D. up to 10 years in prison

3. Which of the following is NOT true about base stations? 3.____

   A. The terrain and location do not affect the function.
   B. A good high-gain antenna improves transmission and reception efficiency.
   C. Multiple frequency capability is available at the base station.
   D. Antenna should be as close as possible to the base station transmitter/receiver.

4. Radio frequencies are designated by cycles per second. 1,000,000 cycles per second equals one 4.____

   A. kilohertz B. megahertz C. gigahertz D. hertz

5. The Federal Communications Commission (FCC) is the agency of the United States government responsible for 5.____

   A. licensing and frequency allocation
   B. establishing technical standards for radio equipment
   C. establishing and enforcing rules and regulations for the operation of radio equipment
   D. all of the above

6. Information relayed to the physician should include all of the following EXCEPT 6.____

   A. patient's age, sex, and chief complaint
   B. pertinent history of present illness
   C. detailed family history
   D. pertinent physical findings

7. True statements regarding UHF band may include all of the following EXCEPT: 7.____

A. It has better penetration in the dense metropolitan area
B. Reception is usually quiet inside the building
C. It has a longer range than VHF band
D. Most medical communications occur around 450 to 470 mhz

8. Which of the following statements is NOT true regarding VHF band? 8.____

A. Low band frequency may have ranges up to 2000 miles, but are unpredictable.
B. VHF band may cause *skip interference,* with patchy losses in communication.
C. High band frequency is wholly free of skip interference.
D. High band frequencies for emergency medical purposes are in the 300 to 3000 mhz range.

9. 1000 cycles per second is equal to one 9.____

A. hertz B. kilohertz C. megahertz D. gigahertz

10. _______ achieves simultaneous transmission of voice and ECG signals over a single radio frequency. 10.____

A. Duplex
B. Multiplex
C. Channel
D. None of the above

11. Radio equipment used for both VHF and UHF band is 11.____

A. frequency modulated
B. amplitude modulated
C. double amplitude modulated
D. all of the above

12. ECG telemetry over UHF frequencies is confined to _____ of a 12 lead ECG. 12.____

A. 1 B. 2 C. 6 D. 12

13. All of the following further clarity and conciseness EXCEPT 13.____

A. understandable rate of speaking
B. knowing what you want to transmit after transmission
C. clear presentation of numbers, names, and dates
D. using phrases and words which are easy to copy

14. The LEAST preferred of the following words is 14.____

A. check B. desire C. want D. advise if

15. All of the following are techniques useful during a call EXCEPT 15.____

A. answering promptly
B. identifying yourself and your department
C. speaking directly into the mouthpiece
D. none of the above

Questions 16-20.

DIRECTIONS: In Questions 16 through 20, match each definition with the term it describes, listed in Column I.

COLUMN I

A. Frequency
B. Noise
C. Patch
D. Duplex
E. Transceiver

16. A radio transmitter and receiver housed in a single unit; a two-way radio 16.____

17. The number of cycles per second of a radio signal, inversely related to the wavelength. 17.____

18. Interference in radio signals. 18.____

19. A radio system employing more than one frequency to permit simultaneous transmission and reception. 19.____

20. Connection between a telephone line and a radio communication system, enabling a caller to get *on the air* by special telephone. 20.____

KEY (CORRECT ANSWERS)

1.	D	11.	A
2.	C	12.	A
3.	A	13.	B
4.	B	14.	C
5.	D	15.	D
6.	C	16.	E
7.	C	17.	A
8.	D	18.	B
9.	B	19.	D
10.	B	20.	C

EXAMINATION SECTION
TEST 1

DIRECTIONS: Each question or incomplete statement is followed by several suggested answers or completions. Select the one that BEST answers the question or completes the statement. *PRINT THE LETTER OF THE CORRECT ANSWER IN THE SPACE AT THE RIGHT.*

1. The term for the place at which the control operator function is performed is the 1.____

   A. operating desk
   B. control point
   C. station
   D. manual control location

2. Before transmitting on any frequency, an operator should 2.____

   A. listen to make sure your signal will be heard
   B. make sure the standing-wave ratio on the antenna feed line is high enough
   C. listen to make sure others are not using the frequency
   D. check the antenna for resonance at the selected frequency

3. The ______ sideband is COMMONLY used for 10-meter phone operation. 3.____

   A. lower
   B. upper
   C. amplitude-compandored
   D. double

4. Which type of system does NOT permit the transmission and reception of any signals to take place at the same time? 4.____

   A. Repeater B. Simplex C. Remote D. Duplex

5. Radio emissions are considered *wideband* if their deviation amounts are greater than a MINIMUM of ______ kHz. 5.____

   A. 10 B. 1 C. 15 D. 5

6. When a signal report is referred to as *three three,* 6.____

   A. its contact is serial number thirty-three
   B. it is unreadable and very weak
   C. it is readable with considerable difficulty
   D. its station is located at thirty-three degrees latitude

7. Generally, the type of communications that are capable of the GREATEST range are ______ band. 7.____

   A. low B. high C. aviation D. side

8. For two-way systems situated in and around an urban area, what block of frequencies are allocated for use by mobile telephone services operated by common carriers? ______ MHz. 8.____

   A. 30 B. 40 C. 470-512 D. 900

9. The basic unit of electrical power is the 9.____

   A. ohm B. ampere C. volt D. watt

10. In the radio transmission of speech, the amplification used at the receiver to maintain the natural balance of high and low speech frequencies is referred to as 10.____

A. preemphasis
B. deemphasis
C. loading
D. squelch

11. An antenna that is mounted horizontally would be MOST suitable for the reception of ______ polarized ______. 11.____

A. horizontally; voltages
B. vertically; waves
C. vertically; voltages
D. horizontally; waves

12. What is the PROPER distress call to use when operating a radiotelephone? 12.____

A. MAYDAY B. HELP C. EMERGENCY D. SOS

13. A two-way FM transmitter should be adjusted for a deviation that will produce a bandwidth ______ AM transmitter. 13.____

A. less than that produced by an equivalently modulated
B. greater than that produced by an equivalently modulated
C. equal to that produced by an equivalently modulated
D. that will not be capable of interacting with an

14. The term for the transmission of signals OUTSIDE the intended band is 14.____

A. spurious emissions
B. off-frequency emissions
C. side tones
D. chirping

15. Which of the following is TRUE of FM radio systems? 15.____

A. The frequency is constant and the amplitude is varied.
B. The amplitude is constant and the frequency is varied.
C. The frequency and the amplitude are varied.
D. Neither the frequency nor the amplitude is modulated.

16. During daytime hours, the BEST band for communications over a distance of 200 miles is the ______-m band. 16.____

A. 160 B. 80 C. 40 D. 6

17. A transmission that disturbs other communications is called 17.____

A. transponder signals
B. unidentified transmissions
C. harmful interference
D. interrupted CW

18. A buzzing or hum in the signal of a high-frequency transmitter is USUALLY caused by 18.____

A. an antenna of the wrong length
B. a bad filter capacitor in the power supply
C. energy from another transmitter
D. a badly-designed power output circuit

19. If an operator's signal is extremely strong and perfectly readable, what adjustment should be made to the transmitter? 19.____

A. Turn on the speech processor
B. Turn down the power output
C. Reduce the frequency
D. Reduce the standing-wave ratio

20. What is generally considered to be the reliable range for UHF communications? _______ km. 20.____

A. 20 B. 40 C. 60 D. 80

21. If a transmitter is operated WITHOUT the cover in place, it may 21.____

A. transmit a weak signal
B. transmit a chirping signal
C. transmit onto unintended bands
D. interfere with other transmitters operating on the same frequency

22. In transmitters used to convey speech, the deviation for the given amplitude 22.____

A. increases as the modulation signal increases
B. decreases as the modulation signal increases
C. remains roughly half of the modulation signal
D. is the same regardless of the frequency of the modulation signal

23. The purpose of a limiter in an FM receiver is to limit the 23.____

A. audio output
B. amplitude of the intermediate frequency signal fed to the detector
C. gain of the radio frequency amplifier
D. amplitude of the detected output signal

24. The FASTEST code speed a repeater may use for automatic identification is _______ words per minute. 24.____

A. 10 B. 20
C. 40 D. no limit

25. The purpose of a squelch control is to 25.____

A. set the sensitivity of the squelch circuit
B. squelch all undesired noise signals
C. set the limit of the noise amplitude
D. squelch interference signals

KEY (CORRECT ANSWERS)

1. B
2. C
3. B
4. B
5. D
6. C
7. A
8. B
9. D
10. B
11. D
12. A
13. C
14. A
15. B
16. C
17. C
18. B
19. B
20. B
21. C
22. D
23. B
24. B
25. A

TEST 2

DIRECTIONS: Each question or incomplete statement is followed by several suggested answers or completions. Select the one that BEST answers the question or completes the statement. *PRINT THE LETTER OF THE CORRECT ANSWER IN THE SPACE AT THE RIGHT.*

1. The basic unit of electrical resistance is the 1.____

   A. watt B. ampere C. volt D. ohm

2. An autopatch is a device that 2.____

   A. automatically selects the strongest signal to be repeated
   B. allows repeater users to make telephone calls from their stations
   C. locks other repeaters out of important, confidential communications
   D. connects a mobile station to the next repeater if it moves out of range

3. Which of the following is NOT an advantage gained by using a crystal in radio equipment? 3.____
   Increased

   A. power generation
   B. frequency stability
   C. overtone generation
   D. frequency accuracy

4. The purpose of a key-operated on/off switch in the main power line of a station is to 4.____

   A. keep the power company from shutting down power during an emergency
   B. protect against failure of the main fuses
   C. turn off the station in the event of an emergency
   D. keep unauthorized persons from using the station

5. For two-way systems situated in and around an urban area, what block of frequencies are allocated for use by citizen two-way users? 5.____
   _______ MHz.

   A. 30 B. 40 C. 470-512 D. 900

6. A reactance tube is used to develop a(n) _______ signal. 6.____

   A. drift-free AM
   B. FM
   C. SSB
   D. TTY

7. Messages concerning a person's well-being that are sent into or out of a disaster area are _______ traffic messages. 7.____

   A. routine
   B. tactical
   C. formal message
   D. health and welfare

8. A(n) _______ is used to measure standing wave ratio. 8.____

   A. SWR meter
   B. current bridge
   C. ammeter
   D. ohmmeter

9. What is the USUAL remedy for an FM hand-held transceiver that is over-deviating? 9.___

A. Talk more loudly into the microphone
B. Change to a higher power level
C. Talk farther from the microphone
D. Allow the transceiver to cool

10. *Backwave radiation* is radiation 10.___

A. from the rear of the antenna
B. leaking from a CW antenna
C. from a CW transmitter with the key open
D. from a phone transmitter during silent periods

11. The input impedance of a grounded-grid amplifer is 11.___

A. low B. moderate C. high D. very high

12. If a dial which reads 4.525 MHz were marked in kilohertz, it would read _______ kHz. 12.___

A. 4,525,000 B. 4525 C. .004525 D. 45.25

13. A _______ system uses a total of three transmission frequencies. 13.___

A. simplex B. duplex C. repeater D. remote

14. The basic unit of frequency is the 14.___

A. hertz
B. ohm
C. ampere
D. wave ratio

15. What type of feedback is required for an oscillator? 15.___

A. Split-phase
B. In-phase
C. Grid-leak
D. Degenerative

16. Cross-band operation of a repeater station is 16.___

A. permitted, but requires a special state license
B. permitted under the regular repeater station license
C. permitted if the repeater receives signals in both bands
D. not permitted under any circumstances

17. If an unlicensed third party is allowed to use your station, what must you do at your center of operations? 17.___

A. Monitor and supervise the third party's participation when communication occurs at below 30 MHz.
B. Continuously monitor and supervise the third party's participation.
C. Key the transmitter and make the station identification.
D. Report the third party to the FCC.

18. Receiver overload is caused by 18.____

A. too much voltage from the power supply
B. interference from a poorly-adjusted volume control
C. too much current from the power supply
D. interference from the signals of a nearby transmitter

19. Equal but opposite signals are required for operating a _______ amplifier. 19.____

A. parallel B. push-pull C. class C D. series

20. The MAIN purpose of shielding a transmitter is to 20.____

A. prevent unwanted radio-frequency radiation
B. keep electronic parts warmer and more stable
C. give low-pass air filter a solid support
D. help the sound quality

21. In an FM signal, whether modulated or unmodulated, the 21.____

A. carrier frequency amplitude is fixed
B. modulating frequency varies
C. carrier frequency varies
D. modulating frequency is fixed

22. For voice operation, the microphone is connected to the 22.____

A. antenna switch B. transceiver
C. power supply D. antenna

23. Harmonic radiation is unwanted signals 23.____

A. that are combined with a 60-Hz hum
B. caused by vibrations from a nearby transmitter
C. at frequencies which are multiples of an operator's chosen frequency
D. which cause skip propagation

24. The LOWEST frequency of electrical energy that is usually known as radio frequency is _______ Hz. 24.____

A. 20 B. 2,000 C. 20,000 D. 200,000

25. What is the term for the kind of interference created by a continuous broad band of numerous unrelated radio frequency pulses? 25.____

A. Chirp B. Oscillation
C. Impulse noise D. Fluctuation noise

KEY (CORRECT ANSWERS)

1.	D	11.	A
2.	B	12.	B
3.	A	13.	B
4.	D	14.	A
5.	C	15.	B
6.	B	16.	D
7.	D	17.	B
8.	A	18.	D
9.	C	19.	B
10.	C	20.	A

21. C
22. B
23. C
24. C
25. D

EXAMINATION SECTION
TEST 1

DIRECTIONS: Each question or incomplete statement is followed by several suggested answers or completions. Select the one that BEST answers the question or completes the statement. *PRINT THE LETTER OF THE CORRECT ANSWER IN THE SPACE AT THE RIGHT.*

1. When a signal report is referred to as *five nine plus 10 db,* 1.____

   A. its bandwidth is 10 decibels above linearity
   B. its relative signal strength reading is 10 decibels greater than strength 9
   C. its signal strength has increased by a factor of 90
   D. it should be repeated at a frequency 10 kHz higher

2. *Chirp* is a(n) 2.____

   A. overload in a receiver's audio circuit whenever CW is received
   B. slight change in a transmitter's frequency each time it is keyed
   C. gradual change in transmitter frequency as the circuit warms up
   D. high-pitched tone received with a CW signal

3. A vertical antenna sends out MOST of its radio energy 3.____

   A. in two opposite directions
   B. high into the air
   C. equally in all horizontal directions
   D. in one direction

4. For correct station identification when using a radiotelephone, FCC rules suggest using ______ as an aid. 4.____

   A. a phonetic alphabet
   B. unique words of the operator's choice
   C. Q signals
   D. a speech compressor

5. A COMMON result of an operator speaking too loudly into a hand-held FM transceiver is 5.____

   A. interference to other stations operating near the operator's frequency
   B. digital interference to computer equipment
   C. atmospheric interference in the air around the antenna
   D. interference to stations operating on a higher frequency band

6. When using a repeater to transmit a two-way radio signal, the operator should pause briefly between transmissions to 6.____

   A. dial up the repeater's autopatch
   B. listen for anyone wanting to break in
   C. prepare for recording possible third-party communications
   D. check the standing-wave ratio of the repeater

7. The USUAL input/output frequency separation for repeaters in the 2-meter band is 7.____

A. 1 MHz B. 5 MHz C. 1.5 MHz D. 600 kHz

8. What is the PROPER way to ask someone's location when using a repeater? 8.____

A. What is your QTH?
B. What is your 20?
C. Where are you?
D. Where's the break?

9. If an ammeter reads 4 amperes, the current flow, in milliamperes, is 9.____

A. .004 B. 4,000,000 C. 4000 D. .0004

10. The purpose of repeater operation is to 10.____

A. cut power costs by linking with another high-power system
B. help mobile and low-power stations extend their ranges
C. transmit signals for observing propagation and reception
D. make calls within a range of 50 miles

11. For two-way systems situated in and around an urban area, what block of frequencies are allocated for use by police, fire, and private industries? _____ MHz. 11.____

A. 30 B. 40 C. 470-512 D. 900

12. What causes the MAXIMUM usable frequency to vary? 12.____

A. The amount of ultraviolet radiation from the sun
B. Windspeed in the upper atmosphere
C. The temperature of the ionosphere
D. The weather just below the ionosphere

13. A transmission line that has no change in voltage or current along its full length has a standing-wave ratio of 13.____

A. less than 1
B. greater than 1
C. 1:1
D. 2:1

14. When a signal is referred to as *full quieting,* it 14.____

A. is not strong enough to be received
B. is being received, but no audio is being heard
C. contains no extraneous sound
D. is strong enough to overcome all receiver noise

15. During transmission, the antenna of a hand-held transceiver should be held pointing 15.____

A. toward the ground
B. away from the operator's head and away from others
C. toward the station the operator means to contact
D. away from the station the operator means to contact

16. A _____ system is MOST at risk of receiving a barrage of calls from different sources at the same time. 16.____

A. duplex B. simplex C. repeater D. remote

17. The device that measures standing wave ratio should be connected between the 17.____

A. transmitter and power supply
B. ground and transmitter
C. feed line and antenna
D. receiver and transmitter

18. Electrical energy at a frequency of 7120 Hz is in the _____ frequency range. 18.____

A. hyper B. audio
C. super-high D. radio

19. The type of system in which the transmitter and receiver are at a different location from the microphone and loudspeaker is the _____ system. 19.____

A. remote B. repeater C. simplex D. duplex

20. In the radio transmission of speech, the amplification added to a signal to prevent degradation of consonant sounds is referred to as 20.____

A. preemphasis B. deemphasis
C. loading D. squelch

21. The bandwidth over which a receiver is capable of receiving signals is referred to as its 21.____

A. monitor band B. sideband
C. skip zone D. acceptance band

22. The output of a transceiver should NEVER be connected to a(n) 22.____

A. antenna switch B. receiver
C. SWR meter D. antenna

23. Which band may NOT be used by earth stations for satellite communications? 23.____

A. 10 meters B. 6 meters
C. 2 meters D. 70 centimeters

24. What is the term for the kind of interference created by sharp bursts of radio frequency voltage? 24.____

A. Chirp B. Oscillation
C. Impulse noise D. Fluctuation noise

25. In repeater operations, a courtesy tone 25.____

A. indicates a waiting message
B. activates a receiver in case of severe weather
C. identifies the repeater
D. indicates that the transmission has been completed

KEY (CORRECT ANSWERS)

1. B
2. B
3. C
4. A
5. A
6. B
7. D
8. C
9. C
10. B
11. A
12. A
13. C
14. D
15. B
16. B
17. C
18. D
19. A
20. A
21. D
22. B
23. B
24. C
25. D

TEST 2

DIRECTIONS: Each question or incomplete statement is followed by several suggested answers or completions. Select the one that BEST answers the question or completes the statement. *PRINT THE LETTER OF THE CORRECT ANSWER IN THE SPACE AT THE RIGHT.*

1. Maximum usable frequency means the _____ frequency signal that _____. 1.____

   A. highest; is most absorbed by the ionosphere
   B. lowest; is most absorbed by the ionosphere
   C. lowest; will reach its intended destination
   D. highest; will reach its intended destination

2. As its wavelength gets LONGER, a signal's frequency 2.____

   A. lengthens B. shortens
   C. stays the same D. disappears

3. The term for voice emissions that are radio-transmitted is 3.____

   A. RTTY B. CW C. data D. phone

4. A ______ is used to inject a frequency calibration signal into a receiver. 4.____

   A. calibrated voltmeter B. calibrated wavemeter
   C. crystal calibrator D. calibrated oscilloscope

5. The basic unit of electric current is the 5.____

   A. volt B. ampere C. watt D. ohm

6. An amateur radiotelephone station operated as a mobile station is identified by 6.____

   A. transmitting the word *mobile* after the call sign
   B. at the end of every ten minutes, transmitting the call sign followed by the word *mobile*
   C. after the call sign, transmitting the word *mobile,* followed by the call sign area in which the station is operating
   D. transmitting the area of operation after the call sign

7. Which type of repeater operation should be DISCOURAGED during commuter rush hours? 7.____

   A. Traffic information networks
   B. Low-power stations
   C. Mobile stations
   D. Third-party networks

8. The MOST effective way of checking the accuracy of a receiver's tuning dial would be to tune to 8.____

   A. one of the frequencies of station WWV or WWVH
   B. a popular amateur network frequency
   C. the frequency of a shortwave broadcasting station
   D. an amateur station and ask what frequency the operator is using

9. A(n) _____ produces a stable, low-level signal that can be set to a desired frequency. 9._____

A. oscilloscope
B. reflectometer
C. signal generator
D. wavemeter

10. What is the PROPER distress call to use when operating continuous-wave? 10._____

A. MAYDAY B. HELP C. QRZ D. SOS

11. What device should be connected to a transmitter's output when an operator is making transmitter adjustments? 11._____

A. Dummy antenna
B. Reflectometer
C. Receiver
D. Multimeter

12. The BEST way to minimize on-air interference during a lengthy transmitter test procedure is by 12._____

A. using a resonant antenna that requires no loading-up
B. using a dummy load
C. using a non-resonant antenna
D. choosing an unoccupied frequency

13. At what point in an operator's station is the transceiver power measured? 13._____

A. At the power supply terminals
B. At the antenna terminals
C. On the antenna
D. At the final amplifier input terminals

14. A(n) _____ meter is used to measure relative signal strength in a receiver. 14._____

A. RST
B. signal deviation
C. S
D. SSB

15. When a signal is referred to as *five seven,* it is 15._____

A. perfectly readable, but weak
B. readable with considerable difficulty
C. perfectly readable and moderately strong
D. readable with a nearly pure tone

16. What is the result of overdeviation in an FM transmitter? 16._____

A. Increased transmitter power
B. Out-of-channel emissions
C. Increased transmitter range
D. Poor carrier suppression

17. For safety, the BEST thing to do with transmitting antennas is 17._____

A. use vertical polarization
B. use horizontal polarization
C. mount them close to the ground
D. mount them where nobody can come near them

18. _____ may be caused by a multi-band antenna connected to a poorly-tuned antenna. 18._____

A. Auroral distortion
B. Parasitic excitation
C. Harmonic radiation
D. Intermodulation

19. Using a final amplifier capable of providing a 100 W output to a transmission line that provides a 10-decibel loss, the antenna will receive _____ W of power. 19._____

A. 1
B. 10
C. 90
D. 100

20. For two-way systems situated in and around an urban area, what block of frequencies are allocated for use by land mobile services? _____ MHz. 20._____

A. 30
B. 40
C. 470-512
D. 900

21. What type of messages are sent into or out of a disaster area and concern the immediate safety of human life? _____ traffic. 21._____

A. Emergency
B. Tactical
C. Formal message
D. Health and welfare

22. 50 hertz means 50 22._____

A. meters per second
B. cycles per meter
C. cycles per second
D. cycles per minute

23. A common result of operating an FM transmitter with the microphone gain set too high is 23._____

A. atmospheric interference in the air around the antenna
B. digital interference to computer equipment
C. interference to other stations operating near the operator's frequency
D. interference to stations operating on a higher frequency band

24. Which is the SIMPLEST type of system for which simultaneous transmission and reception are possible? 24._____

A. Remote
B. Repeater
C. Duplex
D. Simplex

25. *Splatter interference* is caused by 25._____

A. overmodulation of a transmitter
B. keying a transmitter too quickly
C. routing of a transmitter's output signals back to its input circuit
D. a transmitting antenna of the wrong length

KEY (CORRECT ANSWERS)

1. D
2. B
3. D
4. C
5. B
6. C
7. D
8. A
9. C
10. D
11. A
12. B
13. B
14. C
15. C
16. B
17. D
18. C
19. B
20. D
21. A
22. C
23. C
24. B
25. A

EXAMINATION SECTION
TEST 1

DIRECTIONS: Each question or incomplete statement is followed by several suggested answers or completions. Select the one that BEST answers the question or completes the statement. *PRINT THE LETTER OF THE CORRECT ANSWER IN THE SPACE AT THE RIGHT.*

Questions 1-3.

DIRECTIONS: Questions 1 through 3 are to be answered SOLELY on the basis of the following passage.

On May 15 at 10:15 A.M., Mr. Price was returning to his home at 220 Kings Walk when he discovered two of his neighbor's apartment doors slightly opened. One neighbor, Mrs. Kagan, who lives alone in Apartment 1C, was away on vacation. The other apartment, IB, is occupied by Martin and Ruth Stone, an elderly couple, who usually take a walk everyday at 10:00 A.M. Fearing a robbery might be taking place, Mr. Price runs downstairs to Mr. White in Apartment BI to call the police. Police Communications Technician Johnson received the call at 10:20 A.M. Mr. Price gave his address and stated that two apartments were possibly being burglarized. Communications Technician Johnson verified the address in the computer and then asked Mr. Price for descriptions of the suspects. He explained that he had not seen anyone, but he believed that they were still inside the building. Communications Technician Johnson immediately notified the dispatcher who assigned two patrol cars at 10:25 A.M., while Mr. Price was still on the phone. Communications Technician Johnson told Mr. Price that the police were responding to the location.

1. Who called Communications Technician Johnson? 1.____

   A. Mrs. Kagan
   B. Mr. White
   C. Mrs. Stone
   D. Mr. Price

2. What time did Communications Technician Johnson receive the call? 2.____
   _______ A.M.

   A. 10:00
   B. 10:15
   C. 10:20
   D. 10:25

3. Which tenant was away on vacation? 3.____
   The tenant in Apartment

   A. 1C
   B. IB
   C. BI
   D. ID

4. Dispatcher Watkins receives the following information regarding a complaint. 4.____

   Place of occurrence: St. James Park
   Complaint: Large group of intoxicated males throwing beer bottles and playing loud music
   Complainant: Oscar Aker
   Complainant's Address: 13 St. James Square, Apt. 2B

   Dispatcher Watkins is not certain if this incident should be reported to 911 or Mr. Aker's local precinct. Dispatcher Watkins is about to notify his supervisor of the call. Which one of the following expresses the above information MOST clearly and accurately?

A. Mr. Aker, who lives at 13 St. James Square, Apt. 2B, called to make a complaint of a large group of intoxicated males who are throwing beer bottles and playing loud music in St. James Park.
B. Mr. Aker, who lives at 13 St. James Square, called to complain about a large group of intoxicated males, in Apt. 2B. They are throwing beer bottles and playing loud music in St. James Park.
C. Mr. Aker of 13 St. James Square, Apt. 2B, called to complain about loud music. There were a large group of intoxicated males throwing beer bottles in St. James Park.
D. As a result of intoxicated males throwing beer bottles Mr. Aker of 13 St. James Square, Apt. 2B, called to complain. A large group was playing loud music in St. James Park.

5. Communications Operator Davis recorded the following information from a caller: 5.____

Crime:	Rape
Time of Rape:	11:30 A.M.
Place of Rape:	Ralph's Dress Shop, 200 Lexington
Avenue Victim:	Linda Castro - employee at Ralph's Dress Shop
Description of Suspect:	Male, white
Weapon:	Knife

Communications Operator Davis needs to be clear and accurate when relaying information to the patrol car. Which one of the following expresses the above information MOST clearly and accurately?

A. Linda Castro was at 200 Lexington Avenue when she was raped at knife point by a white male. At 11:30 A.M., she is an employee of Ralph's Dress Shop.
B. At 11:30 A.M., Linda Castro reported that she was working in Ralph's Dress Shop located at 200 Lexington Avenue. A white male raped her while she was working at knife point.
C. Linda Castro, an employee of Ralph's Dress Shop, located at 200 Lexington Avenue, reported that at 11:30 A.M. a white male raped her at knife point in the dress shop.
D. At 11:30 A.M., a white male pointed a knife at Linda Castro. He raped an employee of Ralph's Dress Shop, which is located at 200 Lexington Avenue.

Question 6.

DIRECTIONS: Question 6 is to be answered SOLELY on the basis of the following information.

Police Communications Technicians frequently receive low priority calls, which are calls that do not require an immediate police response. When a low priority call is received, the Police Communications Technician should transfer the caller to a tape-recorded message which states *there will be a delay in police response*.

6. Police Communications Technicians should transfer to the low priority taped message a call reporting a 6.____

A. hubcap missing from an auto
B. child has just swallowed poison

C. group of youths fighting with knives
D. woman being assaulted

Questions 7-9.

DIRECTIONS: Questions 7 through 9 are to be answered SOLELY on the basis of the following passage.

On Tuesday, March 20 at 11:55 P.M., Dispatcher Uzel receives a call from a female stating that she immediately needs the police. The dispatcher asks the caller for her address. The excited female answers, *I can not think of it right now.* The dispatcher tries to calm down the caller. At this point, the female caller tells the dispatcher that her address is 1934 Bedford Avenue. The caller then realizes that 1934 Bedford Avenue is her mother's address and gives her address as 3455 Bedford Avenue. Dispatcher Uzel enters the address into the computer and tells the caller that the cross streets are Myrtle and Willoughby Avenues. The caller answers, *I don't live near Willoughby Avenue.* The dispatcher repeats her address at 3455 Bedford Avenue. Then the female states that her name is Linda Harris and her correct address is 5534 Bedford Avenue. Dispatcher Uzel enters the new address into the computer and determines the cross streets to be Utica Avenue and Kings Highway. The caller agrees that these are the cross streets where she lives.

7. What is the caller's CORRECT address? 7.____

A. Unknown
B. 1934 Bedford Avenue
C. 3455 Bedford Avenue
D. 5534 Bedford Avenue

8. What are the cross streets of the correct address? 8.____

A. Myrtle Avenue and Willoughby Avenue
B. Utica Avenue and Kings Highway
C. Bedford Avenue and Myrtle Avenue
D. Utica Avenue and Willoughby Avenue

9. Why did the female caller telephone Dispatcher Uzel? 9.____

A. She needed the cross streets for her address.
B. Her mother needed assistance.
C. The purpose of the call was not mentioned.
D. She did not know where she lived.

Question 10.

DIRECTIONS: Question 10 is to be answered SOLELY on the basis of the following information.

When performing vehicle license plate checks, Operators should do the following in the order given:

I. Request the license plate in question.
II. Repeat the license plate back to the patrol car officers.
III. Check the license plate locally in the computer.
IV. Advise the patrol car officers of the results of the local check.
V. Check the license plate nationally in the computer.
VI. Advise the patrol car officers of the results of the nationwide check.

10. Operator Johnson gets a request from a patrol car officer for a license plate check on a suspicious car. The patrol car officer tells Operator Johnson that the license plate number is XYZ-843, which Operator Johnson repeats back to the patrol car officer. Operator Johnson checks the license plate locally and determines that the car was stolen in the New York City area. 10.____
What should Operator Johnson do NEXT?

A. Repeat the license plate back to patrol car officers.
B. Check the license plate nationally.
C. Advise the patrol car officers of the results of the local check.
D. Advise the patrol ear officers of the results of the nationwide check.

11. Police Communications Technician Hughes receives a call from the owner of The Diamond Dome Jewelry Store, reporting a robbery. He obtains the following information from the caller: 11.____

Place of Occurrence:	The Diamond Dome Jewelry Store, 10 Exchange Place
Time of Occurrence:	10:00 A.M.
Crime:	Robbery of a $50,000 diamond ring
Victim:	Clayton Pelt, owner of The Diamond Dome Jewelry Store
Description of Suspect:	Male, white, black hair, blue suit and gray shirt
Weapon:	Gun

Communications Technician Hughes is about to relay the information to the dispatcher. Which one of the following expresses the above information MOST clearly and accurately?

A. Clayton Pelt reported that at 10:00 A.M. his store, The Diamond Dome Jewelry Store, was robbed at gunpoint. At 10 Exchange Place, a white male with black hair took a $50,000 diamond ring. He was wearing a blue suit and gray shirt.
B. At 10:00 A.M., a black-haired male robbed a $50,000 diamond ring from The Diamond Dome Jewelry Store, which is owned by Clayton Pelt. A white male was wearing a blue suit and gray shirt and had a gun at 10 Exchange Place.
C. At 10:00 A.M., Clayton Pelt, owner of The Diamond Dome Jewelry Store, which is located at 10 Exchange Place, was robbed of a $50,000 diamond ring at gunpoint. The suspect is a white male with black hair wearing a blue suit and gray shirt.
D. In a robbery that occurred at gunpoint, a white male with black hair robbed The Diamond Dome Jewelry Store, which is located at 10 Exchange Place. Clayton Pelt, the owner who was robbed of a $50,000 diamond ring, said he was wearing a blue suit and a gray shirt at 10:00 A.M.

12. Dispatcher Sanders receives the following information from the computer: Place of Occurrence: Bushwick Housing Projects, rear of Building 12B 12.____

Time of Occurrence:	6:00 P.M.
Crime:	Mugging
Victim:	Hispanic female
Suspect:	Unknown

Dispatcher sanders is about to relay the information to the patrol car.
Which one of the following expresses the above information MOST clearly and accurately?

A. In the rear of Building 12B, a Hispanic female was mugged. An unknown suspect was in the Bushwick Housing Projects at 6:00 P.M.
B. At 6:00 P.M., a Hispanic female was mugged by an unknown suspect in the rear of Building 12B, in the Bushwick Housing Projects.
C. At 6:00 P.M., a female is in the rear of Building 12B in the Bushwick Housing Projects. An unknown suspect mugged a Hispanic female.
D. A suspect's identity is unknown in the rear of Building 12B in the Bushwick Housing Project at 6:00 P.M. A Hispanic female was mugged.

Questions 13-15.

DIRECTIONS: Questions 13 through 15 are to be answered SOLELY on the basis of the following passage.

Dispatcher Clark, who is performing a 7:30 A.M. to 3:30 P.M. tour of duty, receives a call from Mrs. Gold. Mrs. Gold states there are four people selling drugs in front of Joe's Cleaners, located at the intersection of Main Street and Broadway. After checking the location in the computer, Dispatcher Clark asks the caller to give a description of each person. She gives the following descriptions: one white male wearing a yellow shirt, green pants, and red sneakers; one Hispanic male wearing a red and white shirt, black pants, and white sneakers; one black female wearing a green and red striped dress and red sandals; and one black male wearing a green shirt, yellow pants, and green sneakers. She also states that the Hispanic male, who is standing near a blue van, has the drugs inside a small black shoulder bag. She further states that she saw the black female hide a gun inside a brown paper bag and place it under a black car parked in front of Joe's Cleaners. The drug selling goes on everyday at various times. During the week, it occurs from 7 A.M. to 1 P.M. and from 5 P.M. to 12 A.M., but on weekends it occurs from 3 P.M. until 7 A.M.

13. Which person was wearing red sneakers? 13.____

A. Black male
B. Hispanic male
C. Black female
D. White male

14. Mrs. Gold stated the drugs were located 14.____

A. under the blue van
B. inside the black shoulder bag
C. under the black car
D. inside the brown paper bag

15. At what time does Mrs. Gold state the drugs are sold on weekends? 15.____

A. 7:30 A.M. - 3:30 P.M.
B. 7:00 A.M. - 1:00 P.M.
C. 5:00 P.M. - 12:00 A.M.
D. 3:00 P.M. - 7:00 A.M.

16. Police Communications Technician Bentley receives a call of an auto being stripped. He obtains the following information from the caller: 16.____

Place of Occurrence:	Corner of West End Avenue and W. 72nd Street
Time of Occurrence:	10:30 P.M.
Witness:	Mr. Simpson
Suspects:	Two white males
Crime:	Auto stripping
Action Taken:	Suspects fled before police arrived

Communications Technician Bentley is about to enter the incident into the computer and send the information to the dispatcher.
Which one of the following expresses the above information MOST clearly and accurately?

A. At 10:30 P.M., Mr. Simpson witnessed two white males stripping an auto parked at the corner of West End Avenue and W. 72nd Street. The suspects fled before the police arrived.
B. An auto was parked at the corner of West End Avenue and W. 72nd Street. Two white males who were stripping at 10:30 P.M. were witnessed by Mr. Simpson. Before the police arrived, the suspects fled.
C. Mr. Simpson saw two white males at the corner of West End Avenue and W. 72nd Street. Fleeing the scene before the police arrived, the witness saw the suspects strip an auto.
D. Before the police arrived at 10:30 P.M. on the corner of West End Avenue and W. 72nd Street, Mr. Simpson witnessed two white males. The suspects, who stripped an auto, fled the scene.

17. 911 Operator Washington receives a call of a robbery and obtains the following information regarding the incident: 17.____

Place of Occurrence:	First National Bank, 45 West 96th Street
Time of Occurrence:	2:55 P.M.
Amount Taken:	$10,000
Description of Suspect:	Male, black, wearing a leather jacket, blue jeans, and white shirt
Weapon:	Gun

911 Operator Washington is about to enter the call into the computer.
Which one of the following expresses the above information MOST clearly and accurately?

A. At 2:55 P.M., the First National Bank, located at 45 West 96th Street, was robbed at gunpoint of $10,000. The suspect is a black male and is wearing a leather jacket, blue jeans, and a white shirt.
B. Ten thousand dollars was robbed from the First National Bank at 2:55 P.M. A black male was wearing a leather jacket, blue jeans, and a white shirt at 45 West 96th Street. He also had a gun.
C. At 2:55 P.M., a male was wearing a leather jacket, blue jeans, and a white shirt. The First National Bank located at 45 West 96th Street was robbed by a black male. Ten thousand dollars was taken at gunpoint.
D. Robbing the First National Bank, a male wore a leather jacket, blue jeans, and a white shirt at gunpoint. A black male was at 45 W. 96th Street. At 2:55 P.M., $10,000 was taken.

Questions 18-20.

DIRECTIONS: Questions 18 through 20 are to be answered SOLELY on the basis of the following passage.

Police Communications Technician Gordon receives a call from a male stating there is a bomb set to explode in the gym of Public School 85 in two hours. Realizing the urgency of the call, the Communications Technician calls the radio dispatcher, who assigns Patrol Car 43A to the scene. Communications Technician Gordon then notifies her supervisor, Miss Smith, who first reviews the tape of the call, then calls the Operations Unit which is notified of all serious incidents, and she reports the facts. The Operations Unit notifies the Mayor's Information Agency and Borough Headquarters of the emergency situation.

18. Who did Communications Technician Gordon notify FIRST? 18.____

A. Supervisor Smith
B. Operations Unit
C. Patrol Car 43A
D. Radio dispatcher

19. The Operations Unit was notified 19.____

A. to inform school personnel of the bomb
B. so they can arrive at the scene before the bomb is scheduled to go off
C. to evacuate the school
D. due to the seriousness of the incident

20. Who did Miss Smith notify? 20.____

A. Patrol Car 43A
B. Operations Unit
C. Mayor's Information Agency
D. Borough Headquarters

KEY (CORRECT ANSWERS)

1.	D	11.	C
2.	C	12.	B
3.	A	13.	D
4.	A	14.	B
5.	C	15.	D
6.	A	16.	A
7.	D	17.	A
8.	B	18.	D
9.	C	19.	D
10.	C	20.	B

TEST 2

DIRECTIONS: Each question or incomplete statement is followed by several suggested answers or completions. Select the one that BEST answers the question or completes the statement. *PRINT THE LETTER OF THE CORRECT ANSWER IN THE SPACE AT THE RIGHT.*

1. A Police Communications Technician receives a call reporting a large gathering. She obtained the following information: 1.____

Place of Occurrence:	Cooper Square Park
Time of Occurrence:	1:15 A.M.
Occurrence:	Youths drinking and playing loud music
Complainant:	Mrs. Tucker, 20 Cooper Square
Action Taken:	Police scattered the crowd

Communications Technician Carter is about to relay the information to the dispatcher. Which one of the following expresses the above information MOST clearly and accurately?

A. The police responded to Cooper Square Park because Mrs. Tucker, who called 911, lives at 20 Cooper Square. The group of youths was scattered due to drinking and playing loud music at 1:15 A.M.
B. Mrs. Tucker, who lives at 20 Cooper Square, called 911 to make a complaint of a group of youths who were drinking and playing loud music in Cooper Square Park at 1:15 A.M. The police responded and scattered the crowd.
C. Loud music and drinking in Cooper Square Park by a group of youths caused the police to respond and scatter the crowd. Mrs. Tucker called 911 and complained. At 1:15 A.M., she lives at 20 Cooper Square.
D. Playing loud music and drinking, Mrs. Tucker called the police. The police scattered a group of youths in Cooper Square Park at 1:15 A.M. Mrs. Tucker lives at 20 Cooper Square.

2. Dispatcher Weston received a call from the owner of a gas station and obtained the following information: 2.____

Place of Occurrence:	Blin's Gas Station, 1800 White Plains Road
Time of Occurrence:	10:30 A.M.
Occurrence:	Left station without paying
Witness:	David Perilli
Description of Auto:	A white Firebird, license plate GEB275
Suspect:	Male, white, wearing blue jeans and a black T-shirt

Dispatcher Weston is about to enter the information into the computer. Which one of the following expresses the above information MOST clearly and accurately?

A. At 10:30 A.M., David Perilli witnessed a white male wearing blue jeans and a black T-shirt leave Blin's Gas Station, located at 1800 White Plains Road, without paying. The suspect was driving a white Firebird with license plate GEB275.
B. Wearing blue jeans and a black T-shirt, David Perilli witnessed a white male leave Blin's Gas Station without paying. He was driving a white Firebird with license plate GEB275. This occurred at 1800 White Plains Road at 10:30 A.M.
C. David Perilli witnessed a male wearing blue jeans and a black T-shirt driving a white Firebird. At 10:30 A.M., a white male left Blin's Gas Station, located at 1800 White Plains Road, without paying. His license plate was GEB275.

D. At 10:30 A.M., David Perilli witnessed a white male leaving Blin's Gas Station without paying. The driver of a white Firebird, license plate GEB275, was wearing blue jeans and a black T-shirt at 1800 White Plains Road.

Questions 3-4.

DIRECTIONS: Questions 3 and 4 are to be answered SOLELY on the basis of the following information.

Police Communications Technicians are required to assist callers who need non-emergency assistance. The callers are referred to non-emergency agencies. Listed below are some non-emergency situations and the agencies to which they should be referred.

Agency	
Local Precinct	Unoccupied suspicious car
Environmental Protection Agency	Open fire hydrant
Sanitation Department	Abandoned car
S.P.C.A.	Injured, stray or sick animal
Transit Authority	Transit Authority travel information

3. Communications Technician Carter received a call from Mr. Cane, who stated that a car without license plates had been parked in front of his house for five days. Mr. Crane should be referred to the 3.____

   A. A.S.P.C.A.
   B. Transit Authority
   C. Sanitation Department
   D. Environmental Protection Agency

4. Mrs. Dunbar calls to report that a dog has been hit by a car and is lying at the curb in front of her house. Mrs. Dunbar should be referred to the 4.____

   A. Sanitation Department
   B. Local Precinct
   C. Environmental Protection Agency
   D. A.S.P.C.A.

5. Operator Bryant received a call of a robbery and obtained the following information: 5.____

Place of Occurrence:	Deluxe Deli, 303 E. 30th Street
Time of Occurrence:	5:00 P.M.
Crime:	Robbery of $300
Victim:	Bonnie Smith, cashier of Deluxe Deli
Description of Suspect:	White, female, blonde hair, wearing black slacks and a red shirt
Weapon:	Knife

Operator Bryant is about to enter this information into the computer.
Which one of the following expresses the above information MOST clearly and accurately?

A. Bonnie Smith, the cashier of the Deluxe Deli reported at 5:00 P.M. that she was robbed of $300 at knifepoint at 303 East 30th Street. A white female with blonde hair was wearing black slacks and a red shirt.
B. At 5:00 P.M., a blonde-haired female robbed the 303 East 30th Street store. At the Deluxe Deli, cashier Bonnie Smith was robbed of $300 by a white female at knifepoint. She was wearing black slacks and a red shirt.
C. In a robbery that occurred at knifepoint, a blonde-haired white female robbed $300 from the Deluxe Deli. Bonnie Smith, cashier of the 303 East 30th Street store, said she was wearing black slacks and a red shirt at 5:00 P.M.
D. At 5:00 P.M., Bonnie Smith, cashier of the Deluxe Deli, located at 303 East 30th Street, was robbed of $300 at knifepoint. The suspect is a white female with blonde hair wearing black slacks and a red shirt.

6. 911 Operator Landers receives a call reporting a burglary that happened in the past. He obtained the following information from the caller: 6.____

Place of Occurrence:	196 Simpson Street
Date of Occurrence:	June 12
Time of Occurrence:	Between 8:30 A.M. and 7:45 P.M.
Victim:	Mr. Arnold Frank
Items Stolen:	$300 cash, stereo, assorted jewelry, and a VCR

911 Operator Landers is about to enter the incident into the computer.
Which one of the following expresses the above information MOST clearly and accurately?

A. Mr. Arnold Frank stated that on June 12, between 8:30 A.M. and 7:45 P.M., someone broke into his home at 196 Simpson Street and took $300 in cash, a stereo, assorted jewelry, and a VCR.
B. Mr. Arnold Frank stated between 8:30 A.M. and 7:45 P.M., he lives at 196 Simpson Street. A stereo, VCR, $300 in cash, and assorted jewelry were taken on June 12.
C. Between 8:30 A.M. and 7:45 P.M. on June 12, Mr. Arnold Frank reported someone broke into his home. At 196 Simpson Street, a VCR, $300 in cash, a stereo, and assorted jewelry were taken.
D. A stereo, VCR, $300 in cash, and assorted jewelry were taken between 8:30 M. and 7:45 P.M. On June 12, Mr. Arnold Frank reported he lives at 196 Simpson Street.

Questions 7-9.

DIRECTIONS: Questions 7 through 9 are to be answered SOLELY on the basis of the following passage.

Communications Operator Harris receives a call from Mrs. Stein who reports that a car accident occurred in front of her home. She states that one of the cars belongs to her neighbor, Mrs. Brown, and the other car belongs to Mrs. Stein's son, Joseph Stein. Communications Operator Harris enters Mrs. Stein's address into the computer and receives information that no such address exists. She asks Mrs. Stein to repeat her address. Mrs. Stein repeats her address and states that gasoline is leaking from the cars and that smoke is coming from their engines. She further states that people are trapped in the cars and then hangs up.

Communications Operator Harris notifies her supervisor, Jones, that she received a call but was unable to verify the address and that the caller hung up. Mrs. Jones listens to the tape of the call and finds that the caller stated 450 Park Place not 415 Park Place. She advises Communications Operator Harris to enter the correct address, then notify Emergency Service Unit to respond to the individuals trapped in the cars, the Fire Department for the smoke condition, and Emergency Medical Service for any possible injuries.

7. Who did Communications Operator Harris notify concerning the problem with the caller's address? 7.____

   A. Mrs. Brown
   B. Joseph Stein
   C. Joseph Brown
   D. Mrs. Jones

8. Which agency was Communications Operator Harris advised to notify concerning individuals trapped in the cars? 8.____

   A. Emergency Medical Service
   B. Fire Department
   C. Emergency Service Unit
   D. NYC Police Department

9. Which agency did Supervisor Jones advise Communications Operator Harris to notify for the smoke condition? 9.____

   A. NYC Police Department
   B. Emergency Medical Service
   C. Fire Department
   D. Emergency Service Unit

Question 10.

DIRECTIONS: Question 10 is to be answered SOLELY on the basis of the following information.

When a Police Communications Technician receives a call concerning a bank robbery, a Communications Technician should do the following in the order given:

I. Get address and name of the bank from the caller.
II. Enter the address into the computer.
III. Use the *Hotline* button to alert the dispatcher of the serious incident going into the computer.
IV. Get back to the caller and get the description of the suspect and other pertinent information.
V. Enter additional information into the computer and send it to the dispatcher.
VI. Upgrade the seriousness of the incident so it appears first on dispatcher's screen.
VII. Notify the Supervising Police Communications Technician of the bank robbery.

10. Police Communications Technician Brent receives a call from Mr. Ross stating that while he was on line at the Trust Bank, at West 34th Street and 9th Avenue, he witnessed a bank robbery. Communications Technician Brent enters the address into the computer, then presses the *Hotline* button and alerts the dispatcher that there was a bank robbery at the Trust Bank on West 34th Street and 9th Avenue. Mr. Ross continues to state that the robber is a white male in his 30's wearing a light blue shirt and blue jeans. After obtaining other pertinent information, the NEXT step Communications Technician Brent should take is to 10.____

A. enter additional information into the computer and send it to the dispatcher
B. upgrade the seriousness of the incident so it appears first on the dispatcher's screen
C. notify his supervisor of the bank robbery
D. use the *Hotline* button to alert the dispatcher of a serious incident going into the computer

11. Dispatcher Wilson receives a call regarding drugs being sold in the lobby of an apartment building. He obtains the following information: 11.____

Place of Occurrence:	305 Willis Avenue
Time of Occurrence:	2:00 P.M.
Witnesses:	Roy Rodriguez and Harry Armstrong
Suspect:	Melvin Talbot, left the scene before the police arrived
Crime:	Drug sale

Dispatcher Wilson is about to enter this incident into the computer.
Which one of the following expresses the above information MOST clearly and accurately?

A. Roy Rodriguez and Harry Armstrong reported that they witnessed Melvin Talbot selling drugs in the lobby of 305 Willis Avenue at 2:00 P.M. The suspect left the scene before the police arrived.
B. In the lobby, Roy Rodriguez reported at 2:00 P.M. he saw Melvin Talbot selling drugs with Harry Armstrong. He left the lobby of 305 Willis Avenue before the police arrived.
C. Roy Rodriguez and Harry Armstrong witnessed drugs being sold at 305 Willis Avenue. Before the police arrived at 2:00 P.M., Melvin Talbot left the lobby.
D. Before the police arrived, witnesses stated that Melvin Talbot was selling drugs. At 305 Willis Avenue, in the lobby, Roy Rodriguez and Harry Armstrong said he left the scene at 2:00 P.M.

12. Operator Rogers receives a call of a car being stolen. He obtains the following information: 12.____

Place of Occurrence:	Parking lot at 1723 East 20th Street
Time of Occurrence:	2:30 A.M.
Vehicle Involved:	1988 Toyota Corolla
Suspects:	Male, Hispanic, wearing a red T-shirt
Crime:	Auto theft
Witness:	Janet Alonzo

Operator Rogers is entering the information into the computer.
Which one of the following expresses the above information MOST clearly and accurately?

A. At 2:30 A.M., wearing a red T-shirt, Janet Alonzo witnessed a 1988 Toyota Corolla being stolen by a male Hispanic in the parking lot at 1723 East 20th Street.
B. A male Hispanic, wearing a red T-shirt, was in the parking lot at 1723 East 20th Street." At 2:30 A.M., Janet Alonzo witnessed a 1988 Toyota Corolla being stolen.
C. At 2:30 A.M., Janet Alonzo witnessed a 1988 Toyota Corolla in the parking lot at 1723 East 20th Street being stolen by a male Hispanic who is wearing a red T-shirt.
D. Janet Alonzo witnessed a 1988 Toyota Corolla in the parking lot being stolen. At 2:30 A.M., a male Hispanic was wearing a red T-shirt at 1723 East 20th Street.

Question 13.

DIRECTIONS: Question 13 is to be answered SOLELY on the basis of the following information.

There are times when Police Communications Technicians have to reassign officers in a patrol car from a less serious incident which does not require immediate police response to an incident of a more serious nature which does require immediate police response. Police Communications Technicians must choose among the assigned patrol cars and determine which one is assigned to the least serious incident, then reassign that one to the situation which requires immediate police response.

Communications Technician Reese is working the 13th Division which covers the 79th Precinct. There are only four patrol cars working in the 79th Precinct. They are assigned as follows:

79A is assigned to a car accident with injuries involving an intoxicated driver.

79B is assigned to a group of teenagers playing loud music in a park.

79C is assigned to a group of teenagers trying to steal liquor in a liquor store, who are possibly armed with guns.

79D is assigned to a suspicious man in a bank, with possible intentions to rob the bank.

13. If Communications Technician Reese receives a call of an incident that requires immediate police response, which patrol car should be reassigned? 13.____

A. 79A B. 79B C. 79C D. 79D

Questions 14-16.

DIRECTIONS: Questions 14 through 16 are to be answered SOLELY on the basis of the following information.

On May 12, at 3:35 P.M., Police Communications Technician Connor receives a call from a child caller requesting an ambulance for her mother, whom she cannot wake. The child did not know her address, but gave Communications Technician Connor her apartment number and telephone number. Communications Technician Connor's supervisor, Ms. Bendel, is advised of the situation and consult's Cole's Directory, a listing published by the Bell Telephone Company, to obtain an address when only the telephone number is known. The telephone number is unlisted. Ms. Bendel asks Communications Technician Taylor to call Telco Security to obtain an address from their telephone number listing. Communications Technician Taylor speaks to Ms. Morris of Telco Security and obtains the address. Communications Technician Connor, who is still talking with the child, is given the address by Communications Technician Taylor. She enters the information into the computer system and transfers the caller to the Emergency Medical Service.

14. What information did Communications Technician Connor obtain from the child caller? 14.____

A. Telephone number and apartment number
B. Name and address
C. Address and telephone number
D. Apartment number and address

15. Communications Technician Taylor obtained the address from 15.____

A. Communications Technician Connor
B. Ms. Morris
C. Supervisor Bendel
D. the child caller

16. The caller's address was obtained by calling 16.____

A. Cole's Directory
B. Telco Security
C. Emergency Medical Service
D. The Telephone Company

Question 17.

DIRECTIONS: Question 17 is to be answered SOLELY on the basis of the following information.

The following incidents appear on the Police Communications Technician's computer screen which were called in by three different callers at the same time:

I. At 3040 Hill Avenue between Worth and Centre Streets, there are two people fighting in the third floor hallway. One of them has a shiny metal object.
II. In a building located on Hill Avenue between Worth and Centre Streets, a man and a woman are having an argument on the third floor. The woman has a knife in her hand.
III. In front of Apartment 3C on the third floor, a husband and wife are yelling at each other. The wife is pointing a metal letter opener at her husband. The building is located on the corner of Hill Avenue and Worth Street.

17. A Police Communications Technician may be required to combine into one incident many calls that appear on the computer screen if they seem to be reporting the same incident. Which of the above should a Police Communications Technician combine into one incident? 17.____

A. I and II
B. I and III
C. II and III
D. I, II, and III

Questions 18-19.

DIRECTIONS: Questions 18 and 19 are to be answered SOLELY on the basis of the following information.

Police Communications Technicians must be able to identify and assign codes to the crimes described in the calls they receive. All crimes are coded by number and by priority. The priority code number indicates the seriousness of the crime. The lower the priority number, the more serious the crime.

Listed below is a chart of several crimes and their definitions. The corresponding crime code and priority code number are given.

CRIME	DEFINITION	CRIME CODE	PRIORITY CODE
Criminal Mischief:	Occurs when a person intentionally damages another person's property	29	6
Harrassment:	Occurs when a person intentionally annoys another person by striking, shoving, or kicking them without causing injury	27	8
Aggravated Harrassment:	Occurs when a person intentionally annoys another person by using any form of communication	28	9
Theft of Service:	Occurs when a person intentionally avoids payment for services given	25	7

18. Communications Technician Rogers received a call from Mrs. Freeman, who stated that her next door neighbor, whom she had an argument with, has thrown a rock through her apartment window. 18.____
Which one of the following is the CORRECT crime code?

A. 29 B. 28 C. 27 D. 25

19. Communications Technician Tucker received a call from a man who stated that he is a waiter at the Frontier Diner. He states that one of his customers was refusing to pay for his meal. 19.____
Which one of the following is the CORRECT priority code number for this crime?

A. 6 B. 7 C. 8 D. 9

Dispatcher Matthews received a call of a bomb threat. He obtained the following information; 19.____

Address of Occurrence: 202 Church Avenue
Location: 2nd floor men's room
Time of Call: 12:00 P.M.
Time of Occurrence: 2:00 P.M.
Terrorist Organization: People *Against Government*

Caller:	Anonymous male member of *People* Against Government
Action Taken:	Supervisor Jones notified of the bomb threat

Dispatcher Matthews is about to enter the information into the computer.
Which one of the following expresses the above information MOST clearly and accurately?

A. An anonymous male called Dispatcher Matthews and told him that a bomb is set to go off at 202 Church Avenue in the 2nd floor men's room at 2:00 P.M. Dispatcher Matthews notified Supervisor Jones that the caller is from *People Against Government* at 12:00 P.M.
B. Dispatcher Matthews received a call in the 2nd floor men's room of a bomb threat from an anonymous male member of the *People Against Government* terrorist organization. He notified Supervisor Jones at 12:00 P.M. that a bomb is set to go off at 2:00 P.M. at 202 Church Avenue.
C. Dispatcher Matthews received a call at 202 Church Avenue from the *People Against Government,* a terrorist organization. An anonymous male stated that a bomb is set to go off at 2:00 P.M. in the 2nd floor men's room. At 12:00 P.M., Dispatcher Matthews notified Supervisor Jones of the call.
D. At 12:00 P.M., Dispatcher Matthews received a call from an anonymous male caller who states that he is from a terrorist organization known as *People Against Government.* He states that a bomb has been placed in the 2nd floor men's room of 202 Church Avenue and is set to go off at 2:00 P.M. Dispatcher Matthews notified Supervisor Jones of the bomb threat.

KEY (CORRECT ANSWERS)

1.	B	11.	A
2.	A	12.	C
3.	C	13.	B
4.	D	14.	A
5.	D	15.	B
6.	A	16.	B
7.	D	17.	D
8.	C	18.	A
9.	C	19.	B
10.	A	20.	D

EXAMINATION SECTION
TEST 1

DIRECTIONS: Each question or incomplete statement is followed by several suggested answers or completions. Select the one that BEST answers the question or completes the statement. *PRINT THE LETTER OF THE CORRECT ANSWER IN TEE SPACE AT THE RIGHT.*

1. Police Communications Technicians must connect the caller to Transit Police when an incident occurs on a subway train or in the subway station. 1.____
   Which one of the following calls should be reported to Transit Police?

   A. The newsstand outside the entrance to the 86th Street subway was just robbed, and the suspects fled down the street.
   B. Soon after James Pike left the Columbus Circle subway station, his chain was snatched on the street corner.
   C. While traveling to work on the *D* line subway train, John Smith was mugged.
   D. A noisy group of school children have just come out of the Times Square subway station and are now annoying passersby on the street.

Question 2.

DIRECTIONS: Question 2 is to be answered SOLELY on the basis of the following information.

When a Police Communications Technician is notified by patrol cars that they are in a vehicular pursuit, the dispatcher should obtain the following in the order given:

I. Location of pursuit
II. Type of vehicle, color of vehicle, and direction of travel
III. Nature of offense
IV. License plate number and state
V. Number of occupant(s) in vehicle
VI. Identity of the patrol car in pursuit

2. Police Communications Dispatcher Johnson is working the 26th Division when an unknown patrol car announces via car radio that he is in pursuit of a white 1986 Cadillac traveling north on Vanbrunt Street from Ainsley Place. Dispatcher Johnson then asks the pursuing patrol car, *What is the car wanted for?* The Officer replies, *The car is wanted for a hit and run.* 2.____
   What information should Dispatcher Johnson obtain NEXT?

   A. The number of occupant(s) in the vehicle
   B. Location of pursuit
   C. License plate number and state
   D. Identity of the patrol car in pursuit

Question 3.

DIRECTIONS: Question 3 is to be answered SOLELY on the basis of the following information.

Robbery - involves the unlawful taking of property from a person by force or attempted use of immediate force.

Robbery in Progress - crime is occurring at the time the call came into 911, 5 minutes in the past or when suspects are still in the area.

3. Which of the following situations would be considered a ROBBERY IN PROGRESS? 3.____

   A. Female calls 911 stating that she has just arrived home and found her apartment has been robbed.
   B. Male calls 911 stating that he just discovered that someone picked his pocket.
   C. Female calls 911 stating that she saw a man grab an elderly woman's purse.
   D. Child calls 911 stating that some man is beating up his mother and is trying to take her purse.

4. On June 20, 2007 at 6:30 P.M., Police Communications Technician White receives a call from an anonymous complainant stating the following facts: 4.____

Incident:	Male with a gun sitting in a blue car
Location of Incident:	In front of 185 Hall St.
Description of Suspect:	Male, Black, bald, approximately 25 years old, dressed in red

Dispatcher White needs to be accurate and clear when transferring above information to the police dispatcher. Which one of the following expresses the above information MOST clearly and accurately?

   A. On June 20, 2007 at 6:30 P.M., a call was received stating that a bald man, dressed in red, was in front of 185 Hall St. A black male, approximately 25 years old, is sitting in a blue car holding a gun.
   B. A call was received on June 20, 2007. at 6:30 P.M. stating that a bald black male, approximately 25 years old, who is dressed in red, is armed with a gun sitting in a blue car in front of 185 Hall St.
   C. A call was received on June 20, 2007 at 6:30 P.M. Sitting in a blue car in front of 185 Hall St. is a Black male, approximately 25 years old. Dressed in red with a bald head, a man is armed with a gun.
   D. A call was received stating that in front of 185 Hall St., a bald male, approximately 25 years old, dressed in red, is sitting in a blue car. A Black male is armed with a gun at 6:30 P.M. on June 20, 2007.

5. Police Communications Technician Dozier receives a call from a female who has just witnessed the following: 5.____

Incident:	White female police officer being assaulted
Location of Incident:	Surf Avenue and West 30th Street, in front of a candy store
Description of Suspectp;	Hispanic female wearing a green dress, possibly armed with a gun

Dispatcher Dozier is about to relay the information to the dispatcher.
Which one of the following expresses the above information MOST clearly and accurately?

   A. A call was received from a female on Surf Avenue and West 30th Street stating that a white female police officer is being assaulted by a Hispanic female wearing a green dress. She is possibly armed with a gun in front of a candy store.
   B. In front of a candy store at Surf Avenue and West 30th Street, a call was received from a female stating that a white female police officer is being assaulted by a Hispanic female wearing a green dress. She is possibly armed with a gun.

C. A call was received from a female stating that at the corner of Surf Avenue and West 30th Street in front of a candy store, there is a white female police officer being assaulted. The suspect is a Hispanic female wearing a green dress, who is possibly armed with a gun.
D. A call was received from a female stating that at the corner of West 30th Street and Surf Avenue, there is a white female police officer in front of a candy store being assaulted. She is wearing a green dress. The Hispanic female is possibly armed with a gun.

Questions 6-8.

DIRECTIONS: Questions 6 through 8 are to be answered SOLELY on the basis of the following passage.

At 10:35 A.M., Police Communications Technician Ross receives a second call from Mrs. Smith who is very upset because she has been waiting for the police and an ambulance since her first call, one hour ago. Mrs. Smith was mugged, and in resisting the attack, her nose was broken. The location of the incident is the uptown side of the subway station for the IND #2 train located at Jay Street and Borough Hall. Operator Ross advises Mrs. Smith to hold on and that she will check the status of her complaint. Operator Ross calls the Emergency Medical Service (EMS) and connects Mrs. Smith to the EMS operator. The EMS operator informs Mrs. Smith that an ambulance is coming from a far distance away and will be at the location at approximately 11:03 A.M. Operator Ross then calls the Transit Authority Police Department (TAPD). The TAPD received Mrs. Smith's first call at 9:37 A.M., and police arrived at location at 9:46 M. However, the police arrived at the downtown side of the subway station for the IND #3 train. TAPD informs Operator Ross that a police car will arrive at the correct location as soon as possible.

6. What is the CLOSEST approximate time that Mrs. Smith made her first call for help? _______ A.M. 6.____

A. 9:35 B. 9:46 C. 10:35 D. 11:03 .

7. The ambulance was delayed because 7.____

A. the ambulance responded to the downtown side of the subway station for the IND #2 train
B. EMS never received Mrs. Smith's request for an ambulance
C. a broken nose is not a priority request for an ambulance
D. the ambulance was coming from a far distance

8. There was a delay in TAPD response to the crime scene because TAPD 8.____

A. was coming from a far distance
B. responded on the uptown side of the subway station for the IND #2 train
C. was waiting for the -Police Department to respond first
D. responded on the downtown side of the subway station for the IND #3 train

9. Extreme care must be taken when assigning solo cars (one police officer in a vehicle) to incidents. If anything in the job indicates that the job may be a potentially violent situation, a solo car should not be assigned. 9._____
In which one of the following incidents should a Police Communications Technician assign a solo car?
A

A. disorderly male carrying a knife
B. house that was broken into two days ago
C. suspiciously occupied auto
D. group of rowdy teenagers throwing beer bottles at passersbys

Question 10.

DIRECTIONS: Question 10 is to be answered SOLELY on the basis of the following information.

On the Police Communications Technician's screen, the following incidents appear which were called in at the same time:

I. Caller states that she is looking out her 10th floor window and sees a man sleeping on the street in front of her home at Crescent Street and 4th Avenue.
II. Caller states that he was driving down the block of Crescent Street between 3rd and 4th Avenues and just witnessed a man being beaten and mugged. The caller thinks that the victim is unconscious.
III. Caller states there is a car accident at Crescent Street and 3rd Avenue, and one of the passengers suffered a broken arm.

10. Which of the above should the operator MOST likely consider as the same incident? 10._____

A. I and II
B. II and III
C. I and III
D. I, II, and III

11. Police Communications Operator Raymond receives a call regarding a rape and obtains the following information: 11._____

Time of Rape:	10:35 P.M.
Place of Rape:	Sam's Laundromat, 200 Melrose Avenue
Victim:	Joan McGraw
Crime:	Rape
Suspect:	Male, Hispanic, carrying a gun

Operator Raymond is about to enter the incident into the computer.
Which one of the following expresses the above information MOST clearly and accurately?

A. At 10:35 P.M., Joan McGraw was raped in Sam's Laundromat, located at 200 Melrose Avenue, by a Hispanic male carrying a gun.
B. A Hispanic male was carrying a gun at 10:35 P.M. Joan McGraw was raped in Sam's Laundromat located at 200 Melrose Avenue.
C. Carrying a gun, Joan McGraw was raped by a Hispanic male. This occurred in Sam's Laundromat located at 200 Melrose Avenue at 10:35 P.M.
D. At 10:35 P.M., Joan McGraw was raped by a Hispanic male carrying a gun. Sam's Laundromat is located at 200 Melrose Avenue.

12. Police Communications Dispatcher Gold receives a call concerning a disorderly male in a local drug store. He obtains the following information: 12.____

Place of Occurrence:	Rapid-Serve Drug Store
Complainant:	George Meyer
Crime:	Threatening gestures and abusive language
Suspect:	Male, white
Action Taken:	The suspect was removed from premises by the police.

Dispatcher Gold is about to enter the incident into the computer.
Which one of the following expresses the above information MOST clearly and accurately?

A. George Meyer called the police because a white male was removed from the Rapid-Serve Drug Store. He was making threatening gestures and using abusive language.
B. George Meyer called the police and was removed from the Rapid-Serve Drug Store. A white male was making threatening gestures and using abusive language.
C. At the Rapid-Serve Drug Store, a white male was making threatening gestures and using abusive language. George Meyer called the police and removed the suspect from the drug store.
D. George Meyer called the police because a white male was making threatening gestures and using abusive language in the Rapid-Serve Drug Store. The suspect was removed from the drug store by the police.

Question 13.

DIRECTIONS: Question 13 is to be answered SOLELY on the basis of the following information.

When dispatching an incident involving a suspicious package, a Police Communications Technician should do the following in the order given:

I. Assign a patrol car and Patrol Sergeant.
II. Enter into the computer additional information received from assigned cars.
III. Notify appropriate Emergency Assistance.
IV. Notify the Bomb Squad.
V. Notify the Duty Captain.

13. Police Communications Technician Berlin receives a call involving a suspicious package located on the corner of Gates Avenue and Blake Street. Dispatcher Berlin promptly assigns a patrol car and a Patrol Sergeant to the incident. Upon arrival, the Sergeant determines that there is a ticking sound coming from the box. The Sergeant immediately advises Dispatcher Berlin of the situation and tells Dispatcher Berlin to call the Fire Department and have them respond. 13.____
What should Dispatcher Berlin to NEXT?

A. Call the Fire Department.
B. Notify the Bomb Squad.
C. Enter additional information received from assigned cars into the computer.
D. Notify the Duty Captain.

Questions 14-16.

DIRECTIONS: Questions 14 through 16 are to be answered SOLELY on the basis of the following passage.

Police Communications Technician Robbins receives a call at 5:15 P.M. from Mr. Adams reporting he witnessed a shooting in front of 230 Eagle Road. Mr. Adams, who lives at 234 Eagle Road, states he overheard two white males arguing with a Black man. He describes one white male as having blonde hair and wearing a black jacket with blue jeans, and the other white male as having brown hair and wearing a white jacket and blue jeans.

Mr. Adams recognized the Black man as John Rivers, the son of Mrs. Mary Rivers, who lives at 232 Eagle Road. At 5:10 P.M., the blonde male took a gun, shot John in the stomach, and dragged his body into the alleyway. The two males ran into the backyard of 240 Eagle Road and headed west on Randall Boulevard. Dispatcher Robbins connects Mr. Adams to the Emergency Medical Service. The Ambulance Receiving Operator processes the call at 5:25 P.M. and advises Mr. Adams that the next available ambulance will be sent.

14. Who was the eyewitness to the shooting? 14.____

A. Dispatcher Robbins
B. Mr. Adams
C. Mrs. Rivers
D. John Rivers

15. In front of what address was John Rivers shot? 15.____
_______ Eagle Road.

A. 230 B. 232 C. 234 D. 240

16. What is the description of the male who fired the gun? A male wearing a _______ jacket and blue jeans. 16.____

A. white blonde-haired; white
B. white brown-haired; black
C. white blonde-haired; black
D. Black brown-haired; white

17. A Police Communications Technician can have several calls for police response on their computer screen at one time. A dispatcher may have to determine which of the calls is the most serious and assign that one to the police first. 17.____
Which one of the following situations should a dispatcher assign to the police FIRST?

A. A robbery which occurred two hours ago, and the suspects have fled the scene
B. A suspicious man offering a child candy to get the child into his van at the time of the call
C. A woman returns to her car and finds her left fender dented
D. A group of youths playing cards in the hallway

18. The following information was obtained by Police Communications Technician Fried regarding a call of an auto accident with injuries: 18.____

Date of Accident:	March 7, 2007
Place of Accident:	50 West 96th Street
Time of Accident:	3:15 P.M.
Drivers:	Susan Green and Nancy White

Injured: Nancy White
Action Taken: Emergency Medical Services (EMS) Operator 600 was notified
Dispatcher Fried is about to enter the above information into the computer.
Which one of the following expresses the above information MOST clearly and accurately?

A. At 50 West 96th Street, Susan Green and Nancy White had an auto accident resulting in an injury to Nancy White. EMS Operator 600 was notifed to send an ambulance at 3:15 P.M. on March 7, 2007.
B. EMS Operator 600 was notified to send an ambulance to 50 West 96th Street due to an auto accident between Nancy White and Susan Green, who was injured on March 7, 2007 at 3:15 P.M.
C. Susan Green and Nancy White were involved in an auto accident at 50 West 96th Street on March 7, 2007. At 3:15 P.M., EMS Operator 600 was notified to send an ambulance for Nancy White.
D. On March 7, 2007 at 3:15 P.M., Susan Green and Nancy White were involved in an auto accident at 50 West 96th Street. EMS Operator 600 was notified to send an ambulance for Nancy White who was injured in the accident.

Questions 19-20.

DIRECTIONS: Questions 19 and 20 are to be answered SOLELY on the basis of the following information.

At the beginning of their tours, Police Communications Technicians need to call the precinct to find out what patrol cars are covering which sections of the precinct and which special assignment cars are being used. Special assignment cars are used instead of regular patrol cars when certain situations arise. Special assignment cars should be assigned before a patrol car when a call comes in that is related to the car's special assignment, regardless of what section the incident is occurring in. Otherwise, a regular patrol car should be assigned.

Police Communications Technician Tanner is assigned to the 83rd Precinct. He calls the precinct and determines the following patrol cars and special assignment cars are being used:

Patrol cars are assigned as follows:
Patrol Car 83A - Covers Sections A, B, C
Patrol Car 83D - Covers Sections D, E, F
Patrol Car 83G - Covers Sections G, H, I

Special assignment cars are assigned as follows:
83SP1 - Burglary Car
83SP2 - Religious Establishment
83SP8 - Anti-Crime (plainclothes officers)

19. Dispatcher Tanner receives a call located in the 83rd Precinct in *E* Section. Which car should be assigned? 19.____

A. 83D B. 83A C. 83SP8 D. 83SP2

20. Dispatcher Tanner receives a call concerning a burglary in *B* Section. Which is the CORRECT car to be assigned? 20.____

A. 83A B. 83G C. 83SP1 D. 83SP2

KEY (CORRECT ANSWERS)

1.	C	11.	A
2.	C	12.	D
3.	D	13.	C
4.	B	14.	B
5.	C	15.	A
6.	A	16.	C
7.	D	17.	B
8.	D	18.	D
9.	B	19.	A
10.	A	20.	C

TEST 2

DIRECTIONS: Each question or incomplete statement is followed by several suggested answers or completions. Select the one that BEST answers the question or completes the statement. *PRINT THE LETTER OF THE CORRECT ANSWER IN THE SPACE AT THE RIGHT.*

1. Police Communications Technician Daniel receives a call stating the following: 1.____
   Date and Time of Call: June 21, 2007 at 12:30 P.M.
   Incident: Shots being fired
   Location: The roof of a building, located between Moore Street and Bushwick Avenue, exact address unknown
   Suspect: Male
   Complainant: Mr. Bernard
   Comments: Mr. Bernard will be wearing a brown coat and will direct officers to location of the incident.
   Dispatcher Daniel is about to enter the information into the computer.
   Which one of the following expresses the above information MOST clearly and accurately?
   On June 21, 2007,

   A. at 12:30 P.M., Dispatcher Daniel receives a call from a complainant stating that a male is on a roof of a building with an unknown address firing a gun, and he is wearing a brown coat. The complainant, Mr. Bernard, will be in front of the building to direct the police to the exact location of the incident.
   B. a male is firing a gun from a roof, stated complainant Mr. Bernard to Dispatcher Daniel. This is at Moore Street and Bushwick Avenue. At 12:30 P.M., the caller will be at the location to direct the police to the building where the male is firing the gun. He is wearing a brown coat.
   C. at 12:30 P.M., Dispatcher Daniel receives a call from a complainant, Mr. Bernard, who states that at a building with an unknown address, located between Moore Street and Bushwick Avenue, a male is firing a gun from a roof. Mr. Bernard will be at the location wearing a brown coat to direct the police to the exact building.
   D. Dispatcher Daniel receives a call from a complainant, Mr. Bernard, who is calling from a building with an unknown address. He informs Dispatcher Daniel that a male is firing a gun from a roof of a building between Moore Street and Bushwick Avenue. At 12:30 P.M., Mr. Bernard will be wearing a brown coat to direct the police to the incident.

Questions 2-4.

DIRECTIONS: Questions 2 through 4 are to be answered SOLELY on the basis of the following passage.

Mrs. Arroyo returns from work one evening to find her door open and loud noise coming from her apartment. She peeks through the crack of the door and sees a white male moving rapidly through her apartment wearing blue jeans and a pink T-shirt. She runs to the nearest public telephone and dials 911. Police Communications Technician Ms. Lopez takes the call. Mrs. Arroyo informs Operator Lopez that there is a strange man in her apartment. The operator asks the caller for her address, apartment number, name, and telephone number, and then puts Mrs. Arroyo on hold. Operator Lopez enters the address in the computer and, realizing it is a high priority call, tries to notify the Radio Dispatcher directly by depressing the *hotline* button.

The Radio Dispatcher does not respond, and Operator Lopez realizes the *hotline* button is not working. The operator then continues to enter the rest of the information into the computer and notifies the caller that the police will respond. Operator Lopez then walks into the dispatcher's room to make sure the dispatcher received the information entered into the computer, and then notifies the supervisor of her malfunctioning equipment.

2. The operator notified her supervisor because 2.____

   A. the suspect was still in the apartment
   B. the *hotline* button was not working
   C. she could not enter the address in the computer
   D. it was a high priority call

3. What was the FIRST action the operator took after putting the complainant on hold? 3.____

   A. Entered the caller's telephone number and name in the computer.
   B. Walked into the dispatcher's room.
   C. Entered the caller's address into the computer.
   D. Tried to notify the Radio Dispatcher by depressing the *hotline* button.

4. Operator Lopez depressed the *hotline* button 4.____

   A. to check if the *hotline* button was working properly
   B. because it was a high priority call
   C. to make sure the dispatcher received the information entered into the computer
   D. because the computer was not working properly

Question 5.

DIRECTIONS: Question 5 is to be answered SOLELY on the basis of the following information.

A Police Communications Technician occasionally receives calls from persons making threats against public officials, visiting dignitaries, or members of the Police Department. When this occurs, the Dispatcher should do the following in the order given:

I. Obtain details of the threat
   (A) Who is being threatened and how
   (B) When it is going to happen
II. Attempt to determine the sex and ethnicity of the caller
III. Try to obtain the identity, address, and telephone number of the caller
IV. Notify the supervisor

5. Police Communications Operator Frye receives a call and obtains from the caller that he is going to shoot the mayor on Election Day. Operator Frye determine the caller to be a male with a heavy Hispanic accent. Operator Frye asks the male for his name, address, and phone number. The caller does not respond and hangs up. 5.____
What should Operator Frye do NEXT?

   A. Obtain details of the threats.
   B. Determine the sex and ethnicity of the caller.
   C. Obtain the identity, address, and phone number of the caller.
   D. Notify the supervisor.

Question 6.

DIRECTIONS: Question 6 is to be answered SOLELY on the basis of the following information.

A Police Communications Technician will call back complainants only under the following conditions:

1. Dispatcher needs clarification of information previously received from the complainant and/or
2. To notify the complainant that police need to gain entry to the location of the incident.

6. In which one of the following situations should a Police Communications Technician call back the complainant? 6.____

   A. While responding to an assigned incident, Patrol Car 79A gets a flat tire. Patrol Car 79A radios the dispatcher and advises the dispatcher to call the complainant and notify the complainant that there will be a delay in police response.
   B. Patrol Car 83B is assigned to an incident that occurred approximately 30 minutes ago. Patrol Car 83B advises the dispatcher that he is coming from a far distance and the dispatcher should call the complainant to find out which is the best way to get to the incident location.
   C. Patrol Car 66B is on the scene of an incident and is having a problem gaining entry into the building. Patrol Car 66B asks the dispatcher to call the complainant and ask him to meet the police officers from the patrol car outside the building.
   D. Patrol Car 90B is assigned to a burglary that occurred in the complainant's private home. It is raining heavily outside, so Patrol Car 90B asks the dispatcher to call and request the complainant to meet the police by the patrol car.

7. Police Communications Dispatcher Blake receives a call reporting a bank robbery and obtains the following information: 7.____

Time of Robbery:	11:30 A.M.
Place of Robbery:	Fidelity Bank
Crime:	Bank Robbery
Suspect:	Male, white, wearing blue jeans, blue jacket, carrying a brown bag
Witness:	Susan Lane of 731 Madison Avenue

   Dispatcher Blake is about to inform his supervisor of the facts concerning the bank robbery.
   Which one of the following expresses the above information MOST clearly and accurately?

   A. At 11:30 A.M., the Fidelity Bank was robbed. Susan Lane lives at 731 Madison Avenue. The witness saw a white male wearing blue jeans, a blue jacket, and carrying a brown bag.
   B. Susan Lane of 731 Madison Avenue witnessed the robbery of Fidelity Bank at 11:30 A.M. The suspect is a white male and was wearing blue jeans, a blue jacket, and carrying a brown bag.
   C. Wearing blue jeans, a blue jacket, and carrying a brown bag, Susan Lane of 731 Madison Avenue saw a white male robbing the Fidelity Bank. The robbery was witnessed at 11:30 A.M.

D. At 11:30 A.M., Susan Lane of 731 Madison Avenue witnessed the robbery of the Fidelity Bank. A white male wore blue jeans, a blue jacket, and carried a brown bag.

8. Police Communications Technician Levine receives an incident for dispatch containing the following information: 8.____

Incident:	A female being beaten
Location:	In front of 385 Wall Street
Victim:	White female
Suspect:	White, male, wearing a grey shirt, possibly concealing a gun underneath his shirt

Dispatcher Levine is about to relay this information to the patrol car.
Which one of the following expresses the above information MOST clearly and accurately?

A. A white female is being beaten by a white male wearing a grey shirt, who is possibly concealing a gun underneath his shirt. This is occurring in front of 385 Wall Street.
B. A white male is beating a white female wearing a grey shirt. He is possibly concealing a gun underneath his shirt in front of 385 Wall Street.
C. A female is being beaten in front of 385 Wall Street. A white male is possibly concealing a gun underneath his shirt. She is white, and the suspect is wearing a grey shirt.
D. In front of 385 Wall Street, a white female is being beaten by a suspect, possibly concealing a gun underneath his shirt. A white male is wearing a grey shirt.

Questions 9-11.

DIRECTIONS: Questions 9 through 11 are to be answered SOLELY on the basis of the following passage.

Police Communications Technician John Clove receives a call from a Social Worker, Mrs. Norma Harris of Presbyterian Hospital, who states there is a 16-year-old teenager on the other line, speaking to Dr. Samuel Johnson, a psychologist at the hospital. The teenager is threatening suicide and claims that she is an out-patient, but refuses to give her name, address, or telephone number. She further states that the teenager took 100 pills of valium and is experiencing dizziness, numbness of the lips, and heart palpitations. The teenager tells Dr. Johnson that she wants to die because her boyfriend left her because she is pregnant.

Dr. Johnson is keeping her on the line persuading her to give her name, telephone number, and address. The Social Worker asks the dispatcher to trace the call. The dispatcher puts the caller on hold and informs his supervisor, Mrs. Ross, of the incident. The supervisor contacts Telephone Technician Mr. Ralph Taylor. Mr. Taylor contacts the telephone company and speaks to Supervisor Wallace, asking him to trace the call between Dr. Johnson and the teenager. After approximately 10 minutes, the dispatcher gets back to the Social Worker and informs her that the call is being traced.

9. Why did the Social Worker call Dispatcher Clove? 9.____

A. A teenager is threatening suicide.
B. Mrs. Ross took 100 pills of valium.

C. Dr. Johnson felt dizzy, numbness of the lips, and heart palpitations.
D. An unmarried teenager is pregnant.

10. Who did Mr. Clove notify FIRST? 10.____

A. Mrs. Norma Harris
B. Dr. Samuel Johnson
C. Mr. Wallace
D. Mrs. Ross

11. The conversation between which two individuals is being traced? 11.____

A. Mrs. Norma Harris and the 16-year-old teenager
B. The Telephone Technician and Telephone Company Supervisor
C. Dr. Johnson and the 16-year-old teenager
D. The dispatcher and the Hospital Social Worker

Question 12.

DIRECTIONS: Question 12 is to be answered SOLELY on the basis of the following information.

On the Police Communications Technician's screen, the following incidents appear which were called in at the same time by three different callers:

I. A fight is occurring at 265 Hall Street between Myrtle and Willoughby Ave. The fight started in Apartment 3C, and the two men are now fighting in the street.
II. A fight took place between a security guard and a suspected shoplifter in a store at Hall St. and Willoughby Ave. The security guard is holding the suspect in the security office.
III. A fight is occurring between two white males on the street near the corner of Hall Street and Myrtle Ave. One of the males has a baseball bat.

12. Which of the above should a Police Communications Technician MOST likely consider as the same incident? 12.____

A. I and II
B. II and III
C. I and III
D. I, II, and III

Questions 13-15.

DIRECTIONS: Questions 13 through 15 are to be answered SOLELY on the basis of the following passage.

Police Communications Technician Flood receives a call from Mr. Michael Watkins, Program Director for *Meals on Wheels,* a program that delivers food to elderly people who cannot leave their home. Mr. Watkins states he received a call from Rochelle Berger, whose elderly aunt, Estelle Sims, is a client of his. Rochelle Berger informed Mr. Watkins that she has just received a call from her aunt's neighbor, Sally Bowles, who told her that her aunt has not eaten in several days and is in need of medical attention.

After questioning Mr. Watkins, Dispatcher Flood is informed that Estelle Sims lives at 300 79th Street in Apartment 6K, and her telephone number is 686-4527; Sally Bowles lives in Apartment 6H, and her telephone number is 678-2456. Mr. Watkins further advises that if there is difficulty getting into Estelle Sims' apartment, to ring Sally Bowies' bell and she will let you in. Mr. Watkins gives his phone number as 776-0451, and Rochelle Berger's phone number is 291-7287. Dispatcher Flood advises Mr. Watkins that the appropriate medical assistance will be sent.

13. Who did Sally Bowles notify that her neighbor needed medical attention? 13.____

A. Dispatcher Flood
B. Michael Watkins
C. Rochelle Berger
D. Estelle Sims

14. If the responding medical personnel are unable to get into Apartment 6K, they should speak to 14.____

A. Rochelle Berger
B. Sally Bowles
C. Dispatcher Flood
D. Michael Watkins

15. Whose telephone number is 686-4527? 15.____

A. Michael Watkins
B. Estelle Sims
C. Sally Bowles
D. Rochelle Berger

16. Police Communications Technicians often receive calls regarding incidents where a response from the Fire Department may be necessary. 16.____
In which one of the following situations would a request from the dispatcher for the Fire Department to respond be MOST critical?
A(n)

A. fire hydrant has been opened by children on a hot August afternoon
B. abandoned auto is parked in front of a fire hydrant
C. neighbor's cat has climbed up a tree and is stuck
D. excited woman smells smoke coming from the floor below

Question 17.

DIRECTIONS: Question 17 is to be answered SOLELY on the basis of the following information.

When a patrol car confirms that a murder has taken place, the Police Communications Technician should notify the following people in the order given:

I. Patrol Sergeant
II. Dispatching Supervisor
III. Operations Unit
IV. Crime Scene Unit
V. Precinct Detective Unit
VI. Duty Captain

17. Police Communications Technician Rodger assigns a patrol car to investigate a man who was shot and killed. The patrol car arrives on the scene and confirms that a murder has taken place. The Patrol Sergeant hears what has happened on his police radio and informs Dispatcher Rodger that he is going to respond to the scene. The Dispatching Supervisor walks over to Dispatcher Rodger and is informed of the situation. 17.____
Who should Dispatcher Rodger notify NEXT?

A. Operations Unit
B. Patrol Sergeant
C. Precinct Detective Unit
D. Crime Scene Unit

18. Police Communications Technician Peterson receives a call from a woman inside the subway station reporting that her purse has just been snatched. Dispatcher Peterson obtained the following information relating to the crime: 18.____

Place of Occurrence: E. 42nd Street and Times Square
Time of Occurrence: 5:00 P.M.
Crime: Purse Snatched
Victim: Thelma Johnson
Description of Suspect: Black, female, brown hair, blue jeans, red T-shirt

Dispatcher Peterson is about to relay the information to the Transit Authority Police Dispatcher.

Which one of the following expresses the above information MOST clearly and accurately?

A. At 5:00 P.M., a brown-haired Black woman snatched a purse inside the subway station at E. 42nd Street and Times Square belonging to Thelma Johnson. She was wearing blue jeans and a red T-shirt.
B. A purse was snatched from Thelma Johnson by a woman with brown hair in the subway station at 5:00 P.M. A Black female was wearing blue jeans and a red T-shirt at E. 42nd Street and Times Square.
C. At 5:00 P.M., Thelma Johnson's purse was snatched inside the subway station at E. 42nd Street and Times Square. The suspect is a Black female with brown hair who is wearing blue jeans and a red T-shirt.
D. Thelma Johnson reported at 5:00 P.M. her purse was snatched. In the subway station at E. 42nd Street and Times Square, a Black female with brown hair was wearing blue jeans and a red T-shirt.

19. Police Communications Technician Hopkins receives a call of an assault and obtains the following information concerning the incident: 19.____

Place of Occurrence: Times Square
Time of Occurrence: 3:15 A.M.
Victim: Peter Polk
Victim's Address: 50 E. 60 Street
Suspect: Male, Hispanic, 5'6", 140 lbs., dressed in black
Injury: Broken nose
Action Taken: Victim transported to St. Luke's Hospital

Dispatcher Hopkins is about to enter the job into the computer system.

Which one of the following expresses the above information MOST clearly and accurately?

A. At 3:15 A.M., Peter Polk was assaulted in Times Square by a Hispanic male, 5'6", 140 lbs., dressed in black, suffering a broken nose. Mr. Polk lives at 50 E. 69 Street and was transported to St. Luke's Hospital.
B. At 3:15 A.M., Peter Polk was assaulted in Times Square by a Hispanic male, 5'6", 140 lbs., dressed in black, who lives at 50 E. 69 Street. Mr. Polk suffered a broken nose and was transported to St. Luke's Hospital.
C. Peter Polk, who lives at 50 E. 69 Street, was assaulted at 3:15 A.M. in Times Square by a Hispanic male, 5'6", 140 lbs., dressed in black. Mr. Polk suffered a broken nose and was transported to St. Luke's Hospital.
D. Living at 50 E. 69 Street, Mr. Polk suffered a broken nose and was transported to St. Luke's Hospital. At 3:15 A.M., Mr. Polk was assaulted by a Hispanic male, 5'6", 140 lbs., who was dressed in black.

20. A Police Communications Technician is required to determine which situations called in to 911 require police assistance and which calls require non-emergency assistance. Which one of the following calls should a dispatcher MOST likely refer to non-emergency assistance? 20.____

A. Mr. Moss threatens the owner of Deluxe Deli with bodily harm for giving him incorrect change of twenty dollars.
B. The manager refuses to take back Mrs. Thompson's defective toaster because she doesn't have a receipt. Mrs. Thompson leaves the store.
C. Mrs. Frank is having a violent argument with the manager of Donna's Dress Shop because he is refusing to exchange a dress she recently purchased.
D. The manager of Metro Supermarket refuses to take back a stale loaf of bread, so the consumer punches him in the face.

KEY (CORRECT ANSWERS)

1.	C	11.	C
2.	B	12.	C
3.	C	13.	C
4.	B	14.	B
5.	D	15.	B
6.	C	16.	D
7.	B	17.	A
8.	A	18.	C
9.	A	19.	C
10.	D	20.	B

EXAMINATION SECTION

TEST 1

DIRECTIONS: Each question or incomplete statement is followed by several suggested answers or completions. Select the one that BEST answers the question or completes the statement. *PRINT THE LETTER OF THE CORRECT ANSWER IN THE SPACE AT THE RIGHT.*

1. You are operating the switchboard and you receive an outside call for an extension line which is busy. 1.____
The one of the following which you should do FIRST is to
   A. ask the caller to try again later
   B. ask the caller to wait and inform him every thirty seconds about the status of the extension line
   C. tell the caller the line is busy and ask him if he wishes to wait
   D. tell the caller the line is busy and that you will connect him as soon as possible

2. A person comes to your work area. He makes comments which make no sense, gives foolish opinions, and tells you that he has enemies who are after him. He appears to be mentally ill. 2.____
Of the following, the FIRST action to take is to
   A. humor him by agreeing and sympathize with him
   B. try to reason with him and point out that his fears or opinions are unfounded
   C. have him arrested immediately
   D. tell him to leave at once

3. You are speaking with someone on the telephone who asks you a question which you cannot answer. You estimate that you can probably obtain the requested information in about five minutes. 3.____
Of the following, the MOST appropriate course of action would be to tell the caller that
   A. the information will take a short while to obtain, and then ask her for her name and number so that you can call her back when you have the information
   B. the information is available now, but she should call back later
   C. you do not know the answer and refer her to another division you think might be of service
   D. she is being placed on *hold* and that you will be with her in about five minutes

4. A person with a very heavy foreign accent comes to your work area and starts talking to you. He is very excited and is speaking too rapidly for you to understand what he is saying. 4.____
Of the following, the FIRST action for you to take is to

A. refer the person to your supervisor
B. continue your work and ignore the person in the hope that he will be discouraged and leave the building
C. ask or motion to the person to speak more slowly and have him repeat what he is trying to communicate
D. assume that the person is making a complaint, tell him that his problem will be taken care of, and then go back to your work

5. Assume that you are responsible for handling supplies. You notice that you are running low on a particular type of manila file folder exceptionally fast. You believe that someone in the precinct is taking the folders for other than official use. 5.____
In this situation, the one of the following that you should do FIRST is to
A. put up a notice stating that supplies have been disappearing and ask for the staff's cooperation in eliminating the problem
B. speak to your supervisor about the matter and let him decide on a course of action
C. watch the supply cabinet to determine who is taking the folders
D. ignore the situation and put in a requisition for additional folders

6. One afternoon, several of the officers ask you to perform different tasks. Each task requires a half day of work. Each officer tells you that his assignment must be finished by 4 P.M. the next day. 6.____
Of the following, the BEST way to handle this situation is to
A. do the assignments as quickly as you can, in the order in which the officers handed them to you
B. do some work on each assignment in the order of the ranks of the assigning officers and hand in as much as you are able to finish
C. speak to your immediate supervisor in order to determine the priority of assignments
D. accept all four assignments but explain to the last officer that you may not be able to finish his job

7. Every morning, several officers congregate around your work station during their breaks. You find their conversations very distracting. 7.____
The one of the following which you should do FIRST is to
A. ask them to cooperate with you by taking their breaks somewhere else
B. concentrate as best you can because their breaks do not last very long
C. reschedule your break to coincide with theirs
D. tell your supervisor that the officers are very uncooperative

8. One evening when you are very busy, you answer the phone and find that you are speaking with one of the neighborhood cranks, an elderly man who constantly complains that his neighbors are noisy. 8.____
In this situation, the MOST appropriate action for you to take is to
A. hang up and go on with your work
B. note the complaint and process it in the usual way
C. tell the man that his complaint will be investigated and then forget about it
D. tell the man that you are very buy and ask him to call back later

9. One morning you answer a telephone call for Lieutenant Jones, who is busy on another line. You inform the caller that Lieutenant Jones is on another line and this party says he will hold. After two minutes, Lieutenant Jones is still speaking on the first call. 9.____
Of the following, the FIRST thing for you to do is to
   A. ask the second caller whether it is an emergency
   B. signal Lieutenant Jones to let him know there is another call waiting for him
   C. request that the second caller try again later
   D. inform the second caller that Lieutenant Jones' line is still busy

10. The files in your office have been overcrowded and difficult to work with since you started working there. One day your supervisor is transferred and another aide in your office decides to discard three drawers of the oldest materials. 10.____
For him to take this action is
   A. *desirable*; it will facilitate handling the more active materials
   B. *undesirable*; no file should be removed from its point of origin
   C. *desirable*; there is no need to burden a new supervisor with unnecessary information
   D. *undesirable*; no file should be discarded without first noting what material has been discarded

11. You have been criticized by the lieutenant-in-charge because of spelling errors in some of your typing. You have only copied the reports as written, and you realize that the errors occurred in work given to you by Sergeant X. 11.____
Of the following, the BEST way for you to handle this situation is to
   A. tell the lieutenant that the spelling errors are Sergeant X's, not yours, because they occur only when you type his reports
   B. tell the lieutenant that you only type the reports as given to you, without implicating anyone
   C. inform Sergeant X that you have been unjustly criticized because of his spelling errors and politely request that he be more careful in the future
   D. use a dictionary whenever you have doubt regarding spelling

12. You have recently found several items misfiled. You believe that this occurred because a new administrative aide in your section has been making mistakes. 12.____
The BEST course of action for you to take is to
   A. refile the material and say nothing about it
   B. send your supervisor an anonymous note of complaint about the filing errors
   C. show the errors to the new administrative aide and tell him why they are errors in filing
   D. tell your supervisor that the new administrative aide makes a lot of errors in filing

13. One of your duties is to record information on a standard printed form regarding missing cars. One call you receive concerns a custom-built auto which has apparently been stolen. There seems to be no place on the form for many of the details which the owner gives you. 13.____

Of the following, the BEST way for you to obtain an adequate description of this car would be to

A. complete the form as best you can and attach another sheet containing the additional information the owner gives you
B. complete the form as best you can and request that the owner submit a photograph of the missing car
C. scrap the form since it is inadequate in this case and make out a report based on the information the owner gives you
D. complete the form as best you can and ignore extraneous information that the form does not call for

14. One weekend, you develop a painful infection in one hand. You know that your typing speed will be much slower than normal, and the likelihood of your making mistakes will be increased. 14.____
Of the following, the BEST course of action for you to take in this situation is to

A. report to work as scheduled and do your typing assignments as best you can without complaining
B. report to work as scheduled and ask your co-workers to divide your typing assignments until your hand heals
C. report to work as scheduled and ask your supervisor for non-typing assignments until your hand heals
D. call in sick and remain on medical leave until your hand is completely healed so that you can perform your normal duties

15. When filling out a departmental form during an interview concerning a citizen complaint, an administrative aide should know the purpose of each question that he asks the citizen. 15.____
For such information to be supplied by the department is

A. *advisable*, because the aide may lose interest in the job if he is not fully informed about the questions he has to ask
B. *inadvisable*, because the aide may reveal the true purpose of the questions to the citizens
C. *advisable*, because the aide might otherwise record superficial or inadequate answers if he does not fully understand the questions
D. *inadvisable*, because the information obtained through the form may be of little importance to the aide

16. Which one of the following is NOT a general accepted rule of telephone etiquette for an administrative aide? 16.____

A. Answer the telephone as soon as possible after the first ring
B. Speak in a louder than normal tone of voice, on the assumption that the caller is hard-of-hearing
C. Have a pencil and paper ready at all times with which to make notes and take messages
D. Use the tone of your voice to give the caller the impression of cooperativeness and willingness to be of service

17. The one of the following which is the BEST reason for placing the date and time of receipt of incoming mail is that this procedure 17.____
   A. aids the filing of correspondence in alphabetical order
   B. fixes responsibility for promptness in answering correspondence
   C. indicates that the mail has been checked for the presence of a return address
   D. makes it easier to distribute the mail in sequence

18. Which one of the following is the FIRST step that you should take when filing a document by subject? 18.____
   A. Arrange related documents by date with the latest date in front
   B. Check whether the document has been released for filing
   C. Cross-reference the document if necessary
   D. Determine the category under which the document will be filed

19. The one of the following which is NOT generally employed to keep tract of frequently used material requiring future attention is a 19.____
   A. card tickler file
   B. dated follow-up folder
   C. periodic transferral of records
   D. signal folder

20. Assume that a newly appointed administrative aide arrives 15 minutes late for the start of his tour of duty. One of his co-workers tells him not to worry because he has signed him in on time. The co-worker assures him that he would be willing to over for him anytime he is late and hopes the aide will do the same for him. The aide agrees to do so. 20.____
This arrangement is
   A. *desirable*; it prevents both men from getting a record for tardiness
   B. *undesirable*; signing in for each other is dishonest
   C. *desirable*; cooperation among co-workers is an important factor in morale
   D. *undesirable*; they will get caught if one is held up in a lengthy delay

21. An administrative aide takes great pains to help a citizen who approaches him with a problem. The citizen thanks the aide curtly and without enthusiasm. 21.____
Under these circumstances, it would be MOST courteous for the aide to
   A. tell the citizen he was glad to be of service
   B. ask the citizen to put the compliment into writing and send it to his supervisor
   C. tell the citizen just what pains he took to render this service so that the citizen will be fully aware of his efforts
   D. make no reply and ignore the citizen's remarks

22. Assume that your supervisor spends a week training you, a newly appointed administrative aide, to sort fingerprint for filing purposes. After doing this type of filing for several day, you get an idea which you believe would improve upon the method in use. 22.____
Of the following, the BEST action for you to take in this situation is to
   A. wait to see whether your idea still look good after you have had more experience
   B. try your idea out before bringing it up with your supervisor

C. discuss your idea with your supervisor
D. forget about this idea since the fingerprint sorting system was devised by experts

23. Which one of the following is NOT a useful filing practice? 23.____
A. Filing active records in the most accessible parts of the file cabinet
B. Filling a file drawer to capacity in order to save space
C. Gluing small documents to standard-size paper before filing
D. Using different colored tab for various filing categories

24. A citizen comes in to make a complaint to an administrative aide. 24.____
The one of the following action which would be the MOST serious example of discourtesy would be for the aide to
A. refuse to look up from his desk even though he knows someone is waiting to speak to him
B. not use the citizen's name when addressing him once his identity has been ascertained
C. interrupt the citizen's story to ask questions
D. listen to the complaint and refer the citizen to a special office

25. Suppose that one of your neighbors walks into the precinct where you are an administrative aide and asks you to make 100 copies of a letter on the office duplicating machine for his personal use. 25.____
Of the following, what action should you take FIRST in this situation?
A. Pretend that you do not know the person and order him to leave the building
B. Call a police officer and report the person for attempting to make illegal use of police equipment
C. Tell the person that you will copy the letter but only when you are off-duty
D. Explain to the person that you cannot use police equipment for non-police work

KEY (CORRECT ANSWERS)

1. C
2. A
3. A
4. C
5. B

6. C
7. A
8. B
9. D
10. D

11. D
12. C
13. A
14. C
15. C

16. B
17. B
18. B
19. C
20. B

21. A
22. C
23. B
24. A
25. D

TEST 2

DIRECTIONS: Each question or incomplete statement is followed by several suggested answers or completions. Select the one that BEST answers the question or completes the statement. *PRINT THE LETTER OF THE CORRECT ANSWER IN THE SPACE AT THE RIGHT.*

Questions 1-6.

DIRECTIONS: Questions 1 through 6 are to be answered on the basis of the information supplied in the chart below.

LAW ENFORCEMENT OFFICERS KILLED
(By Type of Activity)
2012-2021

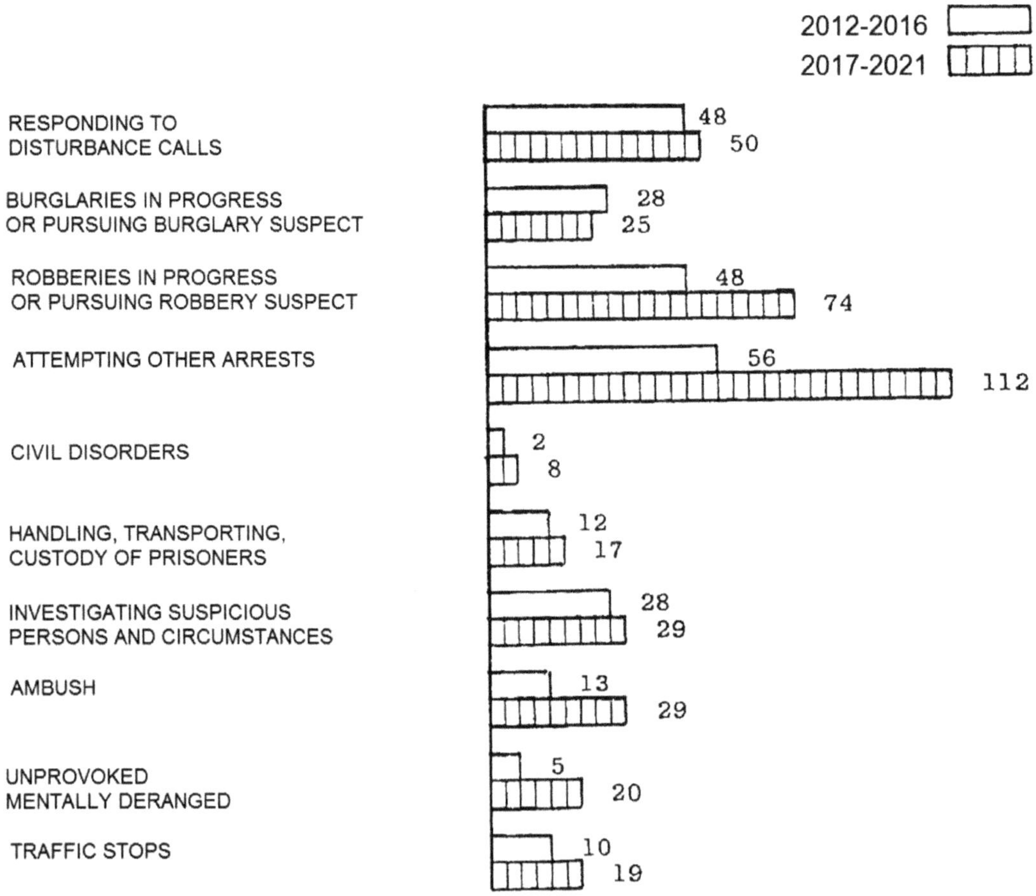

1. According to the above chart, the percent of the total number of law enforcement officers killed from 2012-2021 in activities related to burglaries and robberies is MOST NEARLY _____ percent. 1.____
   A. 8.4 B. 19.3 C. 27.6 D. 36.2

2. According to the above chart, the two of the following categories which increased from 2012–16 to 2017–21 by the same percent are 2.____
   A. ambush and traffic stops
   B. attempting other arrests and ambush
   C. civil disorders and unprovoked mentally deranged
   D. response to disturbance calls and investigating suspicious persons and circumstances

3. According to the above chart, the percentage increase in law enforcement officers killed from the 2012-16 period to the 2017-21 period is MOST NEARLY _____ percent. 3.____
   A. 34 B. 53 C. 65 D. 100

4. According to the above chart, in which one of the following activities did the number of law enforcement officers killed increase by 100 percent? 4.____
   A. Ambush
   B. Attempting other arrests
   C. Robberies in progress or pursuing robbery suspect
   D. Traffic stops

5. According to the above chart, the two of the following activities during which the total number of law enforcement officers killed from 2012 to 2021 was the same are 5.____
   A. burglaries in progress or pursuing burglary suspect and investigating suspicious persons and circumstances
   B. handling, transporting, custody of prisoner and traffic stops
   C. investigating suspicious persons and circumstances and ambush
   D. responding to disturbance calls and robberies in progress or pursuing robbery suspect

6. According to the categories in the above chart, the one of the following statements which can be made about law enforcement officers killed from 2012 to 2016 is that 6.____
   A. the number of law enforcement officers killed during civil disorders equals one-sixth of the number killed responding to disturbance calls
   B. the number of law enforcement officers killed during robberies in progress or pursuing robbery suspect equals 25 percent of the number killed while handling or transporting prisoners
   C. the number of law enforcement officers killed during traffic stops equals one-half the number killed for unprovoked reasons or by the mentally deranged
   D. twice as many law enforcement officers were killed attempting other arrests as were killed during burglaries in progress or pursuing burglary suspect

Questions 7-10.

DIRECTIONS: Assume that all arrests fall into two mutually exclusive categories, felonies and misdemeanors. Last week 620 arrests were made in Precinct A, of which 403 were for felonies. Questions 7 through 10 are to be answered on the basis of this information.

7. The percent of all arrests made in Precinct A last week which were for felonies was _____ percent. 7.____
A. 55 B. 60 C. 65 D. 70

8. If 3/5 of all persons arrested for felonies and 1/4 of all persons arrested for misdemeanors were carrying weapons, then the number of arrests involving persons carrying weapons in Precinct A last week was MOST NEARLY 8.____
A. 135 B. 295 C. 415 D. 525

9. If five times as many men as women were arrested for felonies, and half as many women as men were arrested for misdemeanors, then the number of women arrested in Precinct A last week was APPROXIMATELY 9.____
A. 90 B. 120 C. 175 D. 210

10. If the ratio of arrests made on weekends (Friday through Sunday) to arrests made on weekdays (Monday through Thursday) is 2:1, then the number of arrests made in Precinct A last weekend was 10.____
A. 308 B. 340 C. 372 D. 413

11. The police precincts covering the county receive calls at the average rate of two per minute during the 8 A.M. to 4 P.M. tour, but this rate increases by 50 percent during the 4 P.M. to 12 A.M. tour. However, the initial rate decreases by 50 percent during the 12 A.M. to 8 A.M. tour. 11.____
The number of calls received by the precincts covering the county on this basis is one 24-hour day is
A. 960 B. 1,440 C. 2,880 D. 3,360

12. If an administrative aide is expected to handle 15 calls per hour and Precinct C averages 840 calls during the 4 P.M. to 12 A.M. tour, then the number of aides needed in Precinct C to handle calls during this tour is 12.____
A. 4 B. 5 C. 6 D. 7

13. If in a group of ten administrative aides, four type 40 words per minute, one types 45, two type 50, two type 60, and one types 65, then the average speed in the group is 13.____
A. 49 B. 50 C. 51 D. 52

14. An administrative aide works from midnight to 8 A.M. on a certain day and then is off for 64 hours. 14.____
He is due back at work at
A. 8 A.M. B. 12 noon C. 4 P.M. D. 12 midnight

15. If a certain aide take one hour to type 2 accident reports or 6 missing person reports, then the length of time he will require to finish 7 accident reports and 15 missing persons reports is _____ hours _____ minutes. 15.____
A. 6; 0   B. 6; 30   C. 8; 0   D. 8; 40

16. If one administrative aide can alphabetize 320 reports per hour and another can do 280 per hour, then the number of reports that both could alphabetize during an 8-hour tour is 16.____
A. 4,800   B. 5,200   C. 5,400   D. 5,700

17. If 1,000 candidates applied for administrative aide, and out of those applying 7/8 appear for the written test, and out of those who take the written test 66 2/4 percent pass it, and out of those who pass the written test 85 percent pass the medical exam, then the number of candidates still eligible to become administrative aides will be about 17.____
A. 245   B. 495   C. 585   D. 745

18. If the number of murders in the city in 2018 was 415, and the number of murders has increased by 8 percent each year since that year, then in 2021 we would expect the number of murders to be about 18.____
A. 484   B. 523   C. 548   D. 565

19. If a person reported missing on April 15 was found murdered on July 4, how many days was he missing? (Include April 15 but NOT July 4 in the total.) 19.____
A. 76   B. 80   C. 82   D. 84

20. Suppose that a pile of 96 file cards measures one inch in height and that it takes you ½ hour to file these cards away.
If you are given three piles of cards which measure 2½ inches high, 1¾ inches high, and $3^3/_8$ inches high, respectfully, the time it would take to file the cards is MOST NEARLY _____ hours and _____ minutes. 20.____
A. 2; 30   B. 3; 50   C. 6; 45   D. 8; 15

Questions 21-30.

DIRECTIONS: Questions 21 through 30 test how good you are at catching mistakes in typing or printing. In each question, the name and addresses in Column II should be an exact copy of the name and address in Column I.
Mark your answer:
A. if there is no mistake in either name or address
B. if there is a mistake in both name and address
C. if there is a mistake only in the name
D. if there is a mistake only in the address

	COLUMN I	COLUMN II	
21.	Milos Yanocek 33-60 14 Street Long Island City, NY 11011	Milos Yanocek 33-60 14 Street Long Island City, NY 11001	21.____

22.	Alphonse Sabattelo 24 Minnetta Lane New York, NY 10006	Alphonse Sabbattelo 24 Minetta Lane New York, NY 10006	22.____
23.	Helen Stearn 5 Metroplitan Oval Bronx, NY 10462	Helene Steam 5 Metropolitan Oval Bronx, NY 10462	23.____
24.	Jacob Weisman 231 Francis Lewis Boulevard Forest Hills, NY 11325	Jacob Weisman 231 Francis Lewis Boulevard Forest Hill, NY 11325	24.____
25.	Riccardo Fuente 135 West 83 Street New York, NY 10024	Riccardo Fuentes 134 West 88 Street New York, NY 10024	25.____
26.	Dennis Lauber 52 Avenue D Brooklyn, NY 11216	Dennis Lauder 52 Avenue D Brooklyn, NY 11216	26.____
27.	Paul Cutter 195 Galloway Avenue Staten Island, NY 10356	Paul Cutter 175 Galloway Avenue Staten Island, NY 10365	27.____
28.	Sean Donnelly 45-58 41 Avenue Woodside, NY 11168	Sean Donnelly 45-58 41 Avenue Woodside, NY 11168	28.____
29.	Clyde Willot 1483 Rockaway Avenue Brooklyn, NY 11238	Clyde Willat 1483 Rockaway Avenue Brooklyn, NY 11238	29.____
30.	Michael Stanakis 419 Sheriden Avenue Staten Island, NY 10363	Michael Stanakis 419 Sheraden Avenue Staten Island, NY 10363	30.____

Questions 31-40.

DIRECTIONS: Questions 31 through 40 are to be answered SOLELY on the basis of the following information.

Column I consists of serial numbers of dollar bills. Column II shows different ways of arranging the corresponding serial numbers.

The serial numbers of dollar bills in Column I begin and end with a capital letter and have an eight-digit number in between. The serial numbers in Column I are to be arranged according to the following rules:

First: In alphabetical order according to the first letter.
Second: When two or more serial numbers have the same first letter, in alphabetical order according to the last letter.
Third: When two or more serial numbers have the same first and last letters, in numerical order, beginning with the lowest number.

The serial numbers in Column I are numbered (1) through (5) in the order in which they are listed. In Column II, the numbers (1) through (5) are arranged in four different ways to show different arrangements of the corresponding serial numbers. Choose the answer in Column II in which the serial numbers are arranged according to the above rules.
SAMPLE QUESTION:

COLUMN I		COLUMN II	
(1)	E75044127B	(A)	4, 1, 3, 2, 5
(2)	B96399104A	(B)	4, 1 2, 3, 5
(3)	B93939086A	(C)	4, 3, 2 5, 1
(4)	B47064465H	(D)	3, 2, 5, 4, 1
(5)	B99040922A		

In the sample question, the four serial numbers starting with B should be put before the serial numbers starting with E. The serial numbers starting with B and ending with A should be put before the serial number starting with B and ending with H. The three serial numbers starting with B and ending with A should be listed in numerical order, beginning with the lowest number. The correct way to arrange the serial numbers, therefore, is
(3) B93939086A
(2) B96399104A
(5) B99040922A
(4) B47064465H
(1) B75044127B

Since the order of arrangement is 3, 2, 5, 4, 1, the answer to the sample question is (D).

	COLUMN I			COLUMN II	
31. (1)	P44343324Y	A.	2, 3, 1, 4, 5	31.____
(2)	P44141341S	B.	1, 5, 3, 2, 4	
(3)	P44141431L	C.	4, 2, 3, 5, 1	
(4)	P41143413W	D.	5, 3, 2, 4, 1	
(5)	P44313433H			
32. (1)	D89077275M	A.	3, 2, 5, 3, 1	32.____
(2)	D98073724N	B.	1, 4, 3, 2, 5	
(3)	D90877274N	C.	4, 1, 5, 2, 3	
(4)	D98877275M	D.	1, 3, 2, 5, 3	
(5)	D98873725N			

33.	(1)	H32548137E	A. 2, 4, 5, 1, 3	33.____
	(2)	H35243178A	B. 1, 5, 2, 3, 4	
	(3)	H35284378F	C. 1, 5, 2, 4, 3	
	(4)	H35288337A	D. 2, 1, 5, 3, 4	
	(5)	H32883173B		
34.	(1)	K24165039H	A. 4, 2, 5, 3, 1	34.____
	(2)	F24106599A	B. 2, 3, 4, 1, 5	
	(3)	L21406639G	C. 4, 2, 5, 1, 3	
	(4)	C24156093A	D. 1, 3, 4, 5, 2	
	(5)	K24165593D		
35.	(1)	H79110642E	A. 2, 1, 3, 5, 4	35.____
	(2)	H79101928E	B. 2, 1, 4, 5, 3	
	(3)	A79111567F	C. 3, 5, 2, 1, 4	
	(4)	H79111796E	D. 4, 3, 5, 1, 2	
	(5)	A79111618F		
36.	(1)	P16388385W	A. 3, 4, 5, 2, 1	36.____
	(2)	R16388335V	B. 2, 3, 4, 5, 1	
	(3)	P16383835W	C. 2, 4, 3, 1, 5	
	(4)	R18386865V	D. 3, 1, 5, 2, 4	
	(5)	P18686865W		
37.	(1)	B42271749G	A. 4, 1, 5, 2, 3	37.____
	(2)	B42271779G	B. 4, 1, 2, 5, 3	
	(3)	E43217779G	C. 1, 2, 4, 5, 3	
	(4)	B42874119C	D. 5, 3, 1, 2, 4	
	(5)	E42817749G		
38.	(1)	M57906455S	A. 4, 1, 5, 3, 2	38.____
	(2)	N87077758S	B. 3, 4, 1, 5, 2	
	(3)	N87707757B	C. 4, 1, 5, 2, 3	
	(4)	M57877759B	D. 1, 5, 3, 2, 4	
	(5)	M57906555S		
39.	(1)	C69336894Y	A. 2, 5, 3, 1, 4	39.____
	(2)	C69336684V	B. 3, 2, 5, 1, 4	
	(3)	C69366887W	C. 3, 1, 4, 5, 2	
	(4)	C69366994Y	D. 2, 5, 1, 3, 4	
	(5)	C69336865V		
40.	(1)	A56247181D	A. 1, 5, 3, 2, 4	40.____
	(2)	A56272128P	B. 3, 1, 5, 2, 4	
	(3)	H56247128D	C. 3, 2, 1, 5, 4	
	(4)	H56272288P	D. 1, 5, 2, 3, 4	
	(5)	A56247188D		

Questions 41-48.

DIRECTIONS: Questions 41 through 48 are to be answered SOLELY on the basis of the following passage.

Auto theft is prevalent and costly. In 2020, 486,000 autos valued at over $500 million were stolen. About 28 percent of the inhabitants of federal prisons are there as a result of conviction of interstate auto theft under the Dyer Act. In California alone, auto thefts cost the criminal justice system approximately $60 million yearly.

The great majority of auto theft is for temporary use rather than resale, as evidenced by the fact that 88 percent of autos stolen in 2020 were recovered. In Los Angeles, 64 percent of stolen autos that were recovered were found within two days and about 80 percent within a week. Chicago reports that 71 percent of the recovered autos were found within four miles of the point of theft. The FBI estimates that 8 percent of stolen cars are taken for the purpose of stripping them for parts, 12 percent for resale, and 5 percent for use in another crime. Auto thefts are primarily juvenile acts. Although only 21 percent of all arrests for nontraffic offenses in 2020 were of individuals under 18 years of age, 63 percent of auto theft arrests were of persons under 18. Auto theft represents the start of many criminal careers; in an FBI sample of juvenile auto theft offenders, 41 percent had no prior arrest record.

41. In the above passage, the discussion of the reasons for auto theft does NOT include the percent of 41.____
   A. autos stolen by prior offenders
   B. recovered stolen autos found close to the point of theft
   C. stolen autos recovered within a week
   D. stolen autos which were recovered

42. Assuming the figures in the above passage remain constant, you may logically estimate the cost of auto thefts to the California criminal justice system over a five-year period beginning in 2020 to have been about _____ million. 42.____
   A. $200 B. $300 C. $440 D. $500

43. According to the above passage, the percent of stolen autos in Los Angeles which were not recovered within a week was _____ percent. 43.____
   A. 12 B. 20 C. 29 D. 36

44. According to the above passage, MOST auto thefts are committed by 44.____
   A. former inmates of federal prisons
   B. juveniles
   C. persons with a prior arrest record
   D. residents of large cities

45. According to the above passage, MOST autos are stolen for 45.____
   A. resale
   B. stripping of parts
   C. temporary use
   D. use in another crime

46. According to the above passage, the percent of persons arrested for auto theft who were under 18 46.____
    A. equals nearly the same percent of stolen autos which were recovered
    B. equals nearly two-thirds of the total number of persons arrested for nontraffic offenses
    C. is the same as the percent of persons arrested for nontraffic offenses who were under 18
    D. is three times the percent of persons arrested for nontraffic offenses who were under 18

47. An APPROPRIATE title for the above passage is 47.____
    A. How Criminal Careers Begin
    B. Recovery of Stolen Cars
    C. Some Statistics on Auto Theft
    D. The Costs of Auto Theft

48. Based on the above passage, the number of cars taken for use in another crime in 2020 was 48.____
    A. 24,300
    B. 38,880
    C. 48,600
    D. 58,320

Questions 49-55.

DIRECTIONS: Questions 49 through 55 are to be answered SOLELY on the basis of the following passage.

Burglar alarms are designed to detect intrusion automatically. Robbery alarms enable a victim of a robbery or an attack to signal for help. Such devices can be located in elevators, hallways, homes and apartments, businesses and factories, and subways, as well as on the street in high-crime areas. Alarms could deter some potential criminals from attacking targets so protected. If alarms were prevalent and not visible, then they might serve to suppress crime generally. In addition, of course, the alarms can summon the police when they are needed.

All alarms must perform three functions: sensing or initiation of the signal, transmission of the signal, and annunciation of the alarm. A burglar alarm needs a sensor to detect human presence or activity in an unoccupied enclosed area like a building or a room. A robbery victim would initiate the alarm by closing a foot or wall switch, or by triggering a portable transmitter which would send the alarm signal to a remote receiver. The signal can sound locally as a loud noise to frighten away a criminal, or it can be sent silently by wire to a central agency. A centralized annunciator requires either private lines from each alarmed point, or the transmission of some information on the location of the signal.

49. A conclusion which follows LOGICALLY from the above passage is that 49.____
    A. burglar alarms employ sensor devices; robbery alarms make use of initiation devices
    B. robbery alarms signal intrusion without the help of the victim; burglar alarms require the victim to trigger a switch
    C. robbery alarms sound locally; burglar alarms are transmitted to a central agency
    D. the mechanisms for a burglar alarm and a robbery alarm are alike

50. According to the above passage, alarms can be located 50.____
    A. in a wide variety of settings
    B. only in enclosed areas
    C. at low cost in high-crime areas
    D. only in places where potential criminal will be deterred

51. According to the above passage, which of the following is ESSENTIAL if a signal is to be received in a central office? 51.____
    A. A foot or wall switch
    B. A noise producing mechanism
    C. A portable reception device
    D. Information regarding the location of the source

52. According to the above passage, an alarm system can function WITHOUT a 52.____
    A. centralized annunciating device
    B. device to stop the alarm
    C. sensing or initiating device
    D. transmission device

53. According to the above passage, the purpose of robbery alarms is to 53.____
    A. find out automatically whether a robbery has taken place
    B. lower the crime rate in high-crime areas
    C. make a loud noise to frighten away the criminal
    D. provide a victim with the means to signal for help

54. According to the above passage, alarms might aid in lessening crime if they were 54.____
    A. answered promptly by police
    B. completely automatic
    C. easily accessible to victims
    D. hidden and widespread

55. Of the following, the BEST title for the above passage is 55.____
    A. Detection of Crime By Alarms
    B. Lowering the Crime Rate
    C. Suppression of Crime
    D. The Prevention of Robbery

KEY (CORRECT ANSWERS)

1.	C	11.	C	21.	D	31.	D	41.	A	51.	D
2.	C	12.	D	22.	B	32.	B	42.	B	52.	A
3.	B	13.	A	23.	C	33.	A	43.	B	53.	D
4.	B	14.	D	24.	A	34.	C	44.	B	54.	D
5.	B	15.	A	25.	B	35.	C	45.	C	55.	A
6.	D	16.	A	26.	C	36.	D	46.	D		
7.	C	17.	B	27.	D	37.	B	47.	C		
8.	B	18.	B	28.	A	38.	A	48.	A		
9.	C	19.	B	29.	B	39.	A	49.	A		
10.	D	20.	B	30.	D	40.	D	50.	A		

EXAMINATION SECTION

TEST 1

DIRECTIONS: Each question or incomplete statement is followed by several suggested answers or completions. Select the one that BEST answers the question or completes the statement. *PRINT THE LETTER OF THE CORRECT ANSWER IN THE SPACE AT THE RIGHT.*

Questions 1-6.

DIRECTIONS: Questions 1 through 6 are to be answered SOLELY on the basis of the numbered boxes on the Arrest Report and paragraph below.

ARREST REPORT

1. Arrest Number	2. Precinct of Arrest		3. Date/Time of Arrest	4. Defendant's Name		5. Defendant's Address
6. Defendant's Date of Birth	7. Sex	8. Race	9. Height	10. Weight	11. Location of Arrest	12. Date and Time of Occurrence
13. Location of Occurrence	14. Complaint Number		15. Victim's Name		16. Victim's Address	17. Victim's Date of Birth
18. Precinct of Complaint	19. Arresting Officer's Name		20. Shield Number		21. Assigned Unit Precinct	2. Date of Complaint

On Friday, December 13 at 11:45 P.M., while leaving a store at 235 Spring Street, Grace O'Connell, a white female, 5'2" 130 lbs., was approached by a white male, 5'11", 200 lbs., who demanded her money and jewelry. As the man ran and turned down River Street, Police Officer William James, Shield Number 31724, assigned to the 14th Precinct, gave chase and apprehended him in front of 523 River Street. The prisoner, Gerald Grande, who resides at 17 Water Street, was arrested at 12:05 A.M., was charged with robbery, and taken to the 13th Precinct, where he was assigned Arrest Number 53048. Miss O'Connell, who resides at 275 Spring St., was given Complaint Number 822460.

1. On the basis of the Arrest Report and the above paragraph, the CORRECT entry for Box Number 3 should be 1.____
   A. 11:45 P.M.,12/13
   B. 11:45 P.M., 12/14
   C. 12:05 A.M., 12/13
   D. 12:05 A.M., 12/14

2. On the basis of the Arrest Report and the above paragraph, the CORRECT entry for Box Number 21 should be 2.____
   A. 12th Precinct
   B. 14th Precinct
   C. Mounted Unit
   D. 32nd Precinct

3. On the basis of the Arrest Report and the above paragraph, the CORRECT entry for Box Number 11 should be 3.____
   A. 235 Spring St.
   B. 523 River St.
   C. 275 Spring St.
   D. 17 Water St.

4. On the basis of the Arrest Report and the above paragraph, the CORRECT entry for Box Number 2 should be 4.____
   A. 13th Precinct
   B. 14th Precinct
   C. Mounted Unit
   D. 32nd Precinct

5. On the basis of the Arrest Report and the above paragraph, the CORRECT entry for Box Number 13 should be 5.____
   A. 523 River St.
   B. 17 Water St.
   C. 275 Spring St.
   D. 235 Spring St.

6. On the basis of the Arrest Report and the above paragraph, the CORRECT entry for Box Number 14 should be 6.____
   A. 53048
   B. 31724
   C. 12/13
   D. 82460

Questions 7-10.

DIRECTIONS: Questions 7 through 10 are to be answered SOLELY on the basis of the following information.

You are required to file various documents in file drawers which are labeled according to the following pattern:

DOCUMENTS

MEMOS		LETTERS		REPORTS		INQUIRIES	
File	Subject	File	Subject	File	Subject	File	Subject
84PM1	(A-L)	84PC1	(A-L)	84PR1	(A-L)	84PQ1	(A-L)
84PM2	(M-Z)	84PC2	(M-Z)	84PR2	(M-Z)	84PQ2	(M-Z)

7. A letter dealing with a burglary should be filed in the drawer labeled 7.____
   A. 84PM1
   B. 84PC1
   C. 84PR1
   D. 84PQ2

8. A report on *Statistics* should be found in the drawer labeled 8.____
   A. 84PM1
   B. 84PC2
   C. 84PR2
   D. 84PQ2

9. An inquiry is received about parade permit procedures. It should be filed in the drawer labeled 9.____
   A. 84PM2
   B. 84PC1
   C. 84PR1
   D. 84PQ2

10. A police officer has a question about a robbery report you filed. You should pull this file from the drawer labeled 10.____
    A. 84PM1
    B. 84PM2
    C. 84PR1
    D. 84PR2

Questions 11-18.

DIRECTIONS: Questions 11 through 18 are to be answered SOLELY on the basis of the following information.

Below are listed the code number, name, and area of investigation of six detective units. Each question describes a crime.

For each question, choose the option (A, B, C, or D) which contains the code number for the detective unit responsible for handling that crime.

DETECTIVE UNITS

Unit Code No.	Unit Name	Unit's Area of Investigation
01	Senior Citizens Unit	All robberies of senior citizens 65 years or older
02	Major Case Unit	Any bank robbery; a commercial robbery where value of goods or money stolen is over $25,000
03	Robbery Unit	Any commercial, non-bank robbery where the value of the stolen goods or money is $25,000 or less; robberies of individuals under 65 years of age
04	Fraud and Larceny Unit	Confidence games and pickpockets
05	Special Investigations Unit	Burglaries of premises where the value of goods removed or monies taken is $15,000 or less
06	Burglary Unit	Burglaries of premises where the value of goods removed or monies taken is over $15,000

11. Mrs. Green calls the precinct and reports that her apartment was burglarized while she was on vacation and that precious jewelry and silverware, valued at $27,000, were taken. 11.____
To which unit code number should her complaint be referred?
A. 05 B. 02 C. 03 D. 06

12. Sylvia Bailey, Manager of the Building and Loan Savings Bank, reports that a man handed one of her tellers a note stating, *This is a robbery*. He had a gun and demanded money. The teller gave the man $500 in small bills, and the man then left. 12.____
To which unit code should the complaint be referred?
A. 02 B. 06 C. 03 D. 05

13. Mrs. Miniver, a 67-year-old widow, states that she was beaten and robbed by two men in the elevator of her apartment building. 13.____
To which unit code number should the complaint be referred?
A. 06 B. 01 C. 03 D. 02

14. Mr. Whipple, Manager of T.V.A. Supermarket, reports that during the night someone entered the store and removed merchandise valued at $12,500. 14.____
To which unit code number should the complaint be referred?
A. 05 B. 03 C. 06 D. 02

15. Mr. Gold, owner of Gold's Jewelry Exchange, reports that two men, armed with shotguns, robbed his store and removed money and jewelry valued at $28,000. 15.____
To which unit code number should the complaint be referred?
A. 05 B. 03 C. 06 D. 02

16. Mr. Watson, a 62-year-old man, was walking in Central Park when he was approached by a man with a knife and was robbed of $72. 16.____
To which unit code number should the complaint be referred?
A. 01 B. 06 C. 03 D. 02

17. The Ace Jewelry Manufacturing Company was broken into over the weekend when the building was closed. The owner stated that $35,000 in gold, silver, diamonds, and jewelry were taken. 17.____
To which unit code number should the complaint be referred?
A. 02 B. 03 C. 06 D. 05

18. Mrs. Vargas, 62, reports that she gave Mr. Greene of the Starlite Realty Corporation $1,000 to locate a new apartment for her family. A week went by, and she never heard from Mr. Greene. She called the Starlite Realty Corporation, and they informed her that Mr. Greene never worked for Starlite Realty Corporation and that they have no record of the $1,000 deposit of Mrs. Vargas. 18.____
To which unit code number should the complaint be referred?
A. 04 B. 03 C. 01 D. 05

Questions 19-24.

DIRECTIONS: Questions 19 through 24 consist of sentences which contain examples of correct or incorrect English usage. Examine each sentence with reference to grammar, spelling, punctuation, and capitalization. Choose one of the following options that would be BEST for correct English usage:
A. The sentence is correct.
B. There is one mistake.
C. There are two mistakes.
D. There are three mistakes.

19. Mrs. Fitzgerald came to the 59th Precinct to retreive her property which were stolen earlier in the week. 19.____

20. The two officer's responded to the call, only to find that the perpatrator and the victim have left the scene. 20.____

21. Mr. Coleman called the 61st Precinct to report that, upon arriving at his store, he discovered that there was a large hole in the wall and that three boxes of radios were missing 21.____

22. The Administrative Leiutenant of the 62nd Precinct held a meeting which was attended by all the civilians, assigned to the Precinct. 22.____

23. Three days after the robbery occured the detective apprahended two suspects and recovered the stolen items. 23.____

24. The Community Affairs Officer of the 64th Precinct is the liaison between the Precinct and the community; he works closely with various community organizations, and elected officials. 24.____

Questions 25-32.

DIRECTIONS: Questions 25 through 32 are to be answered on the basis of the following paragraph, which contains some deliberate errors in spelling and/or grammar and/or punctuation. Each line of the paragraph is preceded by a number. There are 9 lines and 9 numbers.

Line No.	Paragraph Line
1	The protection of life and property are, one of
2	the oldest and most important functions of a city.
3	New York city has its own full-time police Agency.
4	The police Department has the power an it shall
5	be there duty to preserve the Public piece,
6	prevent crime detect and arrest offenders, suppress
7	riots, protect the rites of persons and property, etc.
8	The maintainance of sound relations with the community they
9	serve is an important function of law enforcement officers.

25. How many errors are contained in line one? 25.____
A. One B. Two C. Three D. None

26. How many errors are contained in line two? 26.____
A. One B. Two C. Three D. None

27. How many errors are contained in line three? 27.____
A. One B. Two C. Three D. None

28. How many errors are contained in line four? 28.____
A. One B. Two C. Three D. None

29. How many errors are contained in line five? 29.____
A. One B. Two C. Three D. None

30. How many errors are contained in line six? 30.____
A. One B. Two C. Three D. None

31. How many errors are contained in line seven? 31.____
A. One B. Two C. Three D. None

32. How many errors are contained in line eight? 32.____
A. One B. Two C. Three D. None

Questions 33-40.

DIRECTIONS: Questions 33 through 40 are to be answered on the basis of the material contained in the INDEX OF CRIME IN CENTRAL CITY, U.S.A. 2011-2020 appearing below. Certain information is various columns is deliberately left blank.
The correct answer (A, B, C, or D) to these questions requires you to make computations that will enable you to fill in the blanks correctly.

INDEX OF CRIME IN CENTRAL CITY, U.S.A., 2011-2020

	Crime Index Total	Violent Crime[1]	Property Crime[2]	Murder	Forcible Rape	Robbery	Aggra-vated Assault	Burglary	Larceny Theft	Motor Vehicle Theft
2011	8,717	875		19	51	385	420	2,565	4,347	930
2012	10,252	974	9278	20	55	443	456		5,262	977
2013	11,256	1,026	10,230	20		465	485	3,253	5,977	1,000
2014	11,304	986		18	58	420	490	3,089	6,270	959
2015	10,935	1,009	9,926	19	63	405	522	3,053	5,605	968
2016	11,140	1,061	10,079	19	67	417	558	3,104	5,983	992
2017	12,152	1,178	10,974	23	75	466	614	3,299	6,578	1,097
2018	13,294	1,308	11,986	23	83		654	3,759	7,113	1,114
2019	13,289	1,321	11,968	22	82	574	643	3,740	7,154	1,074
2020	12,856	1,285	11,571	22	77	536	650	3,415	7,108	1,048

33. What was the TOTAL number of Property Crimes in 2011? 33.____
A. 9,740 B. 10,252 C. 16,559 D. 7,842

34. What was the TOTAL number of Burglaries for 2012? 34.____
A. 2,062 B. 3,039 C. 3,259 D. 4,001

35. In 2020, the total number of Aggravated Assaults was MOST NEARLY what percent of the total number of Violent Crimes for that year? 35.____
A. 49.1 B. 46.3 C. 50.6 D. 41.7

36. In 2015, Property Crime was MOST NEARLY what percent of the Crime Index Total? 36.____
A. 90.8 B. 9.3 C. 10.1 D. 89.9

37. What was the TOTAL number of Property Crimes for 2014? 37.____
    A. 10,318 B. 11,304 C. 98 D. 10,808

38. What was the TOTAL number of Robberies for 2018? 38.____
    A. 654 B. 571 C. 548 D. 1,202

39. Robbery made up what percent of the TOTAL number of Violent Crimes for 2020? 39.____
    A. 68.8% B. 4.1% C. 21.9% D. 41.7%

40. What was the TOTAL number of Forcible Rapes for 2013? 40.____
    A. 47 B. 56 C. 55 D. 101

KEY (CORRECT ANSWERS)

1.	D	11.	D	21.	A	31.	A
2.	B	12.	A	22.	C	32.	A
3.	B	13.	B	23.	C	33.	D
4.	A	14.	A	24.	B	34.	B
5.	D	15.	D	25.	C	35.	C
6.	D	16.	C	26.	D	36.	A
7.	B	17.	C	27.	C	37.	A
8.	C	18.	A	28.	B	38.	C
9.	D	19.	C	29.	C	39.	D
10.	D	20.	D	30.	B	40.	B

TEST 2

DIRECTIONS: Each question or incomplete statement is followed by several suggested answers or completions. Select the one that BEST answers the question or completes the statement. *PRINT THE LETTER OF THE CORRECT ANSWER IN THE SPACE AT THE RIGHT.*

Questions 1-8.

DIRECTIONS: Each of Questions 1 through 8 consists of three lines of code letters and numbers. The numbers on each line should correspond to the code letters on the same line in accordance with the table below.

Code Letter	X	B	L	T	V	M	P	F	J	S
Corresponding Number	0	1	2	3	4	5	6	7	8	9

On some of the lines, an error exists in the coding. Compare the letters and numbers in each question carefully. If you find an error or errors on:

Only one of the lines in the question, mark your answer A;
Any two of the lines in the question, mark your answer B;
All three lines in the question, mark your answer C;
None of the lines in the question, mark your answer D.

SAMPLE QUESTION: MSXVLPT—5904263
SBFJLTP—9178246
XVMBTPF—8451367

In the above sample, the first line is correct since each code letter listed has the correct corresponding number. On the second line, an error exists because code letter T should have number 3 instead of number 4. On the third line, an error exists because the code letter X should have the number 0 instead of the number 8. Since there are errors on two of the three lines, the correct answer is B.

1. VFSTPLM—4793625 1.____
SBXFLTP—9017236
BT[JFSV—1358794

2. TSLFVPJ—3927468 2.____
JLFTVXS—8273409
MVSXBFL—5490172

3. XFTJSVT—0739843 3.____
VFMTFLB—4753721
LTFJSFM—2378985

4. SJMSJVL—9859742 4.____
VFBXMPF—3710568
PFPXLBS—7670219

5. MFPXVFP—5764076 5.____
PTFJBLX—6378120
VXSVSTB—4094931

6. BXFPVJT—1076483 6.____
STFMVLT—9375423
TXPBTTM—3061335

7. VLSBLVP—4290246 7.____
FPSFBMV—7679154
XTMXMLL—0730522

8. JFVPMTJ—8746538 8.____
TFPMXBL—3765012
TJSFMFX—4987570

Questions 9-18.

DIRECTIONS: Questions 9 through 18 each consists of two columns, each containing four lines of names, numbers and/or addresses. For each question, compare the lines in Column I with the lines in Column II to see if they match exactly, and mark your answer (A, B, C, or D) according to the following instructions:
A. all four lines match exactly
B. only three lines match exactly
C. only two lines match exactly
D. only one line matches exactly

9.	(1)	Earl Hodgson	Earl Hodgson	9.____
	(2)	1409870	1408970	
	(3)	Shore Ave.	Schore Ave.	
	(4)	Macon Rd.	Macon Rd.	
10.	(1)	9671485	9671485	10.____
	(2)	470 Astor Court	470 Astor Court	
	(3)	Halprin, Phillip	Halperin, Phillip	
	(4)	Frank D. Poliseo	Frank D. Poliseo	
11.	(1)	Tandem Associates	Tandom Associates	11.____
	(2)	144-17 Northern Blvd.	144-17 Northern Blvd.	
	(3)	Alberta Forchi	Albert Forchi	
	(4)	Kings Park, NY 10751	Kings Point, NY 10751	
12.	(1)	Bertha C. McCormack	Bertha C. McCormack	12.____
	(2)	Clayton, MO	Clayton, MO	
	(3)	976-4242	976-4242	
	(4)	New City, NY 10951	New City, NY 10951	

13.	(1)	George C. Morill	George C. Morrill	13.____
	(2)	Columbia, SC 29201	Columbia, SD 29201	
	(3)	Louis Ingham	Louis Ingham	
	(4)	3406 Forest Ave.	3406 Forest Ave.	
14.	(1)	506 S. Elliott Pl.	506 S. Elliott Pl.	14.____
	(2)	Herbert Hall	Hurbert Hall	
	(3)	4712 Rockaway Pkway	4712 Rockaway Pkway	
	(4)	169 E. 7 St.	169 E. 7 St.	
15.	(1)	345 Park Ave.	345 Park Pl.	15.____
	(2)	Colman Oven Corp.	Coleman Oven Corp.	
	(3)	Robert Conte	Robert Conti	
	(4)	6179846	6179846	
16.	(1)	Grigori Schierber	Grigori Schierber	16.____
	(2)	Des Moines, Iowa	Des Moines, Iowa	
	(3)	Gouverneur Hospital	Gouverneur Hospital	
	(4)	91-35 Cresskill Pl.	91-35 Cresskill Pl.	
17.	(1)	Jeffery Janssen	Jeffrey Janssen	17.____
	(2)	8041071	8041071	
	(3)	40 Rockefeller Plaza	40 Rockafeller Plaza	
	(4)	407 6 St.	406 7 St.	
18.	(1)	5971996	5871996	18.____
	(2)	3113 Knickerbocker Ave.	3113 Knickerbocker Ave.	
	(3)	8434 Boston Post Rd.	8424 Boston Post Rd.	
	(4)	Penn Station	Penn Station	

Questions 19-22.

DIRECTIONS: Questions 19 through 22 are to be answered by looking at the 4 groups of names and addresses listed below (I, II, III, and IV) and then finding out the number of groups that have their corresponding numbered lines exactly the same.

	Group I	Group II
Line 1	Ingersoll Public Library	Ingersoil Public Library
Line 2	Reference and Research Dept.	Reference and Research Dept.
Line 3	95-12 238 St.	95-12 238 St.
Line 4	East Elmhurst, N.Y. 11357	East Elmhurst, N.Y. 11357

	Group III	Group IV
Line 1	Ingersoll Public Library	Ingersoll Poblic Library
Line 2	Reference and Research Dept.	Referance and Research Dept.
Line 3	92-15 283 St.	95-12 283 St.
Line 4	East Elmhurst, N.Y. 11357	East Elmhurst, N.Y. 1357

19. In how many groups is line one exactly the same? 19.____
    A. Two B. Three C. Four D. None

20. In how many groups is line two exactly the same? 20.____
    A. Two B. Three C. Four D. None

21. In how many groups is line three exactly the same? 20.____
    A. Two B. Three C. Four D. None

22. In how many groups is line four exactly the same? 22.____
    A. Two B. Three C. Four E. None

Questions 23-26.

DIRECTIONS: Questions 23 through 26 are to be answered by looking at the 4 groups of names and addresses listed below (I, II, III, and IV) and then finding out the number of groups that have their corresponding numbered lines exactly the same.

	Group I	Group II
Line 1	Richmond General Hospital	Richman General Hospital
Line 2	Geriatric Clinic	Geriatric Clinic
Line 3	3975 Paerdegat St.	3975 Peardegat St.
Line 4	Loudonville, New York 11538	Londonville, New York 11538

	Group III	Group IV
Line 1	Richmond General Hospital	Richmend General Hospital
Line 2	Geriatric Clinic	Geriatric Clinic
Line 3	3795 Paerdegat St.	3975 Paerdegat St.
Line 4	Loudonville, New York 11358	Loudonville, New York 11538

23. In how many groups is line one exactly the same? 23.____
    A. Two B. Three C. Four D. None

24. In how many groups is line two exactly the same? 24.____
    A. Two B. Three C. Four D. None

25. In how many groups is line three exactly the same? 25.____
    A. Two B. Three C. Four D. None

26. In how many groups is line four exactly the same? 26.____
    A. Two B. Three C. Four D. None

Questions 27-34.

DIRECTIONS: Each of Questions 27 through 34 consists of four or six numbered names. For each question, choose the option (A, B, C, or D) which indicates the order in which the names should be filed in accordance with the following file instructions:

- File alphabetically according to last name, then first name, then middle initial.
- File according to each successive letter within a name.
- When comparing two names where the letters in the longer name are identical with the corresponding letters in the shorter name, the shorter name is filed first.
- When the last names are the same, initials are always filed before names beginning with the same letter.

27. I. Ralph Robinson
    II. Alfred Ross
    III. Luis Robles
    IV. James Roberts
    The CORRECT filing sequence for the above names should be
    A. IV, II, I, III B. I, IV, III, II C. III, IV, I, II D. IV, I, III, II

27.____

28. I. Irwin Goodwin
    II. Inez Gonzalez
    III. Irene Goodman
    IV. Ira S. Goodwin
    V. Ruth I. Goldstein
    VI. M.B. Goodman
    The CORRECT filing sequence for the above names should be
    A. V, II, I, IV, III, VI B. V, II, VI, III, IV, I
    C. V, II, III, VI, IV, I D. V, II, III, VI, I, IV

28.____

29. I. George Allan
    II. Gregory Allen
    III. Gary Allen
    IV. George Allen
    The CORRECT filing sequence for the above names should be
    A. IV, III, I, II B. I, IV, II, III C. III, IV, I, II D. I, III, IV, II

29.____

30. I. Simon Kauffman
    II. Leo Kauffman
    III. Robert Kaufmann
    IV. Paul Kauffman
    The CORRECT filing sequence for the above names should be
    A. I, IV, II, III B. II, IV, I, III C. III, II, IV, I D. I, II, III, IV

30.____

31. I. Roberta Williams
    II. Robin Wilson
    III. Roberta Wilson
    IV. Robin Williams
    The CORRECT filing sequence for the above names should be
    A. III, II, IV, I B. I, IV, III, II C. I, II, III, IV D. III, I, II, IV

31.____

32. I. Lawrence Shultz 32.___
II. Albert Schultz
III. Theodore Schwartz
IV. Thomas Schwarz
V. Alvin Schultz
VI. Leonard Shultz
The CORRECT filing sequence for the above names should be
A. II, V, III, IV, I, VI
B. IV, III, V, I, II, VI
C. II, V, I, VI, III, IV
D. I, VI, II, V, III, IV

33. I. McArdle 33.____
II. Mayer
III. Maletz
IV. McNiff
V. Meyer
VI. MacMahon
The CORRECT filing sequence for the above names should be
A. I, IV, VI, III, II, V
B. II, I, IV, VI, III, V
C. VI, III, II, I, IV, V
D. VI, III, II, V, I, IV

34. I. Jack E. Johnson 34.____
II. R.H. Jackson
III. Bertha Jackson
IV. J.T. Johnson
V. Ann Johns
VI. John Jacobs
The CORRECT filing sequence for the above names should be
A. II, III, VI, V, IV, I
B. III, II, VI, V, IV, I
C. VI, II, III, I, V, IV
D. III, II, VI, IV, V, I

Questions 35-40.

DIRECTIONS: Questions 35 through 40 are to be answered SOLELY on the basis of the following passage.

An aide assigned to the Complaint Room must be familiar with the various forms used by that office. Some of these forms and their uses are:

Complaint Report:	Used to record information on or information about crimes reported to the Police Department.
Complaint Report Follow-Up:	Used to record additional information after the initial complaint report has been filed
Aided Card:	Used to record information pertaining to sick and injured persons aided by the police.
Accident Report:	Used to record information on or information about injuries and/or property damage involving motorized vehicles.
Property Vouch:	Used to record information on or information about property which comes into possession of the Police Department. (Motorized vehicles are not included.)

Auto Voucher: Used to record information on or information about a motorized vehicle which comes into possession of the Police Department.

35. Mr. Brown walks into the police precinct and informs the Administrative Aide that, while he was at work, someone broke into his apartment and removed property belonging to him. He does not know everything that was taken, but he wants to make a report now and will make a list of what was taken and bring it in later. 35.____
According to the above passage, the CORRECT form to use in this situation should be the
A. Property Voucher
B. Complaint Report
C. Complaint Report Follow-Up
D. Aided Card

36. Mrs. Wilson telephones the precinct and informs the Administrative Aide she wishes to report additional property which was taken from her apartment. The Administrative Aide finds a Complaint Report had been previously filed for Mrs. Wilson. 36.____
According to the above passage, the CORRECT form to use in this situation should be the
A. Property Voucher
B. Complaint Report
C. Complaint Report Follow-Up
D. Aided Card

37. Police Officer Jones walks into the Complaint Room and informs the Administrative Aide that, while he was on patrol, he observed a woman fall to the sidewalk and remain there, apparently hurt. He comforted the injured woman and called for an ambulance, which came and brought the woman to the hospital. 37.____
According to the above passage, the CORRECT form on which to record this information should be the
A. Accident Report
B. Complaint Report
C. Complaint Report Follow-Up
D. Aided Card

38. Police Officer Smith informed the Administrative Aide assigned to the Complaint Room that Mr. Green, while crossing the street, was struck by a motorcycle and had to be taken to the hospital. 38.____
According to the above passage, the facts regarding this incident should be recorded on which one of the following forms?
A. Accident Report
B. Complaint Report
C. Complaint Report Follow-Up
D. Aided Card

39. Police Officer Williams reports to the Administrative Aide assigned to the Complaint Room that he and his partner, Police Officer Murphy, found an auto which was reported stolen and had the auto towed into the police garage. 39.____
Of the following forms listed in the above passage, which is the CORRECT one to use to record this information?
A. Property Voucher
B. Auto Voucher
C. Complaint Report Follow-Up
D. Complaint Report

40. Administrative Aide Lopez has been assigned to the Complaint Room. During her tour of duty, a person who does not identify herself hands Ms. Lopez a purse. The person states that she found the purse on the street. She then leaves the station house. 40.____
According to the information in the above passage, which is the CORRECT form to fill out to record the incident?
A. Property Voucher
B. Auto Voucher
C. Complaint Report Follow-Up
D. Complaint Report

KEY (CORRECT ANSWERS)

1.	B	11.	D	21.	A	31.	B
2.	D	12.	A	22.	C	32.	A
3.	B	13.	C	23.	A	33.	C
4.	C	14.	B	24.	C	34.	B
5.	A	15.	D	25.	A	35.	B
6.	D	16.	A	26.	A	36.	C
7.	C	17.	D	27.	D	37.	D
8.	A	18.	C	28.	C	38.	A
9.	C	19.	A	29.	D	39.	B
10.	B	20.	B	30.	B	40.	A

EXAMINATION SECTION

TEST 1

DIRECTIONS: Each question or incomplete statement is followed by several suggested answers or completions. Select the one that BEST answers the question or completes the statement. *PRINT THE LETTER OF THE CORRECT ANSWER IN THE SPACE AT THE RIGHT.*

Questions 1-8.

DIRECTIONS: Each of Questions 1 through 8 consists of a statement which contains a word (one of those underlined) that is either incorrectly used because it is not in keeping with the meaning the quotation is evidently intended to convey or is misspelled. There is only one INCORRECT word in each quotation. Of the four underlined words, determine if the first one should be replaced by the word lettered A, the second replaced by the word lettered B, the third replaced by the word lettered C, or the fourth replaced by the word lettered D. Print the letter of the replacement word you have selected in the space at the right.

1. Whether one depends on fluorescent or artificial light or both, adequate standards should be maintained by means of systematic tests. 1.____
   A. natural B. safeguards C. established D. routine

2. An officer has to be prepared to assume his knowledge as a social scientist in the community. 2.____
   A. forced B. role C. philosopher D. street

3. It is practically impossible to indicate whether a sentence is too long simply by measuring its length. 3.____
   A. almost B. tell C. very D. guessing

4. Strong leaders are required to organize a community for delinquency prevention and for dissemination of organized crime and drug addiction. 4.____
   A. tactics B. important C. control D. meetings

5. The demonstrators, who were taken to the Criminal Courts building in Manhattan (because it was large enough to accommodate them), contended that the arrests were unwarrented. 5.____
   A. exhibitors B. legions C. adjudicate D. unwarranted

6. The were guaranteed a calm atmosphere, free from harassment, which would be conducive to quiet consideration of the indictments. 6.____
   A. guaranteed B. atmospher C. harassment D. inditements

7. The alleged killer was occasionally permitted to excercise in the corridor. 7.____
   A. alledged B. ocasionally C. permited D. exercise

8. Defense <u>counsel</u> stated, in <u>affect</u>, that <u>their</u> conduct was <u>permissable</u> under the First Amendment. 8.____
   A. council B. effect C. there D. permissable

Questions 9-12.

DIRECTIONS: Each of the two sentences in Questions 9 through 12 may be correct or may contain errors in punctuation, capitalization, or grammar. If there is an error only in sentence I, mark your answer A. If there is an error in both sentence I and sentence II, mark your answer C. If both sentence I and sentence II are correct, mark your answer D.

9. I. It is very annoying to have a pencil sharpener, which is not in working order. 9.____
   II. Officer Blake checked the door of Joe's Restaurant and found that the lock has been jammed.

10. I. When you are studying a good textbook is important. 10.____
    II. He said he would divide the money equally between you and me.

11. I. Since he went on the city council a year ago, one of his primary concerns has been safety in the streets. 11.____
    II. After waiting in the doorway for about 15 minutes, a black sedan appeared.

12. I. The question is, "What is the difference between a lawful and an unlawful demonstration?" 12.____
    II. The captain assigned two detectives, John and I, to the investigation.

Questions 13-14.

DIRECTIONS: In each of Questions 13 and 14, the four sentences are from a paragraph in a report. They are not in the right order. Which of the following arrangement is the BEST one?

13. I. Most organizations favor one of the types but always include the others to a lesser degree. 13.____
    II. However, we can detect a definite trend toward greater use of symbolic control.
    III. We suggest that our local police agencies are today primarily utilizing material control.
    IV. Control can be classified into three types: physical, material, and symbolic.
    The CORRECT answer is:
    A. IV, II III, I B. II, I, IV, III C. III, IV, II, I D. IV, I, III, II

14. I They can and do take advantage of ancient political and geographical boundaries, which often give them sanctuary from effective policy activity. 14.____
    II. This country is essentially a country of small police forces, each operating independently within the limits of its jurisdiction.

III. The boundaries that define and limit police operations do not hinder the movement of criminals, of course.
IV. The machinery of law enforcement in America is fragmented, complicated, and frequently overlapping.

The CORRECT answer is

A. III, I, II, IV B. II, IV, I, III C. IV, II, III, I D. IV, III, II, I

15. Generally, the frequency with which reports are to be submitted or the length of the interval which they cover should depend MAINLY on the 15.____
   A. amount of time needed to prepare the reports
   B. degree of comprehensiveness required in the reports
   C. availability of the data to be included in the reports
   D. extent of the variations in the data with the passage of time

16. Suppose you have to write a report on a serious infraction of rules by one of the police administrative aides you supervise. The circumstances in which the infraction occurred are quite complicated. 16.____
   The BEST way to organize this report would be to
   A. give all points equal emphasis throughout the report
   B. include more than one point in a paragraph only if necessary to equalize the size of paragraphs
   C. place the least important points before the most important points
   D. present each significant point in a separate paragraph

17. Suppose that police expenses in the city in a certain year amounted to 7.5% of total expenses. 17.____
   In indicating this percentage on a *pie* or circular chart, which is 360, the size of the angle between the two radiuses would be MOST NEARLY
   A. 3.7 B. 7.5 C. 27 D. 54

18. Suppose that in police precinct A, where there are 4,180 children, 627 children entered a contest sponsored by the Police Community Relations Bureau. In precinct B, where there were 7,840 children, 1,960 children entered the contest. 18.____
   The total percentage of all children in both precincts who entered the contest amounted to MOST NEARLY
   A. 19.5% B. 20% C. 21.5% D. 22.5%

19. If Circle A represents Police Administrative Aides (PAA's) who scored above 85 on a PAA test and Circle B represents PAA's who scored above 85 on a Senior PAA test, then the diagram at the right means that 19.____

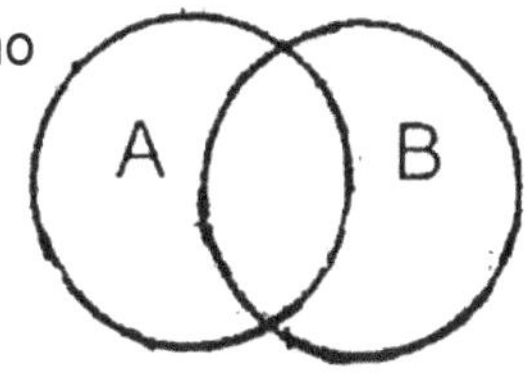

   A. no PAA who scored above 85 on a PAA test scored above 85 on the Senior PAA test
   B. the majority of PAA's who scored above 85 on a PAA test scored above 85 on the Senior PAA test
   C. there were some PAA's who did not take the Senior PAA test
   D. some PAA's who scored above 85 on a PAA test scored above 85 on the Senior PAA test

20. Suppose that in 1912 the city had a population of 550,000 and a police force of 200, and that in 2012 the city had a population of 8,000,000 and a police force of 32,000. 20.____
If the ratio of police to population in 2012 is compared with the same ratio in 1912, what is the resulting relationship of the 2012 ratio to the 1912 ratio?
A. 160:11 B. 160:1 C. 16:1 D. 11:1

Questions 21-24.

DIRECTIONS: Questions 21 through 24 are to be answered SOLELY on the basis of the information contained in the following passage.

Of those arrested in the city in 2019 for felonies or misdemeanors, only 32% were found guilty of any charge. Fifty-six percent of such arrestees were acquitted or had their cases dismissed, 11% failed to appear for trial, and 1% received other dispositions. Of those found guilty, only 7.4% received any sentences of over one year in jail. Only 50% of those found guilty were sentenced to any further time in jail. When considered with the low probability of arrests for most crimes, these figures make it clear that the crime control system in the city poses little threat to the average criminal. Delay compounds the problem. The average case took four appearances for disposition after arraignment. Twenty percent of all cases took eight or more appearances to reach a disposition. Forty-four percent of all cases took more than one year to disposition.

21. According to the above passage, crime statistics for 2019 indicate that 21.____
A. there is a low probability of arrests for all crimes in the city
B. the average criminal has much to fear from the law in the city
C. over 10% of arrestees in the city charged with felonies or misdemeanors did not show up for trial
D. criminals in the city are less likely to be caught than criminals in the rest f the country

22. The percentage of those arrested in 2019 who received sentences of over one year in jail amounted MOST NEARLY to 22.____
A. .237 B. 2.4 C. 23.7 D. 24.0

23. According to the above passage, the percentage of arrestees in 2019 who were found guilty was 23.____
A 20% of those arrested for misdemeanors
B. 11% of those arrested for felonies
C. 50% of those sentenced to further time in jail
D. 32% of those arrested for felonies or misdemeanors

24. According to the above passage, the number of appearances after arraignment and before disposition amounted to 24.____
A. an average of four
B. eight or more in 44% of the cases
C. over four for cases which took more than a year
D. between four and eight for most cases

Questions 25-27.

DIRECTIONS: Questions 25 through 27 are to be answered SOLELY on the basis of the information contained in the following passage.

The traditional characteristics of a police organization, which do not foster group-centered leadership, are being changed daily by progressive police administrators. These characteristics are authoritarian and result in a leader-centered style with all determination of policy and procedure made by the leader. In the group-centered style, policies and procedures are a matter for group discussion and decision. The supposedly modern view is that the group-centered style is the most conducive to improving organizational effectiveness. By contrast, the traditional view regards the group-centered style as an idealistic notion of psychologists. It is questionable, however, that the situation determines the appropriate leadership style. In some circumstances, it will be leader-centered; in others, group-centered. Nevertheless, police supervisors will see more situations calling for a leadership style that, while flexible, is primarily group-centered. Thus, the supervisor in a police department must have a capacity not just to issue orders but to engage in behavior involving organizational leadership which primarily emphasizes goals and work facilitation.

25. According to the above passage, there is reason to believe that with regard to the effectiveness of different types of leadership, the 25.____
   A. leader-centered type is better than the individual-centered type or the group-centered type
   B. leader-centered type is best in some situations and the group-centered type best in other situations
   C. group-centered type is better than the leader-centered type in all situations
   D. authoritarian type is least effective in democratic countries

26. According to the above passage, police administrators today are 26.____
   A. more likely than in the past to favor making decisions on the basis of discussions with subordinates
   B. likely in general to favor traditional patterns of leadership in their organizations
   C. more likely to be progressive than conservative
   D. practical and individualistic rather than idealistic in their approach to police problems

27. According to the above passage, the role of the police department is changing in such a way that its supervisors must 27.____
   A. give greater consideration to the needs of individual subordinates
   B. be more flexible in dealing with infractions of department rules
   C. provide leadership which stresses the goals of the department and helps the staff to reach them
   D. refrain from issuing orders and allow subordinates to decide how to carry out their assignments

Questions 28-31.

DIRECTIONS: Questions 28 through 31 are to be answered SOLELY on the basis of the information contained in the following passage.

Under the provisions of the Bank Protection Act of 1968, enacted July 8, 1968, each Federal banking supervisory agency, as of January 7, 1969, had to issue rules establishing minimum standards with which financial institutions under their control must comply with respect to the installation, maintenance, and operation of security devices and procedures, reasonable in cost, to discourage robberies, burglaries, and larcenies, and to assist in the identification and apprehension of persons who commit such acts. The rules set the time limits within which the affected banks and savings and loan associations must comply with the standards, and the rules require the submission of periodic reports on the steps taken. A violator of a rule under this Act is subject to a civil penalty not to exceed $100 for each day of the violation. The enforcement of these regulations rests with the responsible banking supervisory agencies.

28. The Bank Protection Act of 1968 was designed to 28.____
    A. provide Federal police protection for banks covered by the Act
    B. have organizations covered by the Act take precautions against criminals
    C. set up a system for reporting all bank robberies to the FBI
    D. insure institutions covered by the Act from financial loss due to robberies, burglaries, and larcenies

29. Under the provisions of the Bank Protection Act of 1968, each Federal banking supervisory agency was required to set up rules for financial institutions covered by the Act governing the 29.____
    A. hiring of personnel
    B. punishment of burglars
    C. taking of protective measures
    D. penalties for violations

30. Financial institutions covered by the Bank Protection Act of 1968 were required to 30.____
    A. file reports at regular intervals on what they had done to prevent theft
    B. identify and apprehend persons who commit robberies, burglaries, and larcenies
    C. draw up a code of ethics for their employees
    D. have fingerprints of their employees filed with the FBI

31. Under the provisions of the Bank Protection Act of 1968, a bank which is subject to the rules established under the Act and which violates a rule is liable to a penalty of NOT _____ than $100 for each _____. 31.____
    A. more; violation
    B. less; day of violation
    C. less; violation
    D. more; day of violation

Questions 32-36.

DIRECTIONS: Questions 32 through 36 are to be answered SOLELY on the basis of the information contained in the following passage.

A statement which is offered in an attempt to prove the truth of the matters therein stated, but which is not made by the author as a witness before the court at the particular trial in which it is so offered, is hearsay. This is so whether the statement consists of words (oral or written), of symbols used as a substitute for words, or of signs or other conduct offered as the equivalent of a statement. Subject to some well-established exceptions, hearsay is not generally acceptable as evidence, and it does not become competent evidence just because it is received by the court without objection. One basis for this rule is simply that a fact cannot be proved by showing that somebody stated it was a fact. Another basis for the rule is the fundamental principle that in a criminal prosecution the testimony of the witness shall be taken before the court, so that at the time he gives the testimony offered in evidence he will be sworn and subject to cross-examination, the scrutiny of the court, and confrontation by the accused.

32. Which of the following is hearsay? A(n) 32.____
   A. written statement by a person not present at the court hearing where the statement is submitted as proof of an occurrence
   B. oral statement in court by a witness of what he saw
   C. written statement of what he saw by a witness present in court
   D. re-enactment by a witness in court of what he saw

33. In a criminal case, a statement by a person not present in court is 33.____
   A. *acceptable* evidence if not objected to by the prosecutor
   B. *acceptable* evidence if not objected to by the defense lawyer
   C. *not acceptable* evidence except in certain well-settled circumstances
   D. *not acceptable* evidence under any circumstances

34. The rule on hearsay is founded on the belief that 34.____
   A. proving someone said an act occurred is not proof that the act did occur
   B. a person who has knowledge about a case should be willing to appear in court
   C. persons not present in court are likely to be unreliable witnesses
   D. permitting persons to testify without appearing in court will lead to a disrespect for law

35. One reason for the general rule that a witness in a criminal case must give his testimony in court is that 35.____
   A. a witness may be influenced by threats to make untrue statements
   B. the opposite side is then permitted to question him
   C. the court provides protection for a witness against unfair questioning
   D. the adversary system is designed to prevent a miscarriage of justice

36. Of the following, the MOST appropriate title for the above passage would be 36.____
   A. What is Hearsay
   B. Rights of Defendants
   C. Trial procedures
   D. Testimony of Witnesses

Questions 37-40.

DIRECTIONS: Questions 37 through 40 are to be answered SOLELY on the basis of the following graphs.

BUDGETS FOR POLICE
IN MILLIONS OF DOLLARS
(ACTUAL DOLLARS)
(2017-2021)

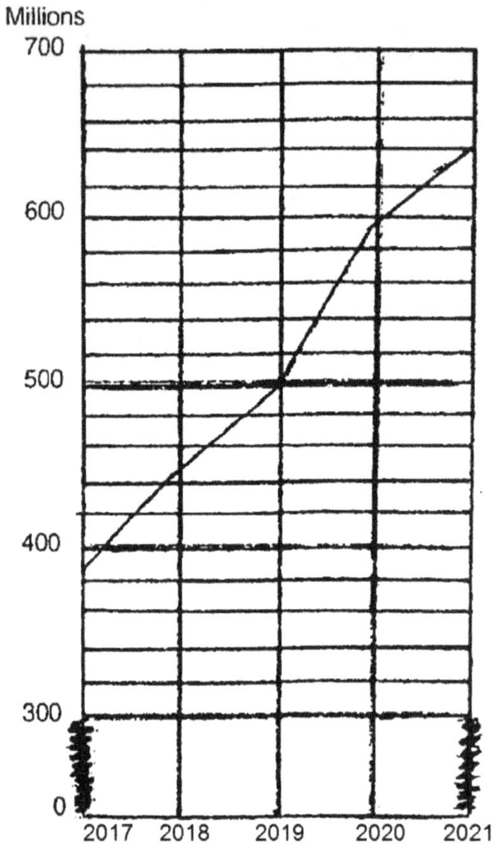

BUDGETS FOR OTHER CRIMINAL
JUSTICE EXPENDITURES IN
MILLIONS OF DOLLARS
(ACTUAL DOLLARS)
2017-2021

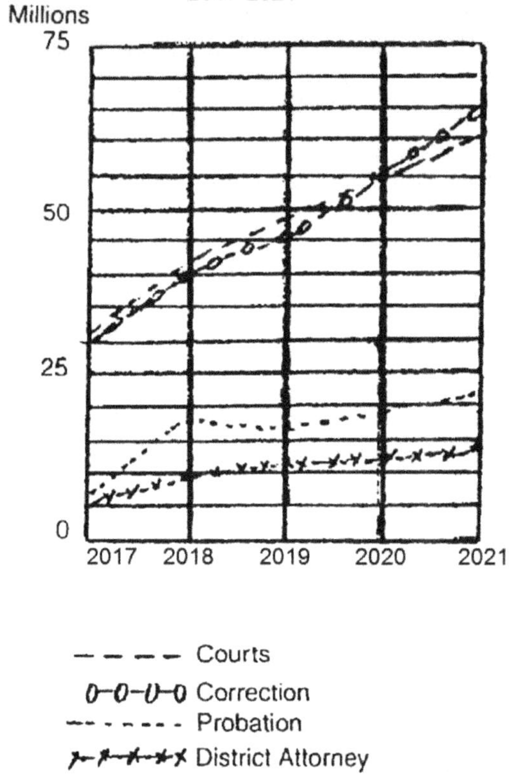

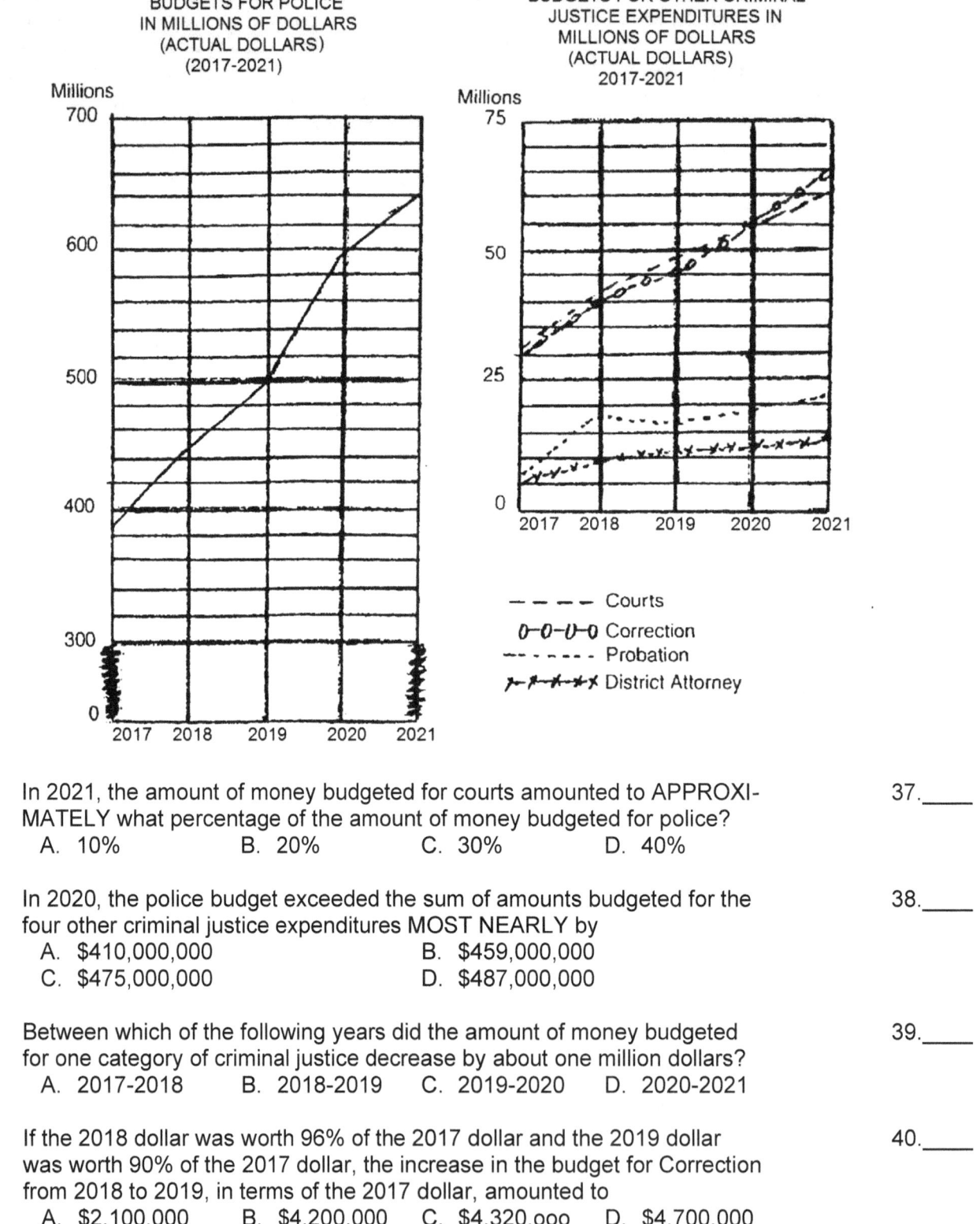

37. In 2021, the amount of money budgeted for courts amounted to APPROXIMATELY what percentage of the amount of money budgeted for police? 37.____
   A. 10% B. 20% C. 30% D. 40%

38. In 2020, the police budget exceeded the sum of amounts budgeted for the four other criminal justice expenditures MOST NEARLY by 38.____
   A. $410,000,000 B. $459,000,000
   C. $475,000,000 D. $487,000,000

39. Between which of the following years did the amount of money budgeted for one category of criminal justice decrease by about one million dollars? 39.____
   A. 2017-2018 B. 2018-2019 C. 2019-2020 D. 2020-2021

40. If the 2018 dollar was worth 96% of the 2017 dollar and the 2019 dollar was worth 90% of the 2017 dollar, the increase in the budget for Correction from 2018 to 2019, in terms of the 2017 dollar, amounted to 40.____
   A. $2,100,000 B. $4,200,000 C. $4,320,ooo D. $4,700,000

KEY (CORRECT ANSWERS)

1.	A	11.	C	21.	C	31.	D
2.	B	12.	B	22.	B	32.	A
3.	B	13.	D	23.	D	33.	C
4.	C	14.	C	24.	A	34.	A
5.	D	15.	D	25.	B	35.	B
6.	C	16.	D	26.	A	36.	A
7.	D	17.	C	27.	C	37.	A
8.	B	18.	C	28.	B	38.	B
9.	C	19.	D	29.	C	39.	B
10.	A	20.	D	30.	A	40.	A

SCANNING MAPS

One section of the exam tests your ability to orient yourself within a given region on a map. Using the map accompanying questions 1 through 3; choose the best way of getting from one point to another.

The New Bridge is closed to traffic because it has a broken span.

MAP 1

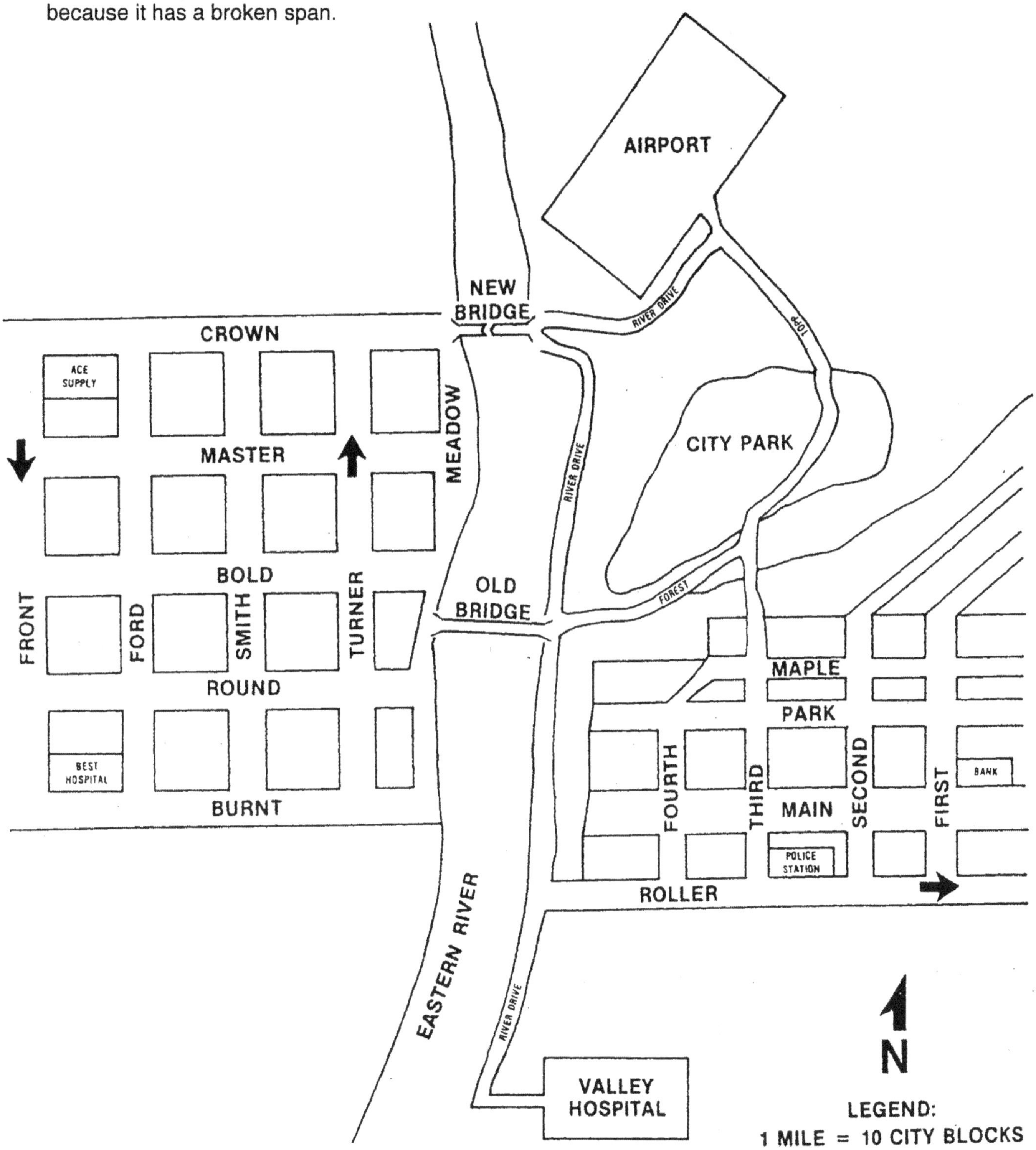

Arrows (→) indicate on-way traffic and direction of traffic. A street marked by an arrow is one way for the entire length of the street.

SAMPLE QUESTIONS

1. Officers in a patrol car which is at the Airport receive a call for assistance at Best Hospital. The shortest route without breaking the law is:
   A. Southwest on River Drive, right on Forest, cross Old Bridge, south on Meadow, and west on Burnt to hospital entrance.
   B. Southwest on River Drive, right on New Bridge, left on Meadow, west on Burnt to hospital entrance.
   C. Southwest on River Drive, right on Old Bridge, left on Turner, right on Burnt to hospital entrance.
   D. North on River Drive to Topp, through City Park to Forest, cross Old Bridge, left on Meadow, west on Burnt to hospital entrance.

2. After returning to the police station, the officers receive a call to pick up injured persons at an accident site (located on the east side of New Bridge) and return to Valley Hospital. The shortest route without breaking the law is:

   A. West on Roller, north on River Drive, left to accident scene at New Bridge, then north on River Drive to hospital entrance.
   B. North on Third, left on Forest, north on River Drive, left to accident scene at new Bridge, then south on River Drive to hospital entrance.
   C. East on Roller, left on First, west on Maple, north on Third, left on Forest, north on River Drive to accident scene at New Bridge, then south on River Drive to hospital entrance.
   D. North on Third, left on Forest, cross Old Bridge, north on Meadow to New Bridge, south on Meadow, east over Old Bridge, then south on River Drive to hospital entrance.

3. While at the Valley Hospital, the officers receive a call asking them to pick up materials at the Ace Supply and return them to the police station. The shortest route without breaking the law is:
   A. North on River Drive, cross New Bridge, west on Crown to Ace Supply, then south on Front, east on Burnt, north on Meadow, cross Old Bridge, east on Forest, south on Third to police station.
   B. North on River Drive, right on Roller to police station, then north on Third, left on Forest, cross Old Bridge, north on Meadow, west on Crown to Ace Supply.
   C. North on River Drive, cross Old Bridge, north on Meadow, west on Crown to Ace Supply, then east on Crown, south on Meadow, cross Old Bridge, east on Forest, south on Third to police station.
   D. North on River Drive, cross Old Bridge, south on Meadow, west on Burnt, north on Front to Ace Supply, then east on Crown, south on Meadow, cross Old Bridge, east on Forest, south on Third to police station.

KEY (CORRECT ANSWERS)

1. A
2. B
3. C

MAP READING
EXAMINATION SECTION
TEST 1

DIRECTIONS: Each question or incomplete statement is followed by several suggested answers or completions. Select the one that BEST answers the question or completes the Statement. *PRINT THE LETTER OF THE CORRECT ANSWER IN THE SPACE AT THE RIGHT.*

Questions 1-5.

DIRECTIONS: Questions 1 through 5 are to be answered SOLELY on the basis of the following information and map.

An employee may be required to assist civilians who seek travel directions or referral to city agencies and facilities.

The following is a map of part of a city, where several public offices and other institutions are located. Each of the squares represents one city block. Street names are as shown. If there is an arrow next to the street name, it means the street is one-way only in the direction of the arrow. If there is no arrow next to the street name, two-way traffic is allowed.

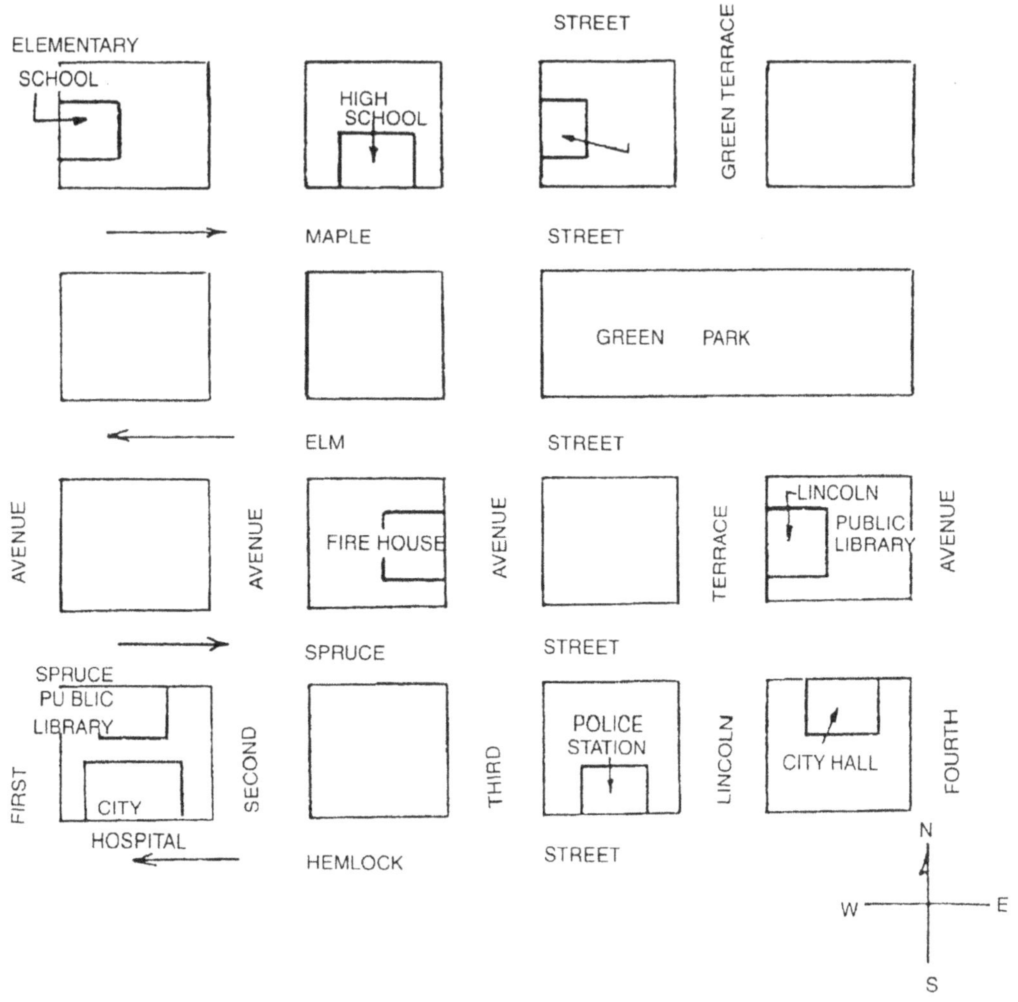

1. A woman whose handbag was stolen from her in Green Park asks a firefighter at the firehouse where to go to report the crime. 1.____
The firefighter should tell the woman to go to the

   A. police station on Spruce Street
   B. police station on Hemlock Street
   C. city hall on Spruce Street
   D. city hall on Hemlock Street

2. A disabled senior citizen who lives on Green Terrace telephones the firehouse to ask which library is closest to her home. 2.____
The firefighter should tell the senior citizen it is the

   A. Spruce Public Library on Lincoln Terrace
   B. Lincoln Public Library on Spruce Street
   C. Spruce Public Library on Spruce Street
   D. Lincoln Public Library on Lincoln Terrace

3. A woman calls the firehouse to ask for the exact location of City Hall. 3.____
She should be told that it is on

   A. Hemlock Street, between Lincoln Terrace and Fourth Avenue
   B. Spruce Street, between Lincoln Terrace and Fourth Avenue
   C. Lincoln Terrace, between Spruce Street and Elm Street
   D. Green Terrace, between Maple Street and Pine Street

4. A delivery truck driver is having trouble finding the high school to make a delivery. The driver parks the truck across from the firehouse on Third Avenue facing north and goes into the firehouse to ask directions. 4.____
In giving directions, the firefighter should tell the driver to go _______ to the school.

   A. north on Third Avenue to Pine Street and then make a right
   B. south on Third Avenue, make a left on Hemlock Street, and then make a right on Second Avenue
   C. north on Third Avenue, turn left on Elm Street, make a right on Second Avenue and go to Maple Street, then make another right
   D. north on Third Avenue to Maple Street, and then make a left

5. A man comes to the firehouse accompanied by his son and daughter. He wants to register his son in the high school and his daughter in the elementary school. He asks a firefighter which school is closest for him to walk to from the firehouse. 5.____
The firefighter should tell the man that the

   A. high school is closer than the elementary school
   B. elementary school is closer than the high school
   C. elementary school and high school are the same distance away
   D. elementary school and high school are in opposite directions

Questions 6-8.

DIRECTIONS: Questions 6 through 8 are to be answered SOLELY on the basis of the following map and information. The flow of traffic is indicated by the arrows. If there is only one arrow shown, then traffic flows in the direction indicated by the arrow. If there are two arrows, then traffic flows in both directions. You must follow the flow of traffic

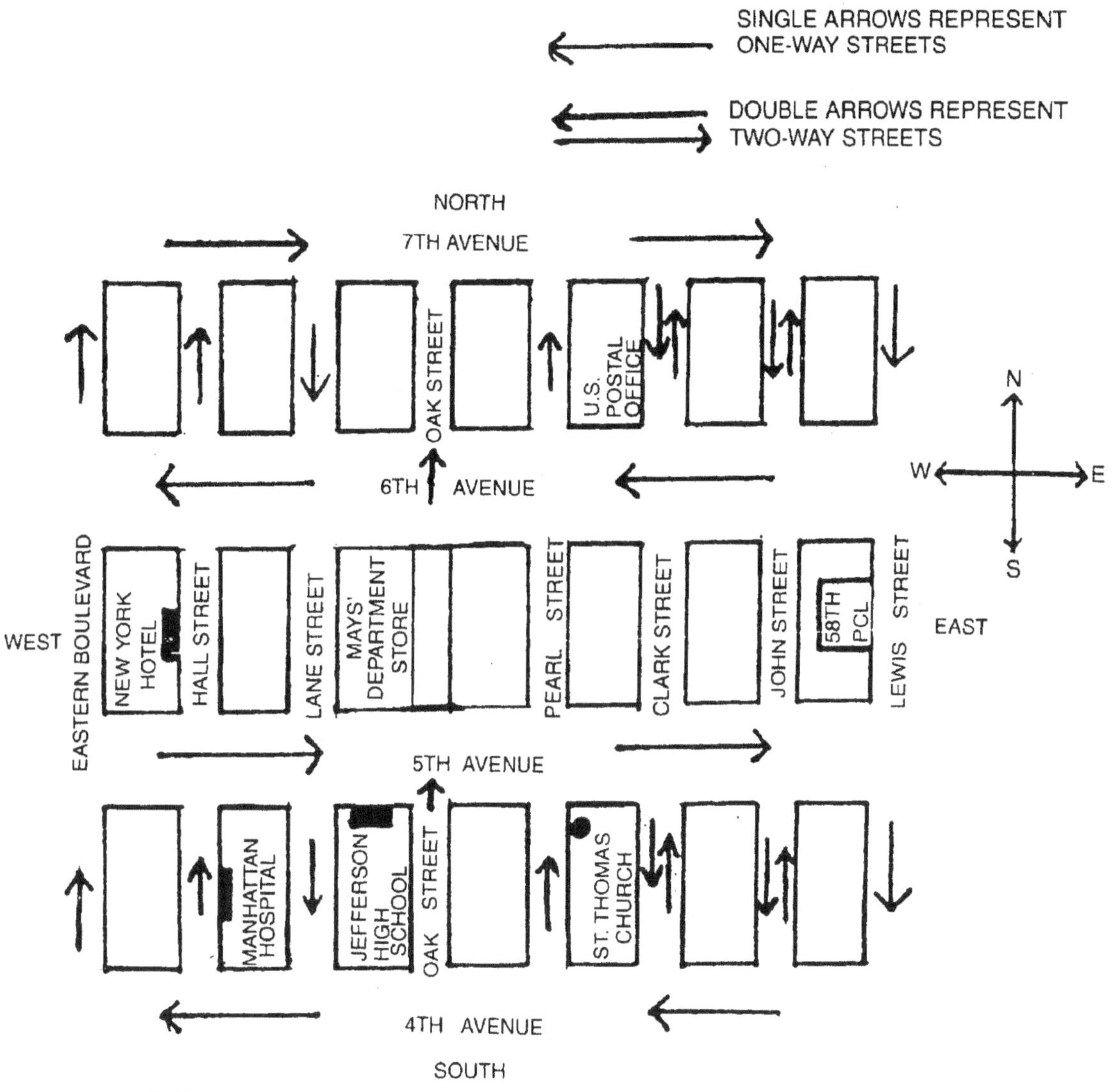

6. Traffic Enforcement Agent Fox was on foot patrol at John Street between 6th and 7th Avenues when a motorist driving southbound asked her for directions to the New York Hotel, which is located on Hall Street between 5th and 6th Avenues. Which one of the following is the SHORTEST route for Agent Fox to direct the motorist to take, making sure to obey all traffic regulations? 6.____
Travel ______ to the New York Hotel.

A. north on John Street, then east on 7th Avenue, then north on Lewis Street, then west on 4th Avenue, then north on Eastern Boulevard, then east on 5th Avenue, then north on Hall Street
B. south on John Street, then west on 6th Avenue, then south on Eastern Boulevard, then east on 5th Avenue, then north on Hall Street

C. south on John Street, then west on 6th Avenue, then south on Clark Street, then east on 4th Avenue, then north on Eastern Boulevard, then east on 5th Avenue, then north on Hall Street
D. south on John Street, then west on 4th Avenue, then north on Hall Street

7. Traffic Enforcement Agent Murphy is on motorized patrol on 7th Avenue between Oak Street and Pearl Street when Lt. Robertson radios him to go to Jefferson High School, located on 5th Avenue between Lane Street and Oak Street. Which one of the following is the SHORTEST route for Agent Murphy to take, making sure to obey all the traffic regulations? 7.____
Travel east on 7th Avenue, then south on ______, then east on 5th Avenue to Jefferson High School.

A. Clark Street, then west on 4th Avenue, then north on Hall Street
B. Pearl Street, then west on 4th Avenue, then north on Lane Street
C. Lewis Street, then west on 6th Avenue, then south on Hall Street
D. Lewis Street, then west on 4th Avenue, then north on Oak Street

8. Traffic Enforcement Agent Vasquez was on 4th Avenue and Eastern Boulevard when a motorist asked him for directions to the 58th Police Precinct, which is located on Lewis Street between 5th and 6th Avenues. 8.____
Which one of the following is the SHORTEST route for Agent Vasquez to direct the motorist to take, making sure to obey all traffic regulations.
Travel north on Eastern Boulevard, then east on ______ on Lewis Street to the 58th Police Precinct.

A. 5th Avenue, then north
B. 7th Avenue, then south
C. 6th Avenue, then north on Pearl Street, then east on 7th Avenue, then south
D. 5th Avenue, then north on Clark Street, then east on 6th Avenue, then south

Questions 9-13.

DIRECTIONS: Questions 9 through 13 are to be answered SOLELY on the basis of the following map and the following information.

Toll collectors answer motorists' questions concerning directions by reading a map of the metropolitan area. Although many alternate routes leading to destinations exist on the following map, you are to choose the MOST direct route of those given.

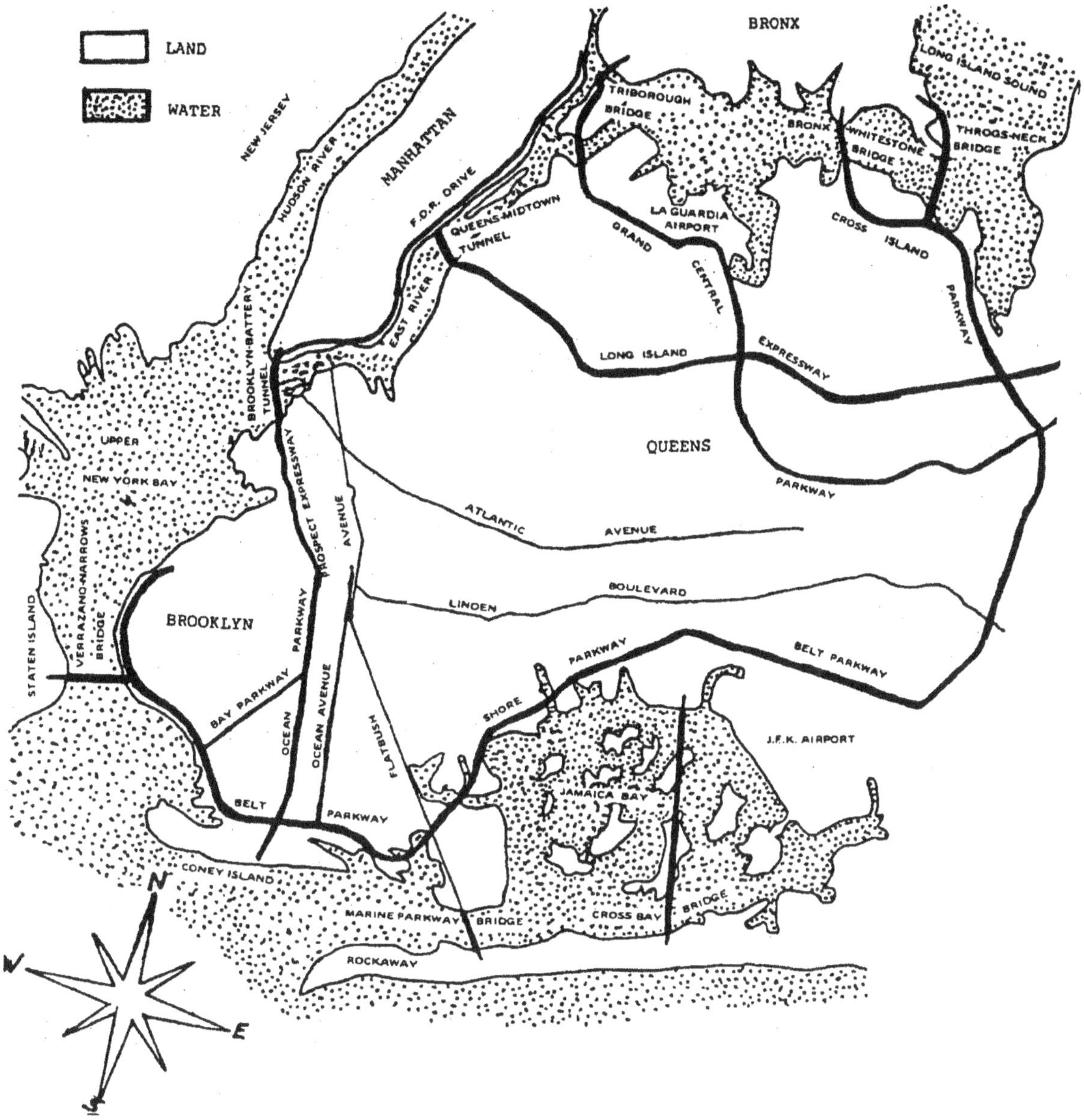

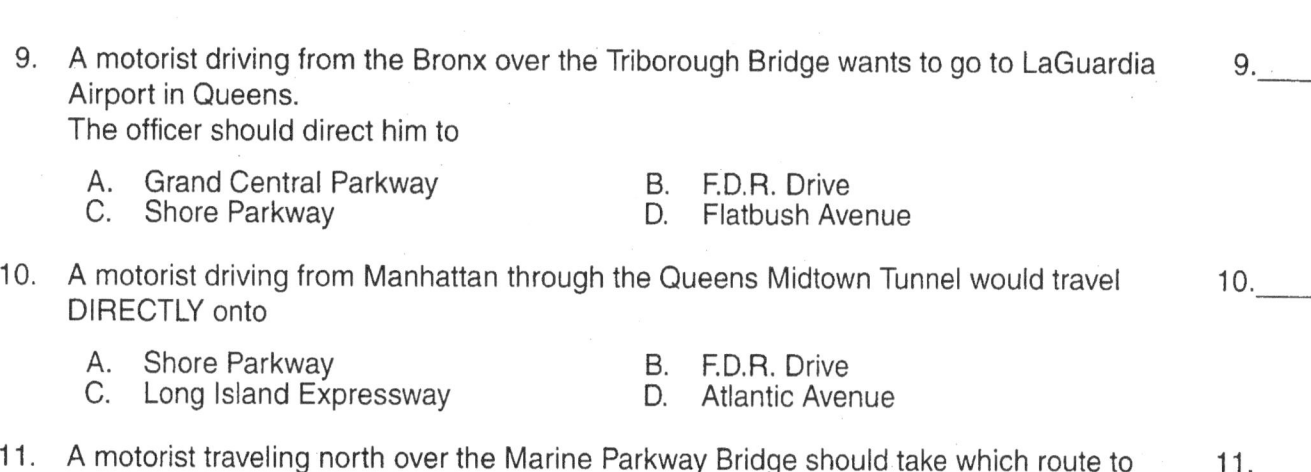

9. A motorist driving from the Bronx over the Triborough Bridge wants to go to LaGuardia Airport in Queens. The officer should direct him to 9.____

   A. Grand Central Parkway
   B. F.D.R. Drive
   C. Shore Parkway
   D. Flatbush Avenue

10. A motorist driving from Manhattan through the Queens Midtown Tunnel would travel DIRECTLY onto 10.____

   A. Shore Parkway
   B. F.D.R. Drive
   C. Long Island Expressway
   D. Atlantic Avenue

11. A motorist traveling north over the Marine Parkway Bridge should take which route to reach Coney Island? 11.____

   A. Shore Parkway East
   B. Belt Parkway West
   C. Linden Boulevard
   D. Ocean Parkway

12. Which facility does NOT connect the Bronx and Queens? 12.____

A. Triborough Bridge
B. Bronx-Whitestone Bridge
C. Verrazano-Narrows Bridge
D. Throgs-Neck Bridge

13. A motorist driving from Manhattan arrives at the toll booth of the Brooklyn-Battery Tunnel and asks directions to Ocean Parkway. 13.____
To which one of the following routes should the motorist FIRST be directed?

A. Atlantic Avenue
B. Bay Parkway
C. Prospect Expressway
D. Ocean Avenue

Questions 14-16.

DIRECTIONS: Questions 14 through 16 are to be answered SOLELY on the basis of the following map. The flow of traffic is indicated by the arrows. If there is only one arrow shown, then traffic flows only in the direction indicated by the arrow. If there are two arrows, then traffic flows in both directions. You must follow the flow of traffic.

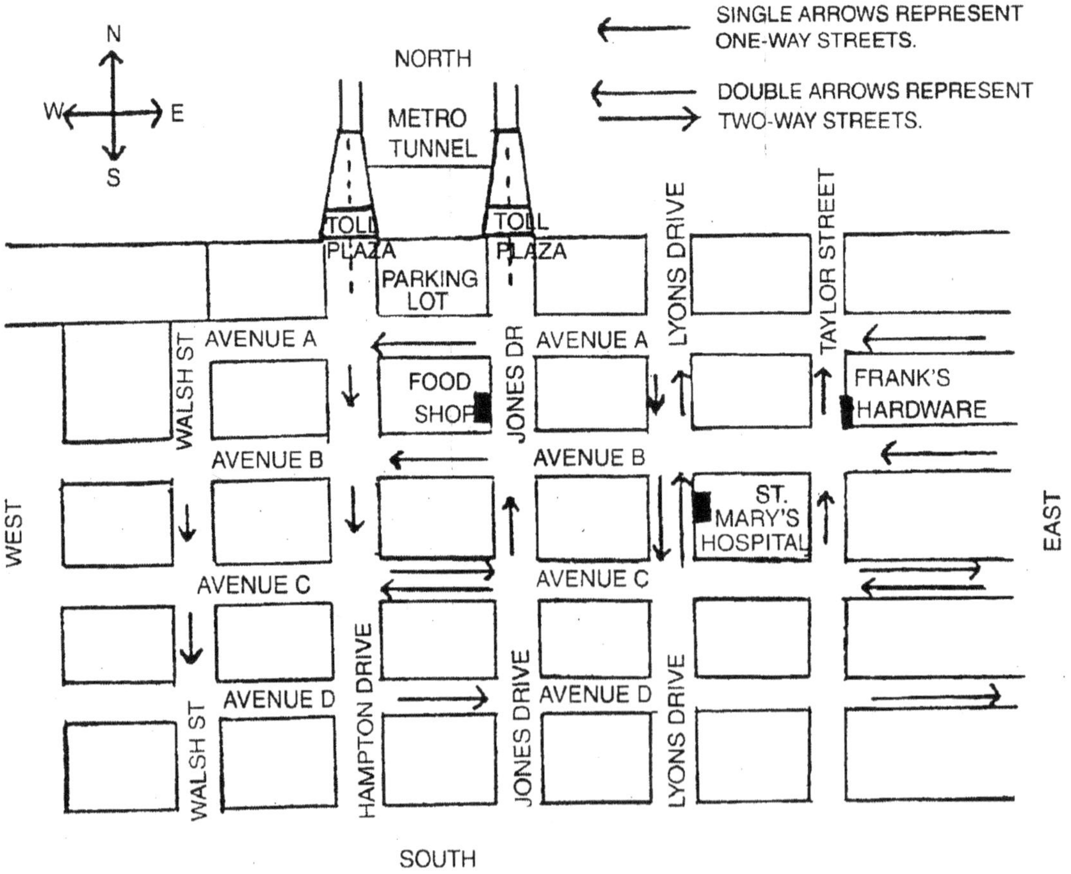

14. A motorist is exiting the Metro Tunnel and approaches the bridge and tunnel officer at the toll plaza. He asks the officer how to get to the food shop on Jones Drive. Which one of the following is the SHORTEST route for the motorist to take, making sure to obey all traffic regulations? 14.____
Travel south on Hampton Drive, then left on ______ on Jones Drive to the food shop.

A. Avenue A, then right
B. Avenue B, then right
C. Avenue D, then left
D. Avenue C, then left

15. A motorist heading south pulls up to a toll booth at the exit of the Metro Tunnel and asks Bridge and Tunnel Officer Evans how to get to Frank's Hardware Store on Taylor Street. Which one of the following is the SHORTEST route for the motorist to take, making sure to obey all traffic regulations? 15.____
Travel south on Hampton Drive, then east on

A. Avenue B to Taylor Street
B. Avenue D, then north on Taylor Street to Avenue B
C. Avenue C, then north on Taylor Street to Avenue B
D. Avenue C, then north on Lyons Drive, then east on Avenue B to Taylor Street

16. A motorist is exiting the Metro Tunnel and approaches the toll plaza. She asks Bridge and Tunnel Officer Owens for directions to St. Mary's Hospital. 16.____
Which one of the following is the SHORTEST route for the motorist to take, making sure to obey all traffic regulations?
Travel south on Hampton Drive, then ______ on Lyons Drive to St. Mary's Hospital.

A. left on Avenue D, then left
B. right on Avenue A, then left on Walsh Street, then left on Avenue D, then left
C. left on Avenue C, then left
D. left on Avenue B, then right

Questions 17-18.

DIRECTIONS: Questions 17 and 18 are to be answered SOLELY on the basis of the map which appears on the following page. The flow of traffic is indicated by the arrows. If there is only one arrow shown, then traffic flows only in the direction indicated by the arrow. If there are two arrows shown, then traffic flows in both directions. You must follow the flow of traffic.

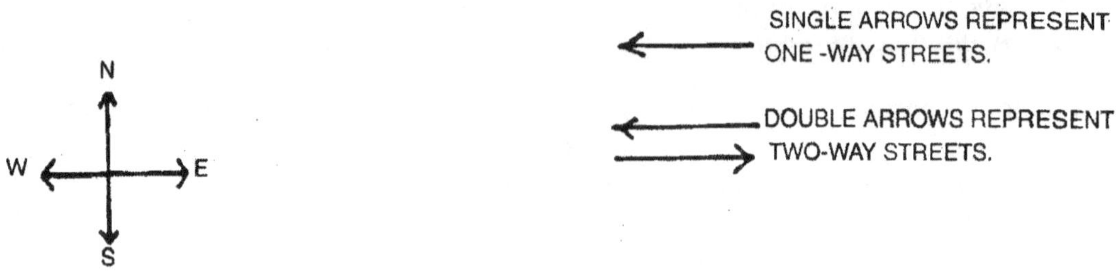

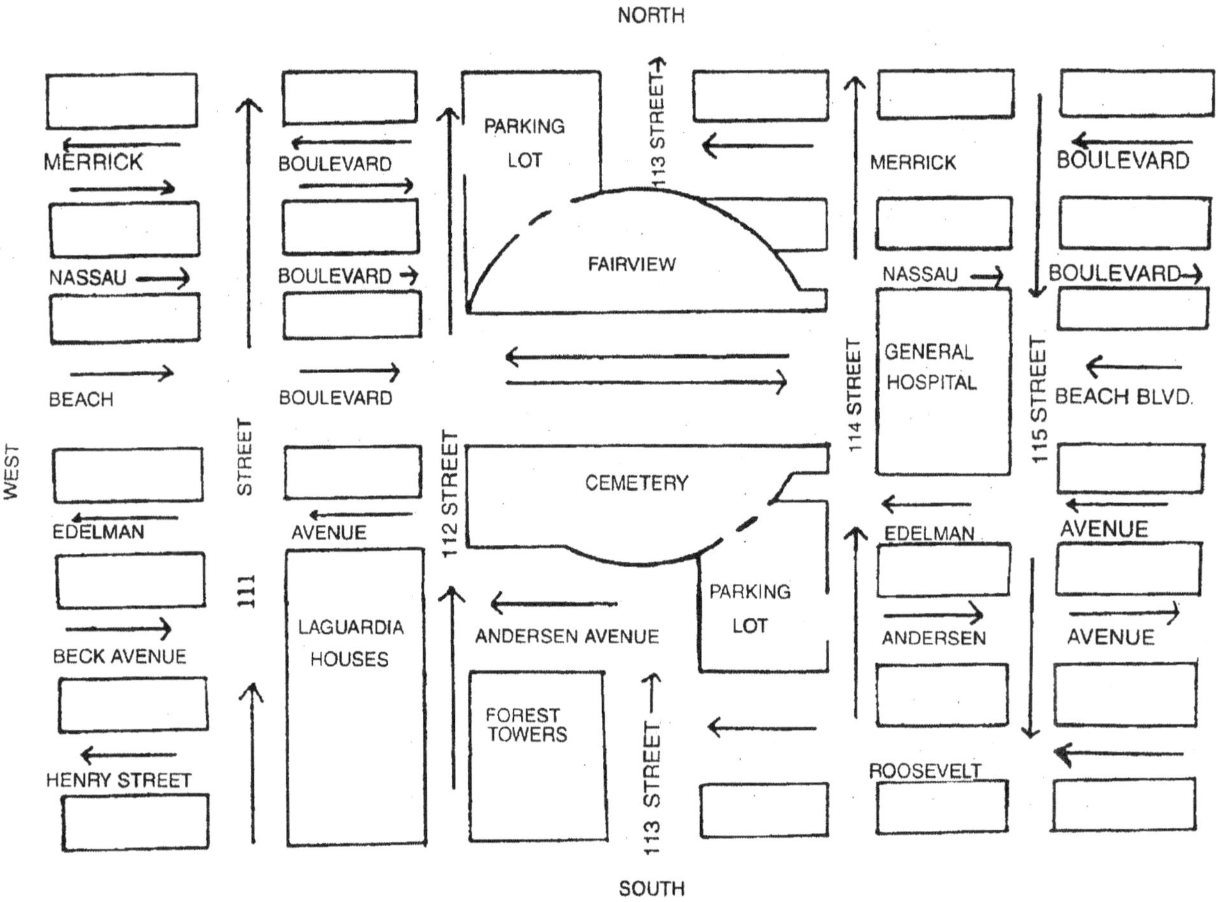

17. Police Officers Glenn and Albertson are on 111th Street at Henry Street when they are dispatched to a past robbery at Beach Boulevard and 115th Street. Which one of the following is the SHORTEST route for the officers to follow in their patrol car, making sure to obey all traffic regulations? Travel north on lllth Street, then east on ______ south on 115th Street. 17.____

A. Edelman Avenue, then north on 112th Street, then east on Beach Boulevard, then north on 114th Street, then east on Nassau Boulevard, then one block
B. Beach Boulevard, then north on 114th Street, then east on Nassau Boulevard, then one block
C. Merrick Boulevard, then two blocks
D. Nassau Boulevard, then south on 112th Street, then east on Beach Boulevard, then north on 114th Street, then east on Nassau Boulevard, then one block

18. Later in their tour, Officers Glenn and Albertson are driving on 114th Street. If they make a left turn to enter the parking lot at Andersen Avenue, and then make a u-turn, in what direction would they now be headed? 18.____

A. North B. South C. East D. West

Questions 19-20.

DIRECTIONS: Questions 19 and 20 are to be answered SOLELY on the basis of the following map. The flow of traffic is indicated by the arrows. If there is only one arrow shown, then traffic flows only in the direction indicated by the arrow. If there are two arrows shown, then traffic flows in both directions. You must follow the flow of traffic.

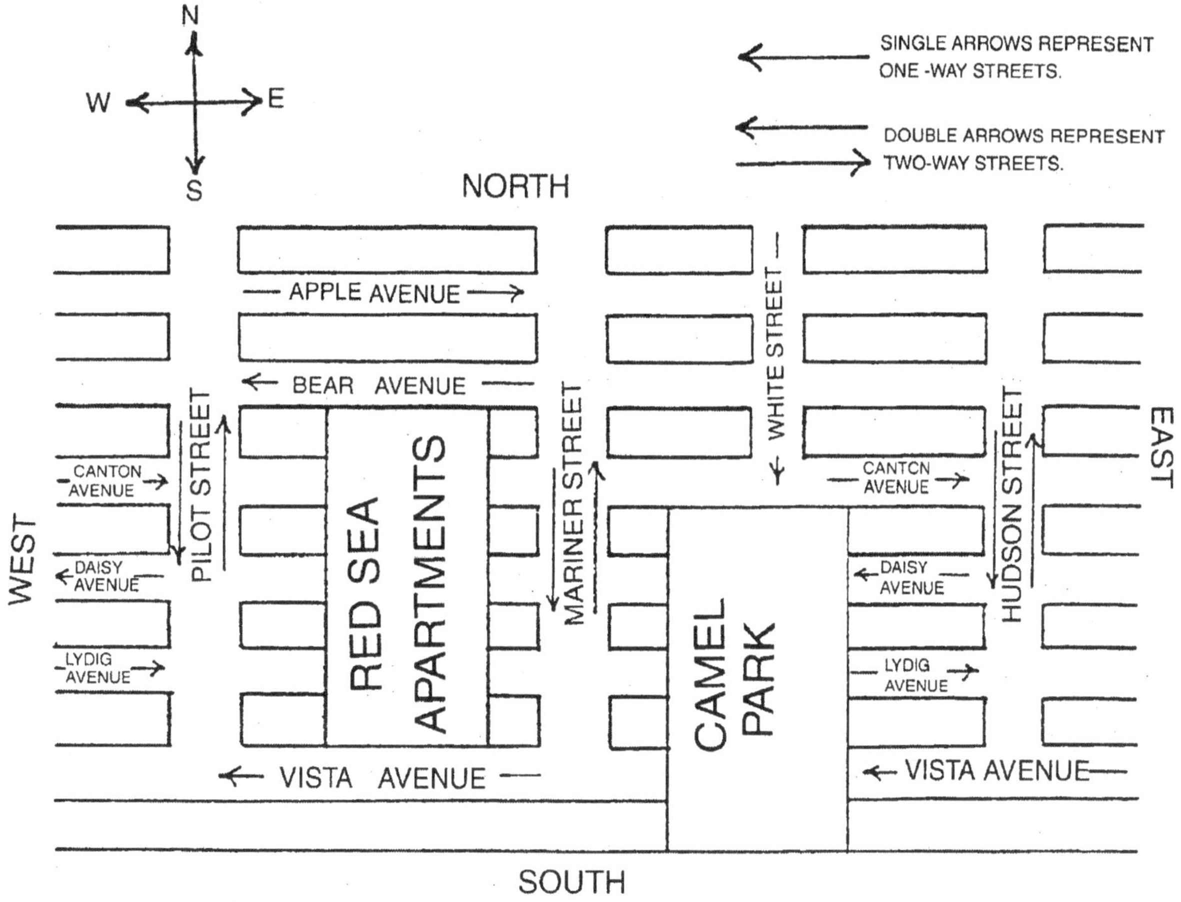

19. You are located at Apple Avenue and White Street. You receive a call to respond to the corner of Lydig Avenue and Pilot Street. 19.____
Which one of the following is the MOST direct route for you to take in your patrol car, making sure to obey all traffic regulations?
Travel _______ on Pilot Street.

A. two blocks south on White Street, then one block east on Canton Avenue, then one block north on Hudson Street, then three blocks west on Bear Avenue, then three blocks south
B. one block south on White Street, then two blocks west on Bear Avenue, then three blocks south

C. two blocks west on Apple Avenue, then four blocks south
D. two blocks south on White Street, then one block west on Canton Avenue, then three blocks south on Mariner Street, then one block west on Vista Avenue, then one block north

20. You are located at Canton Avenue and Pilot Street. You receive a call of a crime in progress at the intersection of Canton Avenue and Hudson Street. 20.____
Which one of the following is the MOST direct route for you to take in your patrol car, making sure to obey all traffic regulations?
Travel

A. two blocks north on Pilot Street, then two blocks east on Apple Avenue, then one block south on White Street, then one block east on Bear Avenue, then one block south on Hudson Street
B. three blocks south on Pilot Street, then travel one block east on Vista Avenue, then travel three blocks north on Mariner Street, then travel two blocks east on Canton Avenue
C. one block north on Pilot Street, then travel three blocks east on Bear Avenue, then travel one block south on Hudson Street
D. two blocks north on Pilot Street, then travel three blocks east on Apple Avenue, then travel two blocks south on Hudson Street

---

KEY (CORRECT ANSWERS)

1.	B	11.	B/D
2.	D	12.	C
3.	B	13.	C
4.	C	14.	D
5.	A	15.	C
6.	D	16.	C
7.	A	17.	B
8.	B	18.	C
9.	A	19.	B
10.	C	20.	D

CLERICAL ABILITIES

EXAMINATION SECTION

TEST 1

DIRECTIONS: Each question or incomplete statement is followed by several suggested answers or completions. Select the one that BEST answers the question or completes the statement. *PRINT THE LETTER OF THE CORRECT ANSWER IN THE SPACE AT THE RIGHT.*

Questions 1-4.

DIRECTIONS: Questions 1 through 4 are to be answered on the basis of the information given below.

The most commonly used filing system and the one that is easiest to learn is alphabetical filing. This involves putting records in an A to Z order, according to the letters of the alphabet. The name of a person is filed by using the following order: first, the surname or last name; second, the first name; third, the middle name or middle initial. For example, *Henry C. Young* is filed under *Y* and thereafter under *Young, Henry C.* The name of a company is filed in the same way. For example, *Long Cabinet Co.* is filed under *L* while *John T. Long Cabinet Co.* is filed under *L* and thereafter under *Long, John T. Cabinet Co.*

1. The one of the following which lists the names of persons in the CORRECT alphabetical order is: 1.____
   - A. Mary Carrie, Helen Carrol, James Carson, John Carter
   - B. James Carson, Mary Carrie, John Carter, Helen Carrol
   - C. Helen Carrol, James Carson, John Carter, Mary Carrie
   - D. John Carter, Helen Carrol, Mary Carrie, James Carson

2. The one of the following which lists the names of persons in the CORRECT alphabetical order is: 2.____
   - A. Jones, John C.; Jones, John A.; Jones, John P.; Jones, John K.
   - B. Jones, John P.; Jones, John K.; Jones, John C.; Jones, John A.
   - C. Jones, John A.; Jones, John C.; Jones, John K.; Jones, John P.
   - D. Jones, John K.; Jones, John C.; Jones, John A.; Jones, John P.

3. The one of the following which lists the names of the companies in the CORRECT alphabetical order is: 3.____
   - A. Blane Co., Blake Co., Block Co., Blear Co.
   - B. Blake Co., Blane Co., Blear Co., Block Co.
   - C. Block Co., Blear Co., Blane Co., Blake Co.
   - D. Blear Co., Blake Co., Blane Co., Block Co.

4. You are to return to the file an index card on *Barry C. Wayne Materials and Supplies Co.* 4.____
Of the following, the CORRECT alphabetical group that you should return the index card to is
A. A to G B. H to M C. N to S D. T to Z

Questions 5-10.

DIRECTIONS: In each of Questions 5 through 10, the names of four people are given. For each question, choose as your answer the one of the four names given which should be filed FIRST according to the usual system of alphabetical filing of names, as described in the following paragraph.

In filing names, you must start with the last name. Names are filed in order of the first letter of the last name, then the second letter, etc. Therefore, BAILY would be filed before BROWN, which would be filed before COLT. A name with fewer letters of the same type comes first, i.e., Smith before Smithe. If the last names are the same, the names are filed alphabetically by the first name. If the first name is an initial, a name with an initial would come before a first name that starts with the same letter as the initial. Therefore, I. BROWN would come before IRA BROWN. Finally, if both last name and first name are the same, the name would be filed alphabetically by the middle name, once again an initial coming before a middle name which starts with the same letter as the initial. If there is no middle name at all, the name would come before those with middle initials or names.

SAMPLE QUESTION: A. Lester Daniels
B. William Dancer
C. Nathan Danzig
D. Dan Lester

The last names beginning with D are filed before the last name beginning with L. Since DANIELS, DANCER, and DANZIG all begin with the same three letters, you must look at the fourth letter of the last name to determine which name should be filed first. C comes before I or Z in the alphabet, so DANCER is filed before DANIELS or DANZIG. Therefore, the answer to the above sample question is B.

5. A. Scott Biala 5.____
B. Mary Byala
C. Martin Baylor
D. Francis Bauer

6. A. Howard J. Black 6.____
B. Howard Black
C. J. Howard Black
D. John H. Black

7. A. Theodora Garth Kingston 7.____
B. Theadore Barth Kingston
C. Thomas Kingston
D. Thomas T. Kingston

8. A. Paulette Mary Huerta 8.____
B. Paul M. Huerta
C. Paulette L. Huerta
D. Peter A. Huerta

9. A. Martha Hunt Morgan 9.____
B. Martin Hunt Morgan
C. Mary H. Morgan
D. Martine H. Morgan

10. A. James T. Meerschaum 10.____
B. James M. Mershum
C. James F. Mearshaum
D. James N. Meshum

Questions 11-14.

DIRECTIONS: Questions 11 through 14 are to be answered SOLELY on the basis of the following information.

You are required to file various documents in file drawers which are labeled according to the following pattern:

DOCUMENTS

MEMOS		LETTERS	
File	Subject	File	Subject
84PM1	(A-L)	84PC1	(A-L)
84PM2	(M-Z)	84PC2	(M-Z)

REPORTS		INQUIRIES	
File	Subject	File	Subject
84PR1	(A-L)	84PQ1	(A-L)
84PR2	(M-Z)	84PQ2	(M-Z)

11. A letter dealing with a burglary should be filed in the drawer labeled 11.____
A. 84PM1 B. 84PC1 C. 84PR1 D. 84PQ2

12. A report on Statistics should be found in the drawer labeled 12.____
A. 84PM1 B. 84PC2 C. 84PR2 D. 84PQS

13. An inquiry is received about parade permit procedures. It should be filed in the drawer labeled 13.____
A. 84PM2 B. 84PC1 C. 84PR1 D. 84PQ2

14. A police officer has a question about a robbery report you filed. You should pull this file from the drawer labeled 14.____
A. 84PM1 B. 84PM2 C. 84PR1 D. 84PR2

Questions 15-22.

DIRECTIONS: Each of Questions 15 through 22 consists of four or six numbered names. For each question, choose the option (A, B, C, or D) which indicates the order in which the names should be filed in accordance with the following filing instructions:

- File alphabetically according to last name, then first name, then middle initial.
- File according to each successive letter within a name.
- When comparing two names in which the letters in the longer name are identical to the corresponding letters in the shorter name, the shorter name is filed first.
- When the last names are the same, initials are always filed before names beginning with the same letter.

15. I. Ralph Robinson 15.____
II. Alfred Ross
III. Luis Robles
IV. James Roberts

The CORRECT filing sequence for the above names should be
A. IV, II, I, III B. I, IV, III, II C. III, IV, I, II D. IV, I, III, II

16. I. Irwin Goodwin 16.____
II. Inez Gonzalez
III. Irene Goodman
IV. Ira S. Goodwin
V. Ruth I. Goldstein
VI. M.B. Goodman

The CORRECT filing sequence for the above names should be
A. V, II, I, IV, III, VI B. V, II, VI, III, IV, I
C. V, II, III, VI, IV, I D. V, II, III, VI, I, IV

17. I. George Allan 17.____
II. Gregory Allen
III. Gary Allen
IV. George Allen

The CORRECT filing sequence for the above names should be
A. IV, III, I, II B. I, IV, II, III C. III, IV, I, II D. I, III, IV, II

18. I. Simon Kauffman 18.____
II. Leo Kaufman
III. Robert Kaufmann
IV. Paul Kauffmann

The CORRECT filing sequence for the above names should be
A. I, IV, II, III B. II, IV, III, I C. III, II, IV, I D. I, II, III, IV

19. I. Roberta Williams 19.____
II. Robin Wilson
III. Roberta Wilson
IV. Robin Williams

The CORRECT filing sequence for the above names should be
A. III, II, IV, I B. I, IV, III, II C. I, II, III, IV D. III, I, II, IV

20. I. Lawrence Shultz 20.____
II. Albert Schultz
III. Theodore Schwartz
IV. Thomas Schwarz
V. Alvin Schultz
VI. Leonard Shultz

The CORRECT filing sequence for the above names should be
A. II, V, III, IV, I, VI B. IV, III, V, I, II, VI
C. II, V, I, VI, III, IV D. I, VI, II, V, III, IV

21. I. McArdle 21.____
II. Mayer
III. Maletz
IV. McNiff
V. Meyer
VI. MacMahon

The CORRECT filing sequence for the above names should be
A. I, IV, VI, III, II, V B. II, I, IV, VI, III, V
C. VI, III, II, I, IV, V D. VI, III, II, V, I, IV

22. I. Jack E. Johnson 22.____
II. R.H. Jackson
III. Bertha Jackson
IV. J.T. Johnson
V. Ann Johns
VI. John Jacobs

The CORRECT filing sequence for the above names should be
A. II, III, VI, V, IV, I B. III, II, VI, V, IV, I
C. VI, II, III, I, V, IV D. III, II, VI, IV, V, I

Questions 23-30.

DIRECTIONS: The code table below shows 10 letters with matching numbers. For each question, there are three sets of letters. Each set of letters is followed by a set of numbers which may or may not match their correct letter according to the code table. For each question, check all three sets of letters and numbers and mark your answer:

A. if no pairs are correctly matched
B. if only one pair is correctly matched
C. if only two pairs are correctly matched
D. if all three pairs are correctly matched

CODE TABLE

T	M	V	D	S	P	R	G	B	H
1	2	3	4	5	6	7	8	9	0

SAMPLE QUESTION: TMVDSP – 123456
RGBHTM – 789011
DSPRGB – 256789

In the sample question above, the first set of numbers correctly match its set of letters. But the second and third pairs contain mistakes. In the second pair, M is correctly matched with number 1. According to the code table, letter M should be correctly matched with number 2. In the third pair, the letter D is incorrectly matched with number 2. According to the code table, letter D should be correctly matched with number 4. Since only one of the pairs is correctly matched, the answer to this sample question is B.

23. RSBMRM – 759262 23.____
GDSRVH – 845730
VDBRTM - 349713

24. TGVSDR – 183247 24.____
SMHRDP – 520647
TRMHSR - 172057

25. DSPRGM – 456782 25.____
MVDBHT – 234902
HPMDBT - 062491

26. BVPTRD – 936184 26.____
GDPHMB – 807029
GMRHMV - 827032

27. MGVRSH – 283750 27.____
TRDMBS – 174295
SPRMGV - 567283

28. SGBSDM – 489542 28.____
MGHPTM – 290612
MPBMHT - 269301

29. TDPBHM – 146902 29.____
VPBMRS – 369275
GDMBHM - 842902

30. MVPTBV – 236194 30.____
PDRTMB – 47128
BGTMSM - 981232

KEY (CORRECT ANSWERS)

1.	A	11.	B	21.	C
2.	C	12.	C	22.	B
3.	B	13.	D	23.	B
4.	D	14.	D	24.	B
5.	D	15.	D	25.	C
6.	B	16.	C	26.	A
7.	B	17.	D	27.	D
8.	B	18.	A	28.	A
9.	A	19.	B	29.	D
10.	C	20.	A	30.	A

TEST 2

DIRECTIONS: Each question or incomplete statement is followed by several suggested answers or completions. Select the one that BEST answers the question or completes the statement. *PRINT THE LETTER OF THE CORRECT ANSWER IN THE SPACE AT THE RIGHT.*

Questions 1-10.

DIRECTIONS: Questions 1 through 10 each consists of two columns, each containing four lines of names, numbers and/or addresses. For each question, compare the lines in Column I with the lines in Column II to see if they match exactly, and mark your answer A, B, C, or D, according to the following instructions:

A. all four lines match exactly
B. only three lines match exactly
C. only two lines match exactly
D. only one line matches exactly

		COLUMN I	COLUMN II	
1.	I.	Earl Hodgson	Earl Hodgson	1.____
	II.	1409870	1408970	
	III.	Shore Ave.	Schore Ave.	
	IV.	Macon Rd.	Macon Rd.	
2.	I.	9671485	9671485	2.____
	II.	470 Astor Court	470 Astor Court	
	III.	Halprin, Phillip	Halperin, Phillip	
	IV.	Frank D. Poliseo	Frank D. Poliseo	
3.	I.	Tandem Associates	Tandom Associates	3.____
	II.	144-17 Northern Blvd.	144-17 Northern Blvd.	
	III.	Alberta Forchi	Albert Forchi	
	IV.	Kings Park, NY 10751	Kings Point, NY 10751	
4.	I.	Bertha C. McCormack	Bertha C. McCormack	4.____
	II.	Clayton, MO	Clayton, MO	
	III.	976-4242	976-4242	
	IV.	New City, NY 10951	New City, NY 10951	
5.	I.	George C. Morill	George C. Morrill	5.____
	II.	Columbia, SC 29201	Columbia, SD 29201	
	III.	Louis Ingham	Louis Ingham	
	IV.	3406 Forest Ave.	3406 Forest Ave.	
6.	I.	506 S. Elliott Pl.	506 S. Elliott Pl.	6.____
	II.	Herbert Hall	Hurbert Hall	
	III.	4712 Rockaway Pkway	4712 Rockaway Pkway	
	IV.	169 E. 7 St.	169 E. 7 St.	

7.	I.	345 Park Ave.	345 Park Pl.	7.____
	II.	Colman Oven Corp.	Coleman Oven Corp.	
	III.	Robert Conte	Robert Conti	
	IV.	6179846	6179846	
8.	I.	Grigori Schierber	Grigori Schierber	8.____
	II.	Des Moines, Iowa	Des Moines, Iowa	
	III.	Gouverneur Hospital	Gouverneur Hospital	
	IV.	91-35 Cresskill Pl.	91-35 Cresskill Pl.	
9.	I.	Jeffery Janssen	Jeffrey Janssen	9.____
	II.	8041071	8041071	
	III.	40 Rockefeller Plaza	40 Rockafeller Plaza	
	IV.	407 6 St.	406 7 St.	
10.	I.	5971996	5871996	10.____
	II.	3113 Knickerbocker Ave.	31123 Knickerbocker Ave.	
	III.	8434 Boston Post Rd.	8424 Boston Post Rd.	
	IV.	Penn Station	Penn Station	

Questions 11-14.

DIRECTIONS: Questions 11 through 14 are to be answered by looking at the four groups of names and addresses listed below (I, II, III, and IV), and then finding out the number of groups that have their corresponding numbered lies exactly the same.

	GROUP I	GROUP II
Line 1.	Richmond General Hospital	Richman General Hospital
Line 2.	Geriatric Clinic	Geriatric Clinic
Line 3.	3975 Paerdegat St.	3975 Peardegat St.
Line 4.	Loudonville, New York 11538	Londonville, New York 11538

	GROUP III	GROUP IV
Line 1.	Richmond General Hospital	Richmend General Hospital
Line 2.	Geriatric Clinic	Geriatric Clinic
Line 3.	3795 Paerdegat St.	3975 Paerdegat St.
Line 4.	Loudonville, New York 11358	Loudonville, New York 11538

1. In how many groups is line one exactly the same? 11.____
   A. Two B. Three C. Four D. None

12. In how many groups is line two exactly the same? 12.____
   A. Two B. Three C. Four D. None

13. In how many groups is line three exactly the same? 13.____
   A. Two B. Three C. Four D. None

14. In how many groups is line four exactly the same? 14.____
    A. Two B. Three C. Four D. None

Questions 15-18.

DIRECTIONS: Each of Questions 15 through 18 has two lists of names and addresses. Each list contains three sets of names and addresses. Check each of the three sets in the list on the right to see if they are the same as the corresponding set in the list on the left. Mark your answers:
- A. if none of the sets in the right list are the same as those in the left list
- B. if only one of the sets in the right list is the same as those in the left list
- C. if only two of the sets in the right list are the same as those in the left list
- D. if all three sets in the right list are the same as those in the left list

15.	Mary T. Berlinger 2351 Hampton St. Monsey, N.Y. 20117	Mary T. Berlinger 2351 Hampton St. Monsey, N.Y. 20117	15.____
	Eduardo Benes 483 Kingston Avenue Central Islip, N.Y. 11734	Eduardo Benes 473 Kingston Avenue Central Islip, N.Y. 11734	
	Alan Carrington Fuchs 17 Gnarled Hollow Road Los Angeles, CA 91635	Alan Carrington Fuchs 17 Gnarled Hollow Road Los Angeles, CA 91685	
16.	David John Jacobson 178 34 St. Apt. 4C New York, N.Y. 00927	David John Jacobson 178 53 St. Apt. 4C New York, N.Y. 00927	16.____
	Ann-Marie Calonella 7243 South Ridge Blvd. Bakersfield, CA 96714	Ann-Marie Calonella 7243 South Ridge Blvd. Bakersfield, CA 96714	
	Pauline M. Thompson 872 Linden Ave. Houston, Texas 70321	Pauline M. Thomson 872 Linden Ave. Houston, Texas 70321	
17.	Chester LeRoy Masterton 152 Lacy Rd. Kankakee, Ill. 54532	Chester LeRoy Masterson 152 Lacy Rd. Kankakee, Ill. 54532	17.____
	William Maloney S. LaCrosse Pla. Wausau, Wisconsin 52136	William Maloney S. LaCross Pla. Wausau, Wisconsin 52146	
	Cynthia V. Barnes 16 Pines Rd. Greenpoint, Miss. 20376	Cynthia V. Barnes 16 Pines Rd. Greenpoint,, Miss. 20376	

18.	Marcel Jean Frontenac 8 Burton On The Water Calender, Me. 01471	Marcel Jean Frontenac 6 Burton On The Water Calender, Me. 01471	18.____
	J. Scott Marsden 174 S. Tipton St. Cleveland, Ohio	J. Scott Marsden 174 Tipton St. Cleveland, Ohio	
	Lawrence T. Haney 171 McDonough St. Decatur, Ga. 31304	Lawrence T. Haney 171 McDonough St. Decatur, Ga. 31304	

Questions 19-26.

DIRECTIONS: Each of Questions 19 through 26 has two lists of numbers. Each list contains three sets of numbers. Check each of the three sets in the list on the right to see if they are the same as the corresponding set in the list on the left. Mark your answers:

A. if none of the sets in the right list are the same as those in the left list
B. if only one of the sets in the right list is the same as those in the left list
C. if only two of the sets in the right list are the same as those in the left list
D. if all three sets in the right list are the same as those in the left lists

19.	7354183476 4474747744 5791430231	7354983476 4474747774 57914302311	19.____
20.	7143592185 8344517699 9178531263	7143892185 8344518699 9178531263	20.____
21.	2572114731 8806835476 8255831246	257214731 8806835476 8255831246	21.____
22.	331476853821 6976658532996 3766042113715	331476858621 6976655832996 3766042113745	22.____
23.	8806663315 74477138449 211756663666	88066633115 74477138449 211756663666	23.____

24.	990006966996 53022219743 4171171117717	99000696996 53022219843 4171171177717	24.____
25.	24400222433004 5300030055000355 20000075532002022	24400222433004 5300030055500355 20000075532002022	25.____
26.	611166640660001116 7111300117001100733 26666446664476518	61116664066001116 7111300117001100733 26666446664476518	26.____

Questions 27-30.

DIRECTIONS: Questions 27 through 30 are to be answered by picking the answer which is in the correct numerical order, from the lowest number to the highest number, in each question.

27. A. 44533, 44518, 44516, 44547
B. 44516, 44518, 44533, 44547
C. 44547, 44533, 44518, 44516
D. 44518, 44516, 44547, 44533

27.____

28. A. 95587, 95593, 95601, 95620
B. 95601, 95620, 95587, 95593
C. 95593, 95587, 95601. 95620
D. 95620, 95601, 95593, 95587

28.____

29. A. 232212, 232208, 232232, 232223
B. 232208, 232223, 232212, 232232
C. 232208, 232212, 232223, 232232
D. 232223, 232232, 232208, 232208

29.____

30. A. 113419, 113521, 113462, 113462
B. 113588, 113462, 113521, 113419
C. 113521, 113588, 113419, 113462
D. 113419, 113462, 113521, 113588

30.____

KEY (CORRECT ANSWERS)

1.	C	11.	A	21.	C
2.	B	12.	C	22.	A
3.	D	13.	A	23.	D
4.	A	14.	A	24.	A
5.	C	15.	C	25.	C
6.	B	16.	B	26.	C
7.	D	17.	B	27.	B
8.	A	18.	B	28.	A
9.	D	19.	B	29.	C
10.	C	20.	B	30.	D

CODING

EXAMINATION SECTION

COMMENTARY

An ingenious question-type called coding, involving elements of alphabetizing, filing, name and number comparison, and evaluative judgment and application, has currently won wide acceptance in testing circles for measuring clerical aptitude and general ability, particularly on the senior (middle) grades (levels).

While the directions for this question usually vary in detail, the candidate is generally asked to consider groups of names, codes, and numbers, and then, according to a given plan, to arrange codes in alphabetic order; to arrange these in numerical sequence; to re-arrange columns of names and numbers in correct order; to espy errors in coding; to choose the correct coding arrangement in consonance with the given directions and examples, etc.

This question-type appear to have few parameters in respect to form, substance, or degree of difficulty.

Accordingly, acquaintance with, and practice in, the coding question is recommended for the serious candidate.

TEST 1

DIRECTIONS: Questions 1 through 8 are to be answered on the basis of the code table and the instructions given below.

Code Letter for Traffic Problem	B	H	Q	J	F	L	M	I
Code Number for Action Taken	1	2	3	4	5	6	7	8

Assume that each of the capital letters on the above chart is a radio code for a particular traffic problem and that the number immediately below each capital letter is the radio code for the correct action to be taken to deal with the problem. For instance, "1" is the action to be taken to deal with problem "B", "2" is the action to be taken to deal with problem "H", and so forth.

In each question, a series of code letters is given in Column 1. Column 2 gives four different arrangements of code numbers. You are to pick the answer (A, B, C, or D) in Column 2 that gives the code numbers that match the code letters in the same order.

SAMPLE QUESTION

Column 1	Column 2
BHLFMQ	A. 125678
	B. 216573
	C. 127653
	D. 126573

According to the chart, the code numbers that correspond to these code letters are as follows: B – 1, M – 2, L – 6, F – 5, M – 7, Q – 3. Therefore, the right answer is 126573. This answer is D in Column 2.

Column 1	Column 2	
1. BHQLMI	A. 123456 B. 123567 C. 123678 D. 125678	1.____
2. HBJQLF	A. 214365 B. 213456 C. 213465 D. 214387	2.____
3. QHMLFJ	A. 321654 B. 345678 C. 327645 D. 327654	3.____
4. FLQJIM	A. 543287 B. 563487 C. 564378 D. 654378	4.____
5. FBIHMJ	A. 518274 B. 152874 C. 528164 D. 517842	5.____
6. MIHFQB	A. 872341 B. 782531 C. 782341 D. 783214	6.____
7. JLFHQIM	A. 465237 B. 456387 C. 4652387 D. 4562387	7.____
8. LBJQIFH	A. 614382 B. 6134852 C. 61437852 D. 61431852	8.____

KEY (CORRECT ANSWERS)

1.	C	5.	A
2.	A	6.	B
3.	D	7.	C
4.	B	8.	A

TEST 2

DIRECTIONS: Each question or incomplete statement is followed by several suggested answers or completions. Select the one that BEST answers the question or completes the statement. *PRINT THE LETTER OF THE CORRECT ANSWER IN THE SPACE AT THE RIGHT.*

Questions 1-5.

DIRECTIONS: Questions 1 through 5 are based on the following list showing the name and number of each of nine inmates.

1. Johnson	4. Thompson	7. Gordon
2. Smith	5. Frank	8. Porter
3. Edwards	6. Murray	9. Lopez

Each question consists of 3 sets of numbers and letters. Each set should consist of the numbers of three inmates and the first letter of each of their names. The letters should be in the same order as the numbers. In at least two of the three choices, there will be an error. On your answer sheet, mark only that choice in which the letters correspond with the numbers and are in the same order. If all three sets are wrong, mark choice D in your answer space.

<u>SAMPLE QUESTION</u>

A. 386 EPM
B. 542 FST
C. 474 LGT

Since 3 corresponds to E for Edwards, 8 corresponds to P for Porter, and 6 corresponds to M for Murray, choice A is correct and should be entered in your answer space. Choice B is wrong because letters T and S have been reversed. Choice C is wrong because the first number, which is 4, does NOT correspond with the first letter of choice C, which is L. It should have been T. If choice A were also wrong, then D would be the correct answer.

1. A. 382 EGS B. 461 TMJ C. 875 PLF 1.____

2. A. 549 FLT B. 692 MJS C. 758 GSP 2.____

3. A. 936 LEM B. 253 FSE C. 147 JTL 3.____

4. A. 569 PML B. 716 GJP C. 842 PTS 4.____

5. A. 356 FEM B. 198 JPL C. 637 MEG 5.____

Questions 6-10.

DIRECTIONS: Questions 6 through 10 are to be answered on the basis of the following information:

In order to make sure stock is properly located, incoming units are stored as follows:

STOCK NUMBERS	BIN NUMBERS
00100 – 39999	D30, L44
40000 – 69999	14L, D38
70000 – 99999	41L, 80D
100000 and over	614, 83D

Using the above table, choose the answer A, B, C, or D, which lists the correct Bin Number for the Stock Number given.

6. 17243 6.____
A. 41L B. 83D C. 14L D. D30

7. 9219 7.____
A. D38 B. L44 C. 614 D. 41L

8. 90125 8.____
A. 41L B. 614 C. D38 D. D30

9. 10001 9.____
A. L44 B. D38 C. 80D D. 83D

10. 200100 10.____
A. 41L B. 14L C. 83D D. D30

KEY (CORRECT ANSWERS)

1.	B	6.	D
2.	D	7.	B
3.	A	8.	A
4.	C	9.	A
5.	C	10.	C

TEST 3

DIRECTIONS: Each question or incomplete statement is followed by several suggested answers or completions. Select the one that BEST answers the question or completes the statement. *PRINT THE LETTER OF THE CORRECT ANSWER IN THE SPACE AT THE RIGHT.*

Questions 1-9.

DIRECTIONS: Assume that the Police Department is planning to conduct a statistical study of individuals who have been convicted of crimes during a certain year. For the purpose of this study, identification numbers are being assigned to individuals in the following manner:

The first two digits indicate the age of the individual.
The third digit indicates the sex of the individual:
1. Male
2. Female

The fourth digit indicates the type of crime involved:
1. criminal homicide
2. forcible rape
3. robbery
4. aggravated assault
5. burglary
6. larceny
7. auto theft
8. other

The fifth and sixth digits indicate the month in which the conviction occurred:
01. January
02. February, etc.

Questions 1 through 9 are to be answered SOLELY on the basis of the above information and the following list of individuals and identification numbers.

Abbott, Richard	271304	Morris, Chris	212705
Collins, Terry	352111	Owens, William	231412
Elders, Edward	191207	Parker, Leonard	291807
George, Linda	182809	Robinson, Charles	311102
Hill, Leslie	251702	Sands, Jean	202610
Jones, Jackie	301106	Smith, Michael	42108
Lewis, Edith	402406	Turner, Donald	191601
Mack, Helen	332509	White, Barbara	242803

1. The number of women on the above list is 1.____
   A. 6 B. 7 C. 8 D. 9

2. The two convictions which occurred during February were for the crimes of 2.____
   A. aggravated assault and auto theft
   B. auto theft and criminal homicide
   C. burglary and larceny
   D. forcible rape and robbery

3. The ONLY man convicted of auto theft was 3.____
   A. Richard Abbott B. Leslie Hill
   C. Chris Morris D. Leonard Parker

4. The number of people on the list who were 25 years old or older is 4.____
   A. 6 B. 7 C. 8 D. 9

5. The OLDEST person on the list is 5.____
   A. Terry Collins B. Edith Lewis
   C. Helen Mack D. Michael Smith

6. The two people on the list who are the same age are 6.____
   A. Richard Abbott and Michael Smith
   B. Edward Elders and Donald Turner
   C. Linda George and Helen Mack
   D. Leslie Hill and Charles Robinson

7. A 28-year-old man who was convicted of aggravated assault in October would have identification number 7.____
   A. 281410 B. 281509 C. 282311 D. 282409

8. A 33-year-old woman convicted in April of criminal homicide would have identification number 8.____
   A. 331140 B. 331204 C. 332014 D. 332104

9. The number of people on the above list who were convicted during the first six months of the year is 9.____
   A. 6 B. 7 C. 8 D. 9

Questions 10-19.

DIRECTIONS: The following is a list of patients who were referred by various clinics to the laboratory for tests. After each name is a patient identification number. Questions 10 through 19 are to be answered on the basis of the information contained in this list and the explanation accompanying it.

The first digit refers to the clinic which made the referral:

1. cardiac
2. Renal
3. Pediatrics
4. Ophthalmology
5. Orthopedics
6. Hematology
7. Gynecology
8. Neurology
9. Gastroenterology

The second digit refers to the sex of the patient:
1. male
2. female

The third and fourth digits give the age of the patient
The last two digits give the day of the month the laboratory tests were performed

LABORATORY REFERRALS DURING JANUARY

Adams, Jacqueline	320917	Miller, Michael	511806
Black, Leslie	813406	Pratt, William	214411
Cook, Marie	511616	Rogers, Ellen	722428
Fisher, Pat	914625	Saunders, Sally	310229
Jackson, Lee	923212	Wilson, Jan	416715
James, Linda	624621	Wyatt, Mark	321326
Lane, Arthur	115702		

10. According to the list, the number of women referred to the laboratory during January was 10.____
A. 4 B. 5 C. 6 D. 7

11. The clinic from which the MOST patients were referred was 11.____
A. Cardiac B. Gynecology
C. Ophthalmology D. Pediatrics

12. The YOUNGEST patient referred from any clinic other than Pediatrics was 12.____
A. Leslie Black B. Marie Cook
C. Arthur Lane D. Sally Saunders

13. The number of patients whose laboratory tests were performed on or before January 16 was 13.____
A. 7 B. 8 C. 9 D. 10

14. The number of patients referred for laboratory tests who are under age 45 is 14.____
A. 7 B. 8 C. 9 D. 10

15. The OLDEST patient referred to the clinic during January was 15.____
A. Jacqueline Adams B. Linda James
C. Arthur Lane D. Jan Wilson

16. The ONLY patient treated in the Orthopedics clinic was 16.____
A. Marie Cook B. Pat Fisher
C. Ellen Rogers D. Jan Wilson

17. A woman, age 37 was referred from the Hematology clinic to the laboratory. Her laboratory tests were performed on January 9. 17.____
Her identification number would be
A. 610937 B. 623709 C. 613790 D. 623790

18. A man was referred for lab tests from the Orthopedics clinic. He is 30 years old and his tests were performed on January 6. 18.____
His identification number would be
A. 413006 B. 510360 C. 513006 D. 513060

19. A 4-year-old boy was referred from the Pediatrics clinic to have laboratory tests on January 23. 19.____
His identification number was
A. 310422 B. 310423 C. 310433 D. 320403

KEY (CORRECT ANSWERS)

1.	B	11.	D
2.	B	12.	B
3.	B	13.	A
4.	D	14.	C
5.	D	15.	D
6.	B	16.	A
7.	A	17.	B
8.	D	18.	C
9.	C	19.	B
10.	B		

TEST 4

DIRECTIONS: Each question or incomplete statement is followed by several suggested answers or completions. Select the one that BEST answers the question or completes the statement. *PRINT THE LETTER OF THE CORRECT ANSWER IN THE SPACE AT THE RIGHT.*

Questions 1-10.

DIRECTIONS: Questions 1 through 10 are to be answered on the basis of the information and directions given below.

Assume that you are a Senior Stenographer assigned to the personnel bureau of a city agency. Your supervisor has asked you to classify the employees in your agency into the following five groups:

A. Employees who are college graduates, who are at least 35 years of age but less than 50, and who have been employed by the City for five years or more;
B. Employees who have been employed by the City for less than five years, who are not college graduates, and who earn at least $32,500 a year but less than $34,500;
C. Employees who have been City employees for five years or more, who are at least 21 years of age but less than 35, and who are not college graduates;
D. Employee who earn at least $34,500 a year but less than $36,000 who are college graduates, and who have been employed by the City for less than five years;
E. Employees who are not included in any of the foregoing groups.

NOTE: In classifying these employees you are to compute age and period of service as of January 1, 2003. In all cases, it is to be assumed that each employee has been employed continuously in City service. In each question, consider only the information which will assist you in classifying each employee Any information which is of no assistance in classifying an employee would not be considered.

SAMPLE: Mr. Brown, a 29-year-old veteran, was appointed to his present position of Clerk on June 1, 2000. He has completed two years of college. His present salary is $33,050.

The correct answer to this sample is B, since the employee has been employed by the City for less than five years, is not a college graduate, and earn at least $32,500 a year but less than $34,500.

Questions 1 through 10 contain excerpts from the personnel records of 10 employees in the agency. In the correspondingly numbered space at the right print the capital letter preceding the appropriate group into which you would place each employee.

1. Mr. James has been employed by the City since 1993, when he was graduated from a local college. Now 35 years of age, he earns $36,000 a year. 1.____

2. Mr. Worth began working in City service early in 1999. He was awarded his college degree in 1994, at the age of 21. As a result of a recent promotion, he now earns $34,500 a year. 2.____

3. Miss Thomas has been a City employee since August 1, 1998. Her salary is $34,500 a year. Miss Thomas, who is 25 years old, has had only three years of high school training. 3.____

4. Mr. Williams has had three promotions since entering City service on January 1, 1991. He was graduated from college with honors in 1974, when he was 20 years of age. His present salary is $37,000 a year. 4.____

5. Miss Jones left college after two years of study to take an appointment to a position in the City service paying $33,300 a year. She began work on March 1, 1997 when she was 19 years of age. 5.____

6. Mr. Smith was graduated from an engineering college with honors in January 1998 and became a City employee three months later. His present salary is $35,810. Mr. Smith was born in 1976. 6.____

7. Miss Earnest was born on May 31, 1979. Her education consisted of four years of high school and one year of business school. She was appointed as a typist in a City agency on June 1, 1997. Her annual salary is $33,500. 7.____

8. Mr. Adams, a 24-year-old clerk, began his City service on July 1, 1999, soon after being discharged from the U.S. Army. A college graduate, his present annual salary is $33,200. 8.____

9. Miss Charles attends college in the evenings, hoping to obtain her degree is 2004, when she will be 30 years of age. She has been a City employee since April 1998, and earns $33,350. 9.____

10. Mr. Dolan was just promoted to his present position after six years of City service. He was graduated from high school in 1982, when he was 18 years of age, but did not go on to college. Mr. Dolan's present salary is $33,500. 10.____

KEY (CORRECT ANSWERS)

1.	A	6.	D
2.	D	7.	C
3.	E	8.	E
4.	A	9.	B
5.	C	10.	E

TEST 5

DIRECTIONS: Questions 1 through 4 each contain five numbers that should be arranged in numerical order. The number with the lowest numerical value should be first and the number with the highest numerical value should be last. Pick that option which indicates the CORRECT order of the numbers.

Examples: A. 9; 18; 14; 15; 27
B. 9; 14; 15; 18; 27
C. 14; 15; 18; 27; 9
D. 9; 14; 15; 27; 18

The correct answer is B, which contains the proper arrangement of the five numbers.

1. A. 20573; 20753; 20738; 20837; 20098 1.____
B. 20098; 20753; 20573; 20738; 20837
C. 20098; 20573; 20753; 20837; 20738
D. 20098; 20573; 20738; 20753; 20837

2. A. 113492; 113429; 111314; 113114; 131413 2.____
B. 111314; 113114; 113429; 113492; 131413
C. 111314; 113429; 113492; 113114; 131413
D. 111314; 113114; 131413; 113429; 113492

3. A. 1029763; 1030421; 1035681; 1036928; 1067391 3.____
B. 1030421; 1029763; 1035681; 1067391; 1036928
C. 1030421; 1035681; 1036928; 1067391; 1029763
D. 1029763; 1039421; 1035681; 1067391; 1036928

4. A. 1112315; 1112326; 1112337; 1112349; 1112306 4.____
B. 1112306; 1112315; 1112337; 1112326; 1112349
C. 1112306; 1112315; 1112326; 1112337; 1112349
D. 1112306; 1112326; 1112315; 1112337; 1112349

KEY (CORRECT ANSWERS)

1. D
2. B
3. A
4. C

TEST 6

DIRECTIONS: The phonetic filing system is a method of filing names in which the alphabet is reduced to key code letters. The six key letters and their equivalents are as follows:

KEY LETTERS	EQUIVALENTS
b	p, f, v
c	s, k, g, j, q, x, z
d	t
l	none
m	n
r	none

A key letter represents itself.
Vowels (a, e, i, o, and u) and the letters w, h, and y are omitted.
For example, the name GILMAN would be represented as follows:

G is represented by the key letter C.
I is a vowel and is omitted.
L is a letter and represents itself.
M is a key letter and represents itself.
A is a vowel and is omitted.
N is represented by the key letter M.

Therefore, the phonetic filing code for the name GILMAN is CLMM.

Answer Questions 1 through 10 based on the information below.

1. The phonetic filing code for the name FITZGERALD would be 1.____
A. BDCCRLD B. BDCRLD C. BDZCRLD D. BTZCRLD

2. The phonetic filing code CLBR may represent any one of the following names EXCEPT 2.____
A. Calprey B. Flower C. Glover D. Silver

3. The phonetic filing code LDM may represent any one of the following names EXCEPT 3.____
A. Halden B. Hilton C. Walton D. Wilson

4. The phonetic filing code for the name RODRIGUEZ would be 4.____
A. RDRC B. RDRCC C. RDRCZ D. RTRCC

5. The phonetic filing code for the name MAXWELL would be 5.____
A. MCLL B. MCWL C. MCWLL D. MXLL

6. The phonetic filing code for the name ANDERSON would be 6.____
A. AMDRCM B. ENDRSM C. MDRCM D. NDERCN

7. The phonetic filing code for the name SAVITSKY would be 7.____
A. CBDCC B. CBDCY C. SBDCC D. SVDCC

8. The phonetic filing code CMC may represent any one of the following names EXCEPT 8.____
   A. James B. Jayes C. Johns D. Jones

9. The ONLY one of the following names that could be represented by the phonetic filing code CDDDM would be 9.____
   A. Catalano B. Chesterton C. Cittadino D. Cuttlerman

10. The ONLY one of the following names that could be represented by the phonetic filing code LLMCM would be 10.____
   A. Ellington B. Hallerman C. Inslerman D. Willingham

KEY (CORRECT ANSWERS)

1.	A	6.	C
2.	B	7.	A
3.	D	8.	B
4.	B	9.	C
5.	A	10.	D

POLICE SCIENCE NOTES

POLICE COMMUNICATIONS

Communication can be defined as the transfer of information from one person to another. It can be accomplished in a variety of ways including the spoken word, written message, signal or electrical device. Geographically, communication involves the transmission of messages from one point to another, either interdepartmentally or intradepartmentally. Any exchange of words, messages, or signals in connection with police action may be classified as police communications.

History

Police communications, contrary to many modern beliefs, are as old as the police service itself. In 17th century England, policemen carried bells or lanterns for identification and as signal devices to give warnings or to summon assistance. The 18th century saw little improvement in police signaling equipment. Police officers in the 19th century utilized whistles, night sticks, and even their pistols as signal devices. The 20th century brought the introduction of electrical devices to the field of police communications. The horn, bell, light, telegraph, telephone, radio-telegraph, radio, radar, and now television, afford communications with infinitely increased efficiency. These developments also have produced great strides in the area of speed, range, and area coverage.

Along with these developments in the technical aspects of police communications, the written reporting system of law enforcement agencies have become considerably more sophisticated with the use of automatic and electronic data storage and processing equipment becoming more and more common. This progress has resulted in more accurate, complete, and easily recoverable information for police use.

The rapid growth of police communication probably is the best indication of its success in police administration. It has enabled a remarkable increase in the promptness and effectiveness of police action, especially in emergencies where time is of utmost importance, and closer and more effective control over patrolmen in the field. Most recently developed and available are: two-way radios small enough to be carried on an officer's belt; printout or screen display devices mounted in patrol cars with computer inquiry capability; and automatic query/response devices which show dispatchers or supervisors the geographic locations of patrol cars by radio direction finding systems. Advances in radio communication render perhaps the most important innovations in police methods since the introduction of fingerprinting.

Present Practice

Today's tools of communication are allowing police departments, both large and small, to increase the extent and efficiency of their service. Hardly a single police action is taken that does not involve some sort of communication. Original complaints are usually made to the police department by use of citizen-placed telephone calls. The information is relayed to police dispatchers or other appropriate personnel by use of interoffice phones or by use of mechanical devices, such as the pneumatic tube. In many cases two-way radio is used to relay information to patrol vehicles or to other police departments.

Also helping to stretch the police potential are systems of communication involving teletype, radiotelegraph, land-wire telegraph, long-distance phone circuits, interconnected computer and photo transmitting machines.

These are but a sample of what make up the network of communication found in most police departments. These tools plus proper techniques are invaluable in accomplishing the necessary steps to deal with natural disasters or nuclear attacks. Therefore, knowledge of such tools and techniques are imperative to successful actions of local police auxiliary units.

Telephone Procedures

The citizen's first contact with the police department is often a telephone conversation with an officer. On the telephone you are the police department's voice and whatever you say and how you say it creates for the citizen an impression of the department to that citizen. Every time you pick up the phone you are doing a public relations job. It may be good, bad, or indifferent. Why not always try for the good public relations job?

When considering proper procedures for the use of the telephone, courtesy and consideration are always the keywords. Even when receiving calls from persons who are agitated or excited the proper action remains much the same as in normal telephone calls. Since a large part of police telephone work is receiving calls the following procedures are essential ones.

1. Identify yourself immediately after answering.
2. Speak courteously.
3. Have pad and pencil handy-makes notes when necessary.

On the other hand, when *you* make a call follow the same basic guides of courtesy and consideration. This may be stated as follows:

1. Have in mind what you wish to know or say when your call is answered.
2. Identify yourself and state your business.
3. Have pad and pencil available-make notes when necessary.

Reaching for a telephone is one of our most frequent and familiar gestures. However, this does not guarantee good telephone usage. Proper procedures can result in good telephone usage and are important to proper police work.

Radio Procedure

Two-way radio might well be considered the backbone of police communications. In many instances the proper use of this instrument may well mean the difference between success or failure in any given situation. In general, the same guides apply as did to good telephone procedures, namely, courtesy and consideration. However, a few specific guides are identified for your use.

To transmit a message:

1. Be certain the dispatcher is not busy transmitting other messages.
2. Contact dispatcher, giving your identification, and then wait for dispatcher to answer.
3. Begin your message after the dispatcher has answered you.

While transmitting a message:

1. Speak distinctly into the microphone as in ordinary conversation. Too loud a voice distorts the reception.
2. Speak slowly.
3. Keep messages brief.
4. Mentally rehearse your message before transmitting.
5. Never use vulgar language.

The final rule cannot be overemphasized. Not only is such language in poor taste, but is prohibited by regulations of the FCC. Furthermore, any excess language used, and vulgar language is excess, may well confuse or distort the meaning of your message.

In learning to use radio communications effectively it is necessary to master the codes and specific procedures in effect in your local police department. Appendix II gives some samples of such procedures.

Emergency Information Media

In addition to the telephone and radio communications of the police service, during a CD emergency the auxiliary policeman will need to receive and act on messages disseminated by public information media (radio and television broadcasts, newspapers, etc.) as part of the emergency information program. Although these messages will be intended for the general public, they will also convey information of value to the auxiliary policeman in the performance of his duties. For example, in many local civil defense plans provision is made for certain radio stations to remain on the air as part of the Emergency Broadcasting System, and their broadcasts will convey official information on such matters as warning conditions and last-minute instructions regarding movement to shelters or relocation areas.

POLICE COMMUNICATIONS & TELETYPE OPERATIONS

TABLE OF CONTENTS

		Page
I.	COMMUNICATIONS	1
	a. Radio in Automobiles	1
	b. Police Radio Messages	1
	c. Tampering with Private Communications	1
	d. Failing to Report Criminal Telephone or Telegraph Communications	1
	e. Unlawfully Obtaining Communications Information	2
	f. Tampering with Letters, Mail, etc.	2
II.	OFFENSES IN USE OF COMMUNICATION MEDIA	2
	a. Party Lines	2
	b. Annoying or Alarming Communications	2
	c. Jamming, Other Non-Legitimate Phone Calls	3
	d. Theft of Services (Telephone, Telegraph)	3
III.	INVESTIGATIONS	3
IV.	POLICE RADIO COMMUNICATIONS	4
	a. General Requirements for Proper Transmissions	4
	i. Ten-Signal Code	5
	ii. Word Code	6
	b. Headquarters Transmissions	7
	c. Field Transmissions	7
	d. Listeners	7
	e. Authority	7
	f. Radio Logs	7
V.	POLICE TELETYPE NETWORKS	8
	a. Description of "cops"	8
	b. Computer Control	8
	c. Operating Rules and Procedures	9
	d. Teletype Messages Required by Law	9
	e. Persons Wanted	9
	f. Warrant and Extradition	10
	g. Retention of Teletype Message Copies	11
	h. Cases Involving Property	11
	i. Stolen Cars	11
	j. Emergency Messages	11
	k. Criminal Record Requests – New York State	11
	l. Firearms Records	11
	m. Definitions	12
	n. Authorized Abbreviations	13

VI. PREPARING TELETYPE MESSAGES 15
a. Message Form 15
b. Message Example 15
c. File 1 and File 16 Messages 17
d. Punctuation 19
e. Numbers in Messages 20
f. Added Information, Correction, Reply, Cancellation 20
g. Code Signals 20
h. Fifth Line, Other Original Messages 20
i. Body of Message 20
j. Authority for Messages 21
k. File Classification Chart 22
l. Data Available on Persons or Property 25
m. Comparison of NCIC, NYIIS, COPS Data 25
n. Entering Data and Making Inquiries 26
o. Message Record Sheet 26
p. Cancellations and Corrections 27

POLICE COMMUNICATIONS & TELETYPE OPERATIONS

I. COMMUNICATIONS

A. RADIOS IN AUTOMOBILES

It is an Unclassified misdemeanor for any person who is not a peace officer to either equip an automobile with or knowingly use an automobile equipped with a radio receiving set capable of receiving signals on the frequencies allocated to police use. Excepted are holders of Federal amateur radio operator's licenses operating a receiver in connection with a mobile transmitter (V&T Sec. 397).

B. POLICE RADIO MESSAGES

It is a like misdemeanor to in any way knowingly interfere with the transmission of radio messages by police without first having secured a permit to do so from the person authorized to issue such a permit by the local municipal governing body or board. Offenses are punishable by fine not over $1,000, imprisonment not more than 6 months, or both (V&T Sec. 397).

The law excepts persons who hold a valid amateur radio operator's license issued by the Federal Communications Commission and who operate a duly licensed portable transmitter-receiver on frequencies allocated by the Federal Communications Commission to licensed radio amateurs (V&T Sec. 397).

C. TAMPERING WITH PRIVATE COMMUNICATIONS

A person is guilty of Tampering with Private Communications when, knowing that he does not have the consent of the sender or receiver, he obtains or attempts to obtain from an employee, officer or representative, of a telephone or telegraph corporation, by connivance, deception, intimidation or in any other manner, information with respect to the contents or nature thereof of a telephonic or telegraphic communication (P.L. Sec. 250.25, subd. 3).

A person is also guilty of Tampering with Private Communications when, knowing that he does not have the consent of the sender or receiver, and being an employee, officer or representative of a telephone or telegraph corporation, he knowingly divulges to another person the contents or nature thereof of a telephonic or telegraphic communication. The provisions of this subdivision do not apply to such person when he acts to report a criminal communication under the requirements of Penal Law Section 250.35 (see next paragraph) (P.L. Sec. 250.25, subd. 4). Tampering with Private Communications is a Class B misdemeanor.

D. FAILING TO REPORT CRIMINAL TELEPHONE OR TELEGRAPH COMMUNICATIONS

It is the duty of a telephone or telegraph corporation and of any employee, officer or representative thereof having knowledge that the facilities of such corporation are being used to conduct any criminal business, traffic or transaction, to furnish or attempt to furnish to an appropriate law enforcement officer or agency, all pertinent information within his possessionrelating to such matter, and to cooperate fully with any law enforcement officer or agency investigating such matter. A person is guilty of Failing to Report Criminal Communications when he knowingly violates any duty prescribed in this section (P.L. Sec. 250.35).

Failing to Report Criminal Communications is a Class B misdemeanor.

The prohibitions in Section 250.25, Penal Law do not apply to a law enforcement officer who obtains information from a telephone or telegraph corporation pursuant to Section 250.35 of the Penal Law (P.L. Sec. 250.25, subd.3).

E. UNLAWFULLY OBTAINING COMMUNICATIONS INFORMATION

A person is guilty of Unlawfully Obtaining Communications Information when, knowing that he does not have the authorization of a telephone or telegraph corporation, he obtains or attempts to obtain, by deception, stealth or in any other manner, from such corporation or from any employee, officer or representative thereof:

1. Information concerning identification or location of any wires, cables, lines, terminals or other apparatus used in furnishing telephone or telegraph service; or
2. Information concerning a record of any communication passing over telephone or telegraph lines of any such corporation (P.L. Sec. 250.30).

Unlawfully Obtaining Communications Information is a Class B misdemeanor.

F. TAMPERING WITH LETTERS, MAIL, ETC.

A person is guilty of Tampering with Private Communications when:

1. Knowing that he does not have the consent of the sender or receiver, he opens or reads a sealed letter or other sealed private communication (P.L. Sec. 250.25, subd. 1); or
2. Knowing that a sealed letter or other sealed private communication has been opened or read in violation of subdivision one of this section, he divulges, without the consent of the sender or receiver, the contents of such letter or communication, in whole or in part, or a resume of any portion of the contents thereof (P.L. Sec. 250.25, subd. 2).

Tampering with Private Communications is a Class B misdemeanor.

It is a Federal crime, punishable by $2,000 fine or 5 years imprisonment or both, to take a letter, postcard or package out of any post office or authorized depository or from a mail carrier or to take such thing which has been in the mails before it is delivered to a person to whom directed, with intent to obstruct the correspondence or to pry into the business or secrets of another. This violation includes taking mail left by the carrier, including from private mail boxes where deposited by the carrier.

It is also a Federal violation to steal or obtain mail by fraud from the post office or any postal facility.

These Federal violations are investigated by U.S. Postal Inspectors, who should be promptly notified of offenses (Title 18 U.S. Code, Secs. 1703, 1708).

II. OFFENSES IN USE OF COMMUNICATION MEDIA

A. PARTY LINES

A person commits the crime of Unlawfully Refusing to Yield a Party Line when being informed that a party line is needed for an emergency call, he refuses to immediately relinquish the line (P.L. Sec 270.15, subd. 2).

Unlawfully Refusing to Yield a Party Line is a Class B misdemeanor. A "party line" is a subscriber's line telephone circuit, consisting of two or more main telephone stations connected therewith, each station with a distinctive ring or telephone number (P.L. Sec. 270.15, subd. 1-a). An "emergency call" is a telephone call to a police or fire department, or for medical aid or ambulance service, necessitated by a situation in which human life or property is in jeopardy and prompt summoning of aid is essential (P.L. Sec. 270.15, subd. 1-b).

B. ANNOYING OR ALARMING COMMUNICATIONS

It is the crime of Aggravated Harassment to communicate with a person anonymously or otherwise, by telephone, telegraph, mail or any other form of communication, in a manner likely to cause annoyance or alarm, with intent to harass, annoy or alarm another (P.L. Sec. 240.30, subd.1). Aggravated Harassment is a Class A misdemeanor.

C. JAMMING, OTHER NON-LEGITIMATE PHONE CALLS

It is also Aggravated Harassment for any person to make a telephone call, whether or not a conversation ensues, with no purpose of legitimate communication and with intent to harass, annoy or alarm another (P.L. Sec. 240.30, subd. 2).

D. THEFT OF SERVICES (TELEPHONE, TELEGRAPH)

A person is guilty of Theft of Services when, with intent to avoid payment by himself or another person of the lawful charge for any telecommunications service, he obtains or attempts to avoid payment therefor by himself or another person by means of:

1. Tampering or making connection with the equipment of the supplier, whether by mechanical, electrical, acoustical, or other means, or
2. Any misrepresentation of fact which he knows to be false, or
3. Any other artifice, trick,deception, code or device (P.L. Sec. 165.15, subd. 4).

Theft of Services is a Class A misdemeanor. It includes use of illicit credit cards

III. INVESTIGATIONS

In any case involving police-frequency radio in automobiles, care must be taken to ensure that an actual test of the illicit receiver is made, to establish receipt of police frequencies. In addition, an expert in radio matters should make an examination of the radio, for expert testimony that the radio could receive police frequencies.

In taking complaints dealing with Tampering with Private Communications, the officer must be certain to pin down specific facts and details of the matter divulged, with exact times, dates and facts as to identification of violators.

In cases involving *"jamming"* telephones, it is proper to take detailed written statements from complaints, setting down the time and date of the calls and specific words said. Any factual information the victim may have to identify the offender should be obtained in detail. Where positive proof of identity is lacking, obtain permission to monitor the victim's telephone and consider obtaining an order to monitor the telephone of any suspect. Telephone companies may be able to offer valuable technical assistance in respect to crimes of this kind and the possibilities should be explored with ranking telephone company officals in proper cases.

In party line telephone cases, the officer must establish that the offender was in fact informed that the line was needed for an emergency call and that the emergency met the terms of the statute. A factor of identification of the offender is always present and if the complainant is not familiar with the offender, arrangements may be made for telephone and personal confrontation of the complainant and each potential user of the party line who could be the offender, for identification purposes. Officers should not overlook the value of proper interrogation of suspects in this kind of case.

In cases involving Theft of Services, officers should always work closely with telephone company sections assigned responsibility for attempting to determine to whom calls should properly be billed, since these persons are frequently able to make associations of persons and numbers which cannot be done by anyone not constantly working with such things.

IV. POLICE RADIO COMMUNICATIONS

Police radio transmitters must be licensed by the Federal Communications Commission (FCC). Each Base Station transmitter must be licensed. All mobile stations are included under the main license. The FCC will assign appropriate frequencies and call letters. Police radio falls in the category of "Public Safety Radio Services" in FCC terminology and is covered by FCC Rules and Regulations, Part 89.

All adjustments and tests which may affect the proper operation of police radios must be made only by holders of first or second class commercial radio operator's licenses. Such license holders may be either a department member or an outsider, such as a radio shop owner or employee.

Police officers and dispatchers broadcasting over police voice radios are not required to have individual licenses.

FCC Rules and Regulations, Sec. 89.151, require that all police transmissions, regardless of their nature, shall be restricted to the minimum practical transmission time.

In all police agencies with radio broadcasting systems, clear general instructions should be in effect to ensure that the headquarters transmitter is in charge of the air and may order other units silenced for priority messages, regardless of the rank of persons using mobile equipment, including radio cars, in the field.

In an emergency, the headquarters transmitter can temporarily transfer command of the air to a ranking officer in the field. This should be a rare occasion and should be done on a formal basis. There should be no informal monopolizing of the air by mobile units in the field.

A list of emergency telephone numbers should be maintained at the dispatcher's desk. The list should be regularly checked and kept current and complete. It should include hospitals, ambulance service, doctors available for emergencies, fire departments, coroner and medical examiners, garages, etc.

A. GENERAL REQUIREMENTS FOR PROPER TRANSMISSIONS

All transmission must be clearly enunicated. The microphone should be held exactly in front of the speaker's lips and about two inches away. The voice should always be free of emotion or stress. The speaker must be certain that a very brief pause is made after pressing the transmitter button and before speaking and that another very brief pause is made before releasing the button after speaking, to avoid chopping off parts of the transmission.

Inexperienced officers commonly fail to clearly enunciate and often chop off parts of their transmissions by pressing or releasing the transmitter button too late or too soon. All officers using any transmitter should receive substantial training to ensure that they use it properly. (A microphone-amplifier-loudspeaker or a tape recorder set-up should be used in training and not any actual radio transmissions.)

Training should include practice in the use of established radio procedure of the department and in brief, clear wording of transmissions, whether information messages, requests for information or instructions.

Headquarters radio transmitters are distinguishable by sound from the mobile transmitters. It is thus not necessary for headquarters to always identify itself. FCC rules require only that the main station shall identify itself with its assigned call letters at least once each thirty minutes during each period of operation. Mobile transmitters (radio cars, walkie-talkies, etc.) must identify themselves with the geographic name of the governmental subdivision under whose name the main station is licensed (e.g., car two of the Southton, N.Y., Police Department would call itself "Southton two").

A usual, clear and brief routine would thus be: "Car two" (from headquarters); "Southton two" (from the mobile unit), "Compliant, Mrs. John Doe, one Main Street, family disturbance" (from Headquarters); "Southton two okay" (from the mobile unit). With these brief messages, headquarters has located car two "in service," issued instructions to investigate a family disturbance based on a complaint, given the identity of the complainant and the location of the disturbance and has been informed by car two that the message was understood and that the instructions would be complied with.

Established procedures should also include routing for mobile units to inform headquarters when they go into service at the beginning of a tour of duty and when they go out of service from time to time during the tour. The initial call at the beginning of the tour will automatically give a check of the operating condition of the mobile units' radio equipment. The officer or officers using the equipment during the tour should be identified in this initial call.

A usual routing would be: "Southton two" (from the mobile unit); "Car two" (from headquarters); "In service, occupant 113" (from the mobile unit); "'Okay two" (acknowledgment from headquarters, specifying which car is being acknowledged).

"Occupant 113" identifies the officers in Southton Car two in the preceding example. It is best to use numbers, usually badge or shield numbers, to identify officers on the air. It is more secure against unauthorized listeners and is more accurate and brief than using names. The headquarters radioman should of course have a complete list of officers' names and numbers, arranged in numerical sequence and also in name order. He should record the mobile units in use and the officers using them, as they call in.

In larger departments, where air-time is limited, due to the large number of mobile units requiring air-time, it is desirable to use a code to save time on the air. The *"ten-signal"* code is widely used. It provides codes for a major part of the information constituting police radio traffic, thus cutting down words and saving substantial amounts of air-time. Some departments may add security to their use of radio by assigning numbers "post numbers") to key locations in their territory and then describing locations by giving distance and direction from a post number. The following are frequently used *"ten-signals"* of the system recommended by the Associated Public Safety Communications Officers, Inc. (APCO);

TEN-SIGNAL CODE

10-1	Unable to copy, change your location
10-2	Signals good
10-3	Stop transmitting
10-4	Acknowledgment
10-5	Relay
10-6	Busy, stand by unless urgent
10-7	Out of service atreport (give location or telephone number)
10-16	Domestic trouble at
10-17	Meet complainant at
10-18	Complete assignment quickly
10-19	Return to
10-20	My location is (or what is your location)
10- 8	In Service
10- 9	Repeat, please
10-10	Fight in progress at
10-11	Dog case (describe - e.g., *"fight," "biting," "rabid")*
10-12	Stand by (or "stop")
10-13	Weather and road
10-14	Report of prowler at
10-15	Civil disturbance at
10-48	Traffic standard needs repairs at
10-49	Traffic light out at
10-50	Accident (Kind, location)
10-51	Wrecker needed at

10-21 Call by telephone
10-22 Disregard
10-23 Arrived at scene
10-24 Assignment completed
10-25 Report in person to (meet)
10-26 Holding subject - expedite reply
10-27 Diver's license information
10-29 Check records for wanted
10-30 Illegal use of radio
10-31 Crime in progress at
10-32 Man with gun at
10-33 Emergency
10-36 Correct time is
10-37 Investigate suspicious vehicle (describe)
10-38 Stopping suspicious vehicle (Give description and location before stopping)
10-41 Beginning tour of duty
10-42 Ending tour of duty
10-43 Inform me about
10-44 Request permission to leave patrol for
10-45 Animal carcass in lane at
10-46 Assist motorist at
10-47 Emergency road repairs needed at
or stolen

10-52 Ambulance needed at
10-53 Road blocked at
10-54 Livestock on highway
10-55 Intoxicated driver
10-56 Intoxicated pedestrian
10-57 Hit-and-run (fatal personal injury, property damage)
10-58 Direct traffic at
10-59 Convoy or escort (specify)
10-62 Reply to message
10-63 Prepare to make written copy
10-64 Message for local delivery
10-65 Net message assignment
10-66 Message cancellation
10-67 Clear to read net message
10-68 Dispatch information
10-69 Message received
10-70 Fire alarm at
10-74 Negative
10-75 In contact with
10-76 En Route
10-77 Estimated time of arrival
10-78 Need assistance at
10-90 Bank alarm at
10-94 Drag racing at
10-96 Mental subject
10-99 Records indicate wanted

Accuracy is of prime importance in radio work. Names should be spelled out in any instance where a file check is required or it is otherwise important that the correct spelling be known. Names should be spelled with a word-code by the officer transmitting. The following word code is good:

WORD CODE

A	Adam	I	Ida	R	Robert
B	Boy	J	John	S	Sam
C	Charles	K	King	T	Tom
D	David	L	Lincoln	U	Union
E	Edward	M	Mary	V	Victor
F	Frank	N	Nora	W	William
G	George	O	Ocean	X	X-ray
H	Henry	P	Paul	Y	Young
		Q	Queen	Z	Zebra

In using the word-code for spelling, transmit as follows:

"... JONES, J-JOHN, O-OCEAN, N-NORA, E-EDWARD, S-SAM." Do not say: "J AS IN JOHN" or "J LIKE IN JOHN" or similar wordy recitals.

In cases where numbers must be transmitted, such as license and serial numbers, the receiving officer should repeat each completed number on the air so that the sending officer can verify that it was correctly heard and understood.

B. HEADQUARTERS TRANSMISSIONS

A ranking officer should always be in command of headquarters radio. A dispatcher trained in radio procedures may be permitted to send out routine complaints or other items as received, but all important messages, including instructions to make arrests, alarms of major crimes and similar things should be screened by the ranking officer to insure that proper instructions are issued, that important instructions are not overlooked and that problems of identification, force to be used, road blocks and similar matters requiring police skill and experience are correctly handled. It should be the ranking officer's duty to also coordinate closely the work of the radio dispatcher and any complaint desk or officer, if complaint duties are not handled by the radio dispatcher.

C. FIELD TRANSMISSIONS

In order to keep transmission brief, officers should eliminate the use of unnecessary expressions or formal courtesies, such as "Roger," "Wilco," "Over and out," "Do you want to," "Will you please," "Yes, sir," "Thank you," and so on. Transmissions must be brief, businesslike and impersonal.

D. LISTENERS

It must always be remembered that police frequencies may be overheard by anyone on a large number of radio receivers purchasable almost anywhere. Consequently, matters of a confidential nature should not be put over the air except in extreme emergencies.

E. AUTHORITY

Standing instructions should exist in all departments having radio as to the authority of the headquarters dispatcher to make assignments of mobile units and officers and procedures for instances where mobile units have current assignments when they are called by the dispatcher to take a new assignment, or to take some police action of higher priority.

Generally speaking, the dispatcher should have final and complete authority as to assignments and all should understand that he is working closely with and expressing the instructions of the ranking officer in charge of communications.

The dispatcher should log all assignments as made and the exact time, for immediate reference and for a permanent record.

F. RADIO LOGS

Federal Communications Commission rules require that a radio log be maintained at each base (fixed) station from which transmissions are made (Federal Communications Commission Rules and Regulations, Section 89.175). Maintaining a log is also in accordance with proper police practice and procedure. Logs maintained by police agencies should include all transmissions and messages received and the exact time of each. Abbreviations may be used to reduce the work involved. These logs should also contain notations of exact time station identifying call letters were broadcast, and the full signature of the operator, showing time at beginning and end of his period of responsibility or tour of duty.

Mobile unit operators should not be required to keep radio logs. It is dangerous, since they will often be driving while receiving or transmitting.

V. POLICE TELETYPE NETWORKS

Chapter 533, Laws of 1931, established a basic system of coordinated teletypewriter communications, "for the purpose of prompt collection and distribution of information throughout the State of New York as the police problems of the state may require" (Exec. L. Sec. 217).

The Superintendent of State Police is responsible for the system's installation, operation and maintenance. The system is available for use by any department or division of the government of New York State, or by any municipal, county, town, village, railroad or other special police department lawfully maintained by any New York corporation (Exec. L. Sec. 219).

The original "basic system" has been expanded over the years since it was established. The current system is operated in conjunction with computers which do both data recording and message routing. Its modern and current name is "Computer Oriented Police information System," and it is commonly referred to by police officers as "COPS."

The COPS teletype network connects with and is part of the Nationwide Law Enforcement Teletype System (known to police as "LETS" or "N-LETS"). LETS covers the 48 continental states (not Alaska or Hawaii).

COPS is also directly connected to the National Crime Information Center ("NCIC") operated by the FBI in Washington, DC, and the NCIC computers. These computers store crime data from throughout the United States.

A. DESCRIPTION OF "COPS"

The Computer Oriented Police-information System of New York is a teletype network divided into districts, under the control of New York State Police Headquarters. Each district is generally co-extensive with the territory assigned to the various State Police stations. State and Troop Headquarters are "control points."

"Control points" control the teletypewriter circuits in the geographical area assigned them. The individual circuits have varying numbers of teletype machines and stations. All circuits terminate in the computer located at State Police Headquarters in Albany. The teletypewriter stations are located in municipal police departments, sheriff's offices, and other law enforcement agencies, including, of course, New York State Police installations.

All teletypewriter machines on the COPS system are equipped with "selective coding equipment" which permits each teletype machine to receive only those messages addressed to it.

Messages to police departments and other law enforcement agencies not on the COPS network are sent to the station nearest or most accessible to the department to which directed, to be forwarded by telephone or personal delivery. No special instructions in messages are required to secure this service. However, it will only be done in case of messages sent direct to or for the attention of a particular department. An "All Points Bulletin" ("APB") will be sent only to stations on the COPS network. If it is desired that one or more police agencies not on COPS receive an alarm, an individual direction to such agency(ies) is necessary.

B. COMPUTER CONTROL

The entire COPS network is under the control of its computer in Albany. All messages are transmitted by the computer exactly as received from the sending machines. It is thus essential that every person preparing teletype messages for sending via a COPS teletypewriter shall make certain that only correct messages are delivered to communications personnel for sending.

1. Through selective coding and automatic switching by the computer, the various teletype machines receive only messages addressed to them, except that "control points" receive also all messages on the "circuits" which they control.

2. The computer is designed to hold up and store teletype traffic for any station when the station is out of service due to routine maintenance, mechanical or electronic trouble, change of paper, etc. It will then send the traffic when the station returns to service.

C. OPERATING RULES AND PROCEDURES

Operating rules and detailed procedures for sending messages on the basic system are set out in the COPS Operating Manual. Copies may be obtained from the New York State Police. Operating rules and procedures must be strictly adhered to. Unless there is exact adherence to proper message construction and-to proper codes, the computer will not accept or will misdirect messages.

1. Officers must be familiar with and comply with the following basic Regulations:
   a. Message traffic shall be brief and in the form prescribed.
   b. No message may be sent without proper authorization.
   c. All message traffic must be official business.
   d. Only the messages of duly authorized member agencies shall be transmitted.
   e. Member stations shall transmit official messages without charge for State Police personnel and for members of police departments without teletypewriter service.
   f. Requests of military authorities for use of system to report the arrest of deserters or other military personnel shall be honored.
   g. All messages are confidential and shall not be divulged to unauthorized persons.
   h. The official time of the system is Eastern Standard except that Daylight Saving Time shall be used whenever it is officially in effect.

D. TELETYPE MESSAGES REQUIRED BY LAW

When any peace officer or police agency in New York receives a complaint that a felony has been committed and if the perpetrator thereof has not been apprehended within five hours after such complaint was received, such police agency must cause information of such felony to be dispatched over the police communications system. Police agencies not connected with basic system must transmit such information to the nearest or most convenient teletypewriter station, from where it will be immediately dispatched in conformity with the regulations governing the system (Exec. L. Sec. 221).

1. The paramount consideration in respect to the messages sent in compliance with this law is that they shall accurately inform all police agencies that criminals are abroad and could be in any one of their jurisdictions.

2. Any classification of teletype which conforms to COPS regulations will comply with this law.

E. PERSONS WANTED

Section 173 of the Criminal Procedure Law provides that when a warrant has been issued in New York for the arrest of a person for a crime or offense, any officer having received a communication in the official course of business of the existence of such warrant may arrest such person, although the officer does not have the warrant in his possession at the time of arrest, if the arrest would otherwise have been proper if the officer had the warrant in his possession. The officer must advise the person arrested of the crime or offense charged and of the fact that a warrant has been issued.

Any officer originating any communication in the official course of business involving the commission of a misdemeanor or lesser offense must include therein the fact that a warrant of arrest has or has not been issued and further indicate, when appropriate, that the warrant has been endorsed for "nighttime" and Sunday execution."

Messages on persons wanted from police agencies in states other than New York are covered by Section 843 of the Criminal Procedure Law, which permits arrest without a warrant upon reasonable information that the defendant stands charged in the courts of another state with a crime punishable by death or imprisonment for a term exceeding one year. The official teletype message will constitute "reasonable information."

1. Messages on persons wanted from Canada or any foreign country must be handled in accordance with Federal law. Defendants can only be extradited by Canada or other foreign countries through the government of the United States, in accordance with Federal statute, treaties and conventions. Section 3184 of Title 18, United States Code, provides that any justice or judge of the United States, any United States Commissioners authorized by a US District Court or any New York judge of a court of record of general jurisdiction may, on complaint made under oath, issue a warrant of arrest for a person charged with a crime in the jurisdiction of any foreign government, if the crime is one provided for by treaty or convention between the United States and that foreign government. The teletype message may be used as the basis for complaint by New York officers in such cases.

F. WARRANT AND EXTRADITION

All messages on persons wanted (whether File 5, or other classifications) must state whether a warrant has been issued or facts justifying arrest without a warrant. If no warrant has been issued and one is required, the message must state "CHECKING ON WARRANT."

1. If a message is directed outside New York State, it must also state whether the requesting authority will extradite (e.g., "WARRANT ISSUED, WILL EXTRADITE," or "WAREX") and, if this fact has not been determined, must state "CHECKING ON EXTRADITION."
2. No message concerning a person wanted will be relayed outside New York State unless it has a statement as to warrant and extradition.
3. An "ADDED INFORMATION" message should be directed to the same points as the original message as soon as the facts have been ascertained as to warrant and extradition if the original message stated "CHECKING ON WARRANT" or "CHECKING ON WARRANT AND EXTRADITION" or "WARRANT ISSUED, CHECKING ON EXTRADITION."
4. Wording such as "HOLD FOR INVESTIGATION," "DETAIN FOR THIS DEPARTMENT," etc., cannot be used in any messages on persons wanted, and messages containing such phrases will not be forwarded.

Messages on persons wanted should include all available information required to accurately identify the persons to be taken into custody, including the exact time of the crime or incident, when known, in order to protect arresting officers.

1. When the fingerprint classification (abbreviated "FPC") of a wanted person is known, it must be included in the person wanted message.
2. Such messages shall also include any information known that wanted persons are armed with a dangerous weapon or are otherwise dangerous or have suicidal tendencies.

G. RETENTION OF TELETYPE MESSAGE COPIES

The printed message or "printout" which teletype machines produce (both inquiries of and answers from the computer or other agencies) is a necessary link in establishing "probable cause" warranting the arrest of an individual and should be preserved with the case file. It is not critical whether the document preserved is the original or the copy, but the original is best. The printout should go directly into the file of the agency taking arrest action, to be preserved for any necessary future use.

If a police agency having no teletypewriter terminal of its own has an officer who stops a suspicious car and the officer communicates with a police agency which has a terminal, and is told moments later that he has a "hit," the terminal employee who answers the officer's inquiry should note in writing on the printout sheet how, when and to whom he furnished the information. He should initial his notation, and then forward the printout to the inquiring officer's agency for retention in that agency's case file. This establishes a chain of evidence for the official police communication.

There is no set time as to how long a message printout should be retained. It should be retained as long as there is any chance the defendant will raise a question on the probable cause for his arrest. Some persons arrested and prosecuted in state courts, after arrest on a printout, may receive long sentences and be confined in a penitentiary for several years. Subsequently they may decide to raise the question of arrest in Federal Court on an appeal of some kind. Permanent retention of the printout would seem to be the most desirable rule in any case where an actual arrest is made based on the message.

H. CASES INVOLVING PROPERTY

In any case involving property in which the complainant's only or primary interest is recovery of the property, a message must not be sent unless a warrant has been issued. This rule is for the protection of arresting officers.

I. STOLEN CARS

Whenever a stolen car is reported by a message on the basic system, and is recovered, it should not be released to any person unless and until a full cancellation of the message reporting it stolen has been sent by the department which originated the stolen message and has been received by the department which recovered the car.

J. EMERGENCY MESSAGES

Emergency messages may include only matters requiring immediate transmission and attention, such as hit-and-run, armed robbery, temporary whereabouts of wanted persons, or other urgent matters.

K. CRIMINAL RECORD REQUESTS

New York State Identification and Intelligence System (NYSIIS). - Requests directed to NYSIIS for record information will be sent to and handled by NYSHS, day or night, seven days a week.

1. NYSIIS does its utmost to handle teletypewriter messages requesting information on an immediate basis. It is an imposition to request and in most cases, an impossibility for them to check and reply to a long list of names on a teletype request. Except in a rare case of extreme emergency, lengthy lists of names to be checked should be sent by mail or otherwise and not over the "COPS" system.

L. FIREARMS RECORDS

New York State Police Headquarters (Pistol Permit Section) maintains records of all pistol licenses issued in New York. It also keeps a lost or stolen weapons file, licensed pistol registration file and records of weapons purchased and sold by gun dealers (except gun dealers' records on purchases and sales in New York City). These files will be searched on request. Messages should be directed to "SP ALBANY, ATTN: PISTOL PERMIT SECTION." Requests to check New York City files on gun dealers' purchases and sales should be directed to the New York City Police Department.

M. DEFINITIONS

A full list of definitions applicable to all phases of operation of the basic system is published in the COPS Manual; however, the following teletype terms should be understood by all officers:

ACKNOWLEDGMENT - act by which an operator or machine signifies that a message has been received.

ADDED INFORMATION - message sent to supplement an original message and referred thereto.

APB (ALL POINTS BULLETIN) - a general alarm, to all terminals.

AUTHORITY - person responsible for the origination of a message.

BROADCAST - the transmission of a message on all circuits.

CANCELLATION - a message sent to cancel an original alarm.

CDC (CALL DIRECTING CODE) - directs message to its proper destination.

CORRECTION - a message sent to amend a previous message.

DIRECT MESSAGE - a message addressed to a specific agency or receiver.

EMERGENCY CANCELLATION - a message sent to cancel, without delay, previous message.

FINGERPRINT CLASSIFICATION - a listing of the kinds of fingerprint patterns, ridge counts and tracings and missing fingers in a subject's fingerprints, using a code notation for each of the ten fingers.

JUNK - any message or part thereof which is unintelligible by reason of mechanical or electrical difficulties.

MESSAGE NUMBER - numerals in the upper left-hand corner of a teletypewriter communication to distinguish it from other communications having the same point of origin.

MESSAGE TIME - the figures placed on a message after the sender's name, to indicate the time the typing was completed. Time based on the conventional time designator of ante meridian (AM) and post meridian (PM) (noon and midnight designated as 12-00 N and 12-00 MID, respectively). Eastern Standard Time used except when Daylight Saving Time is in effect.

PART CANCELLATION - a message sent by the originating station to cancel some portion of an original and/or previous message, using a new message number and the same file classification as the original.

REFERENCE - data by which an original message is identified, i.e., the message and file numbers, place and date of origin, message direction and subject.

REPLY - a message that answers a previous teletype message; must refer to the original and be designated by the word "REPLY."

SENDER - surname of operator who originally transmits a message.

N. AUTHORIZED ABBREVIATIONS

The following abbreviations may be used in teletype messages:

AA	Control Point, Troop "A," Batavia
ADDED INFO	Added information
AKA	Also known as
AM	Ante Meridian - (Between Midnight and Noon)
APB	All Points Bulletin
ASSIGN	Assignment
ASST	Assistant
ATL	Attempt to locate
ATTN	Attention
AUTH	Message sent on authority of
BB	Control Point, Troop "B," Malone
BCI	Bureau of Criminal Investigation
BLD	Build
BLK	Black
BRN	Brown
CC	Control Point, Troop "C," Sidney
C (in description)	Chinese
CANCEL	Cancellation
CAPT	Captain
CCT	Circuit
CHIEF INSPR	Chief Inspector
CODE SIG	Code Signal
COL	Colonel
COMP	Complexion
CORRECT	Correction
CP	Chief of Police
CPL	Corporal
CT/SGT	Chief Technical Sergeant
DD	Control Point, Troop "D," Oneida
DATA	We request owner's name, address, make of car, motor number, etc., on the following registration
DCT	Direct
DEP	Deputy
DK	Dark
DMV	Department of Motor Vehicles, Albany, NY
DOA	Dead on arrival
DOB	Date of birth
EE	Control Point, Troop "E," Canandaigua

ETA	Estimated time of arrival
F	Female
FF	Control Point, Troop "F," Middletown
FILE	File classification number
F/SGT	First Sergeant
FOA	For other authorities
FPC	Fingerprint classification
GG	Control Point, Troop "G," Loudonville
HQ	Division Headquarters, Albany
I	Indian
INV	Investigator
INSPR	Inspector
J	Japanese
KK	Control Point, Troop "K," Hawthorne
LETS	Nationwide Law Enforcement Teletype System
LIC	License number
LIEUT	Lieutenant
M	Male
MAJ	Major
MED	Medium
MESA	Referring to your message
MEX	Mexican
MID	Midnight
MOT	Motor
NCIC	National Crime Information Center
NFC	Negative file check
NYSIIS	New York State Identification and Intelligence System
NMN	No middle name
NYS	New York State
O (in description)	Other (meaning any other racial abbreviation not listed herein)
OFF	Officer
OPR	Operator
PART CANCEL	Partial cancellation
PD	Municipal Police Department
PD NYC	Police Department, City of New York
PM	Post Meridian (Between Noon and Midnight)
PTL	Patrolman
QQ	Control Point, Division Headquarters, Albany
REF	Please refer to our message
REG	Registration number
ROIR	Reply only if record
RP	Message repeated by
SER	Serial
SGT	Sergeant
SO	Sheriff
SP	State Police
SR INV	Senior Investigator
S/SGT	Staff Sergeant
SUPT	Superintendent
TT	Control Point, Troop "T," Elsmere
TOT	Turned over to
TPR	Trooper
T/SGT	Technical Sergeant
TWX	Teletypewriter Exchange System

UNK	Unknown
VIN	Vehicle Identification Number
VOID	Cancel our message
W	White
WAREX	Warrant issued will extradite
Z/SGT	Zone Sergeant

The permissible abbreviations for states of the United States, and for foreign countries, Canadian Provinces and Mexican states are set out In the COPS manual, phone book and postal directory.

VI. PREPARING TELETYPE MESSAGES

All messages for transmission over the basic system must be in the prescribed form and as brief as possible without losing clarity. Conformance with instructions for message construction set out in the COPS Manual is not only essential for use on the basic system of New York State but also permits the message to be correctly carried to other states in the continental United States over the Nationwide Law Enforcement Teletype System (LETS) and to the National Crime Information Center (NCIC) computers at the FBI in Washington, DC.

COPS Manuals may be found at all stations on the basic system, including local police stations as well as State Police stations and may be procured from the New York State Police at Albany.

A. MESSAGE FORM

Messages which do not conform (in construction or content) to the requirements set out in the COPS Manual will not be sent but will be returned to the point of origin for correction. Conformity is necessary so that every department in the state may operate with a minimum of delay and to give maximum protection to the individual officer who acts on the basis of information received in a teletype message over the basic system.

B. MESSAGE EXAMPLE

All messages on the basic system must have a heading, a body, an authority and a sender, in the form indicated by the following example:

EXAMPLE:
Line 1 ... NYAZ
Line 2 ... 6214 FILE 12 PD NYC APR 4-10 REPLY
Line 3 ... TO PD JAMESTOWN NY CODE 77
Line 4 ...
Line 5 ... MESA 381 FILE APR 3-10 APB UNK W M
Line 6 ... SUSPECT HARRY ROE WAS AT QUEENS COUNTY ADDRESS FROM 8-30 AM TO 12-00 MID APR 2-10 ACCORDING TO RELIABLE WITNESSESNO FURTHER INVESTIGATION BEING CONDUCTED. WRITTEN REPORT FOLLOWS.
2nd line below
body ..... AUTH LT MURPHY BROWN 6-17 PM
3rd line below
body NY03030

1. File 1 Messages (Stolen Motor Vehicles, Trailers or Motorcycles) and File 16 Messages (Lost and Stolen License Plates) are the only exceptions to the preceding rule as to form of teletype messages. They must be prepared in a special format, as shown later in this ongoing section.

2. All departments have been assigned NCIC code numbers, whether or not they have teletype facilities on the basic system are assigned two-letter call directing codes ("CDC's"). Both NCIC codes and CDC's are listed in the COPS Manual.
3. The individual lines of the sample message were prepared in accordance with the following rules:
   a. Line 1 contains a message's "call directing codes" (or "CDC's"). These are the means by which the computer determines the destination of the message. The police officer preparing the message must decide on its destination and use. It is the responsibility of the teletype operator to translate these into the proper CDC's (and "Function Codes," if any -the Function Codes give instructions as to computer activity in respect to the message). CDC's and Function Codes are all set out in the COPS Manual.
      (1) The first two letters in the example, on Line 1, are the CDC for the agency originating the message (i.e,. NY for New York City Police Department). The next two letters are the CDC for the department to which the message is destined (i.e. AZ for Jamestown Police Department). The correct CDC must always be ascertained from the COPS Manual
      (2) The CDC "SP" will send the message to all New York State Police teletype stations. The CDC "PD" will send it to all police agencies and sheriff's offices in New York. If a message is to go out of New York to an out-of-state law enforcement agency, the CDC for out-of-state is "IS" and must be followed by the CDC for the out-of-state destination.
      (3) If a message has an inquiry of or information for the New York State Identification and Intelligence System (NYSIIS), the proper CDC for NYSIIS is "QC."
   b. Lines 2 and 3 constitute the "heading" of the message. They show the identity of the message and its origin and destinations, spelled out in words and abbreviations. In the example, the message is the 6,214th message sent by the Police Department, New York City. It is a "File 12" (message concerning homicide). Line 3 (the second line of the heading) shows the message's destination and the code signal for special handling desired ("Code 77").
      (1) Every message must be designated by a number (in the example, "6214"). For every teletype station on the basic system, message numbering always begins with "1" for the first message sent after midnight of December 31 annually and messages are thereafter numbered consecutively throughout the year, straight through the last message sent on the following December 31st.
   c. Line 4 is always left blank
   d. Line 5 is always the reference line, if a reference is required and shows to what prior message, if any, the message relates.
   e. Line 6 and following are the body of the message. The body always begins on line 6 unless there is no reference, when it begins on line 5.
   f. The authority, sender and time sent are the next to last line of every message (in the example, this line is marked "2nd line below body" to show its placement when teletyped). The "authority" is the identity and rank of the officer who authorized the message, "Lt. Murphy" in the

example. "Brown" in the example is the teletype operator who sent the message.

g. The last line of the message is the "NCIC Code" of the sending agency. Frequently a sending agency is not one with a station on the basic system and thus has no CDC. The NCIC code will be its identifier. In the example this is "NY 03030," marked "3rd. line below body" to show its placement when typed on the teletype machine.

C. FILE 1 AND FILE 16 MESSAGES

File 1 (Stolen Motor Vehicles, Trailers, and Motorcycles) and File 16 (Lost or Stolen License Plates) messages have a special format of their own. All the data on the stolen or lost item which the message sets out are automatically entered in the memory banks of the computer the instant the teletype message is received by it when the proper function code is included with the call directing codes (CDC's). Examples of a proper File 1 and a proper File 16 original message are as follows:

EXAMPLE, File 1:
Line 1 ... KORESPPDQLQJNX
Line 2 ... 235 FILE 1 SP CLAVERACK NY MAY 1-10
Line 3 ... TO APB
Line 4 ...
Line 5 ... 4A7528.NY.10..
Line 6 ... 09ME44217CO.
Line 7 ... 09.MERC.COU.2T. GRN/LGR
Line 8 ... 050170
Line 9 ... NY11001
Line 10 .. K0235.
Line 11 .. STOLEN GHENT NY 9 TO 11 PM-OWNER CHARLES A. DOE-
1 MAIN-CLAVERACK NY 2nd line below
body ..... AUTH SGT ROE GREEN 11-50 PM
3rd line below body ..... NY 11001

EXPLANATION

1. The above message concerns a 2009 Mercury Cougar, color top green over light green body, hardtop, two-door, 2010 New York license plates 4A7528, owned by Charles A. Doe, 1 Main Street, Claverack, NY, and stolen at Ghent, NY, sometime between 9:00 and 11:00 PM on May 1, 2010. The individual lines of the example were prepared under the following rules:
   a. Line 1 contains the "CDC's" and "KO" is the CDC for the State Police at Claverack. In addition, this line has the function code "RE," a direction to the computer to include the data in the message in the computer memory bank. Function code "RE" is the same for all File 1 messages. "SP" is the CDC for all State Police installations with teletype. "PD" is the CDC for all police and sheriffs' offices with teletype installations. "QL" is the CDC for the New York State Motor Vehicle Department at Albany; "QJ" is the CDC for New York State Police Communications Headquarters, Albany, and "NX" is the CDC for the National Auto Theft Bureau (NATB) in New York City.
   b. Line 2 is the same as any other message and carries the message number, the "file, originating agency and date sent."

c. Line 3 is the same as any other message, showing the distribution desired - in the example, APB (the abbreviation for "all points bulletin" to all teletype installations on the basic system).
d. Line 4 is left blank as in other messages.
e. Line 5 gives the license plate data. These are always set out in this order: plate number, issuing state and year, followed by two periods for a private plate or an appropriate abbreviation from the COPS Manual for any other kind of plate (e.g., "DL" for dealers' plates, "OB" for passenger bus plates, "TK" for truck plates, etc.). Only private passenger automobile plates are represented solely by two periods, as in the example.
f. Line 6 gives the stolen vehicle's identification number its "VIN."
g. Line 7 sets out the description of the vehicle, using the codes set out in the COPS Manual for motor vehicles, always in the following order: year, make, model, style, color. In the example, these are: "09," "Merc" for Mercury, "COU" for Cougar model, "2T" for two-door hardtop style, and GRN/LGR for green top, light green body. Periods must be used in line 7 just as shown in the example (see paragraph on "Punctuation" later in this section).
h. Line 8 is the date of occurrence of the incident . The date must be set out with numerals for month, day and year. If the month or day is a single numeral it is preceded by 0. February third would thus be entered 0203, followed by the year or "020304" for February 3, 2004. October 20, 2004, would be "102004."
i. Line 9 carries the NCIC code of the originating police agency (SP Claverack is "NY 11001").
j. Line 10 is always the CDC of the originating agency and the message number (KO is the CDC for SP Claverack and the message number is 235).
k. Line 11 carries any pertinent information desired as to the theft, such as owner, time of theft, place of theft. Such data are restricted to a total of 42 characters and nothing past the 42 characters will be entered into the computer, although anything past 42 characters will be transmitted to all receiving an actual copy of the message. This is similar to the "body" of other teletype messages. Any readily recognizable abbreviations pertinent and suitable may be used in the 42 characters, contrary to the general rules that only authorized abbreviations may be used in other messages.
    (1) To include material information in 42 characters requires some thought and economy of phrasing but is not difficult. For example, the characters "ARMED V M" indicate an armed white male, the characters "STOLEN 32 CAL COLT REV GLV COMPT" indicate a .32 caliber Colt revolver which was in the glove compartment was stolen.
l. Second line below the body is the same as other messages, showing the authority for the message and the sender.
m. Third line below the body is also the same as in other messages, carrying the NCIC Code for the originating agency (same as Line 9 of File 1's).

EXAMPLE, File 16:

Line 1 ... KORGQLQJ
Line 2 ... 236 FILE 16 SP CLAVERACK NY MAY 1-10
Line 3 ... TO APB
Line 4 ...
Line 5 ... .2A2314.NY.10..1.
Line 6 ... 050110
Line 7 ... NY11001.
Line 8 ... K0236
Line 9 ... STOLEN GHENT
2nd line below
body ..... AUTH SGT ROE GREEN 11-52 PM
3rd line below body NY11001

EXPLANATION

1. The above message concerns the loss of a single license plate at 7:00 p.m. in Ghent, NY. The license plate is numbered "2A2314" and is a 2010 New York Plate, The individual lines of the message conform to rules as follows:
   a. Line 1 contains the CDC of the originating agency ("KO" for SP, Claverack) and the function code for the computer of "RG" which directs the computer to store the data in its memory bank and is the same for all File 16's. "QL" and "QJ" are the CDC's for the New York State Department of Motor Vehicles and the Communications Headquarters of the State Police, both at Albany.
   b. Line 2 is the same as both prior message examples.
   c. Line 3 is the same as both prior message examples, i.e. shows the destination of the message.
   d. Line 4 is blank, same as prior message example.
   e. Line 5 is same as in a File 1 message, showing the license plate in order of plate number, state of issue and year of issue. The periods indicated in the example must be used in all messages. The example shows one lost or stolen plate. If both plates had been lost or stolen, Line 5 would be: "2A2314.NY.10..2.".
   f. Line 6 shows date lost or stolen, same as Line 8 of a File 1 message.
   g. Line 7 shows the NCIC Code of the originating agency, same as Line 9 of a File 1 message.
   h. Line 8 shows the CDC of the originating agency and its message number, same as Line 10 of a File 1 message.
   i. Line 9 carries any pertinent information desired on the lost or stolen plates, usually in briefest form, as not over 11 characters will be included in the computer memory bank.
   j. Second line below body is authority and sender, same as any other message.
   k. Third line below body is NCIC Code for originating agency, same as any other message, and is same as in Line 7 of the example.

D. PUNCTUATION

In sending messages, the usual punctuation marks cannot be used. Instead of commas, colons, semi-colons and periods, a dash must be used, except in File 1 message lines 5, 6, 7, 8, 9 and 10 and File 16 message lines 5, 6, 7 and 8. The reason for use of periods in File 1 and File 16 messages is that the data they contain on the indicated lines must be fed into the computer in specific segments and the segments must be separated and indicated by periods. If a necessary character is missing from any one of the segments, a period must be put in its place in the message.

NUMBERS IN MESSAGES

All numbers used in teletype messages must be in numerals (e.g., 1, 2, 10, etc.) and not spelled out (e.g. "one," "two," "ten," etc.) except that decimals and fractions must be spelled out in words (e.g. "one-half," "ten and sixteen hundredths," etc., instead of "1/2," "10 16/100," etc.

F. ADDED INFORMATION, CORRECTION, REPLY, CANCELLATION

Every message except an original message must show in Line 2, as in the first message example herein, whether it is an "Added Information," "Correction," "Reply" or a "Cancellation." The proper designation, of course, is determined by the purpose or nature of the message.

G. CODE SIGNALS

A Code Signal is a number which, when included on Line 3 of a message ("CODE 77" in the first example prior), directs certain specific handling of the message by addressees. More than one code signal may be used in a message. Approved code signals and their meanings may be found in the COPS Manual.

H. FIFTH LINE, OTHER THAN ORIGINAL MESSAGES

The fifth line of all messages other than original messages is the reference line. The reference line shall show: (1) whether the message relates to a prior message from the sending station ("REF," or "VOID" on cancellations), or from another station ("MESA"); (2) the message number of the original message; (3) the date of the original message; (4) whether the original message was sent direct ("DCT") or to all points ("APB"); and (5) the subject of the original message, including the name of persons first listed on the fifth line of the original message (if any such listing in the original).

1. The license plate number of any stolen motor vehicle, motorcycle, trailer or lost or stolen plate must be on line five of any message relating to stolen vehicles or lost or stolen plates ("File 1" or "File 16" messages).

I. BODY OF MESSAGE

The body of every message should be as brief as possible. All messages are required to be clear and accurate. Telegraph style must be used in messages, leaving out all connecting words and other words not essential to clarity.

CONTENT

1. The first word in the body of every original message should where possible, indicate the purpose of the message, e.g., "STOLEN," "WANTED," "BURGLARY," "RECOVERED," etc. This rule does not apply to File 1 or File 16 messages.
2. The crime involved must be specified by name in all original messages relating to crimes. The pertinent section of the Penal Law, Criminal Procedure Law, etc., may be added for clarity where deemed necessary.
3. Where the bare name of the crime is not sufficiently descriptive, a brief notation of what the crime involved may be added, e.g., "CRIMINALLY NEGLIGENT HOMICIDE-HUNTING."
4. Messages concerning persons wanted or missing should list the persons' full names or brief descriptions, if names are unknown (e.g., "unknown white male," "unknown colored female"), and the license plate number of any vehicle in their possession, on the fifth line of the message.
5. Stolen motor vehicle, trailer or motorcycle ("File 1") messages must carry the license plate number as the first item on line five in all such messages.

6. The license number shall be shown on the fifth line of all messages dealing with vehicles used in or connected with a crime.
7. The plate number of lost or stolen license plates must be shown as the first item on the fifth line of all messages dealing with such plates ("File 16" messages).

The time and place of the crime must always be set out in an original message. They should be set out in the first part of the message.

Information in the body of a message shall be set out in the following sequence, when applicable:

SEQUENCE

1. Name of subject (unless listed above the body of the message on the fifth line of an original message or in the reference line of any other message).
2. Name and brief facts of crime.
3. Time and place of crime.
4. Warrant data, whether will extradite.
5. Description of persons, with items of description set out in the following order:
   Racial description (White, Colored, American Indian, Chinese, etc.);
   Sex, age, height, weight, color hair and eyes;
   Complexion, build;
   Clothing, marks and scars, peculiarities;
   Addresses, occupation, relatives.
   EXAMPLE:
   "W-F-28-5-5-120 LIGHT BRN HAIR-BRN EYES-FAIR COMP-MED BLD-BLUE PLAID KERCHIEF ON HEAD-BLK TOPCOAT-DK GREEN DRESS-BLK LOW HEEL SHOES-BLK BAG OVER SHOULDER-NO MARKS OR SCARS-UNDER MENTAL STRAIN-RESIDES 1 MAIN STREET-COHOES NY-UNEMPLOYED-MOTHER MRS JOHN R. DOE-SAME ADDRESS"
6. Description of Motor Vehicles, with items of description set out in the following order: License plate number, motor number and/or vehicle serial or identification number, year, make, model, color, distinguishing marks.
7. Description of Property, with items of description set out in the following order: Name, make, model, serial number, color, material, size, peculiarities and markings.
   EXAMPLES:
   TYPEWRITER-ROYAL PORTABLE-SER 1J4813996-GREEN PLASTIC FRAME-CHEMICAL SYMBOLS ON KEYBOARD-NO CASE
   WRISTWATCH-WALTHAM-SPRITE-SER UNK-WHITE GOLD-SMALL BAGUETTE DIAMONDS EACH SIDE-BRAIDED NARROW YELLOW GOLD WRIST BAND-ENGRAVED ON BACK CASE-TO JANE WITH LOVE

J. AUTHORITY FOR MESSAGES

Every message must show the rank and surname of the police member authorizing and responsible for the message (and his department if different from the department sending the message). "Authority" is shown by typing at left margin, on the second line below the body of the message, the abbreviation "AUTH" followed by the rank and name of authorizing officer.

K. FILE CLASSIFICATION CHART

The following File Classification Chart is required to be posted at every teletypewriter location associated with the basic system. This chart must be rigidly adhered to and the proper File Classification Number placed on every message. The File Classification Number assigned an original message must be used on all subsequent messages pertaining to and sent in connection with the same case. The File Classification number is used for message filing.

FILE CLASSIFICATION CHART

FILE	CLASSIFICATION
1	STOLEN MOTOR VEHICLES AND MOTORCYCLES
2	MOTOR VEHICLES - INFORMATION REQUESTS
3	EMERGENCY REPORTS TO DIVISION HEADQUARTERS
4	HIT AND RUN DRIVER
5	PERSONS - WANTED OR ESCAPED
6	PERSONS - MISSING
7	BURGLARY
8	ROBBERY AND HOLD UP
9	PROPERTY - LOST OR MISSING
10	PROPERTY - STOLEN (LARCENY)
11	ASSAULT
12	HOMICIDE
13	GENERAL POLICE INFORMATION
14	ORDERS AND ADMINISTRATIVE MESSAGES
15	REQUESTS FOR INFORMATION (MISC.)
16	LOST OR STOLEN LICENSE PLATES
20	CRIMINAL INVESTIGATIONS (BCI ONLY)
24	LEGAL BULLETINS AND OPINIONS
25	MISCELLANEOUS MESSAGES
26	TROUBLE REPORTS
27	WEATHER BUREAU FALLOUT DATA
28	ROAD CONDITIONS AND WEATHER REPORTS
44	TEST MESSAGES

DESCRIPTION

FILE 1: Use for all messages reporting stolen motor vehicles, trailers or motorcycles. In some agencies associated with the basic system, outside New York, stolen car messages are filed by license number and in others by motor, serial or identification number. It is thus necessary that all cancellations of File 1 messages list not only the license number but also the motor, serial or identification number, exactly as set out in the original message. The license plate number of the stolen vehicle must always be the first item on line five of any File 1 message except cancellations.

FILE 2: Use only for messages involving requests for motor vehicle, trailer, motorcycle or drivers' license information either from outside New York or from the New York State Department of Motor Vehicles. Whenever possible, File 2 messages must include the subject's full name, including middle name or initial and his address and date of birth.

1. Where a message is sent to the New York State Department of Motor Vehicles concerning only a check of a name, the message should be directed to one of

three sections of that Department, depending on the first letter of the subject's last name, as follows:
"TO DMV SEC 1" (for A through G)
"TO DMV SEC 2" (for H through O)
"TO DMV SEC 3" (for P through Z)

2. Whenever a license plate number check is desired, the direction should be merely "TO DMV."
3. Department of Motor Vehicles conviction records are maintained on electronic data processing equipment and it takes several days to furnish complete information, as the data tapes are not updated every day, but at stated intervals. Accurate and prompt service can only be provided if the Department is given accurate and complete information. The subject's name, date of birth, sex and license identification number must be furnished exactly as they appear on the person's operator's or chauffeur's license.
4. The following information should be considered as a guide to requesting information from the New York State Department of Motor Vehicles files to avoid unnecessary work and delayed communications:
   a. Where only the previous record for Driving While Intoxicated or while Ability is Impaired is required, do not request complete record of all convictions.
   b. Where only data on previous suspension or revocation of license are wanted, do not request complete record of all convictions.
   c. Where only convictions in past 18 months are wanted, so specify.
   d. In requesting check on nonresidents, specify that the subject is a nonresident, and pinpointing information desired. DMV maintains a file specifically showing speeding convictions and all vehicle and traffic misdemeanors involving nonresidents arrested in New York.
5. The electronic data processing includes only moving violations, vehicle and traffic misdemeanors and suspension and revocation data. Equipment violations, overload violations and non-moving violations (other than misdemeanors) are not included.
6. Where a complete accident and conviction record (known as a "safety record") is desired on a driver, the message should be sent promptly after the driver's arrest since the limitations of the electronic data processing will delay the reply. The request should specify "COMPUTER ABSTRACT REQUIRED."

Photostats from Department of Motor Vehicles: When photostats of drivers' licenses or any records are desired from the Department of Motor Vehicles, they should be requested directly of the Department by mail and no teletype message should be sent requesting photostats.

FILE 3: This classification is only used by the Few York State Police.

FILE 4: This classification is solely for hit-and-run (leaving the scene of accident) motor vehicle or motorcycle violations. Original messages must always include as much information as possible pertinent to the wanted motor vehicle and driver. File 4 classification applies whether the hit-and-run involves property damage, personal injury or both.

FILE 5: Use for messages concerning crimes other than assaults, burglaries, homicides and robberies (which are File 11, File 7, File 12 and File 8 respectively). File 5 should also be used for messages requesting arrest or announcing that persons are wanted and subject to arrest, including escapees from prisons, jails and mental institutions. File 5 sconcerning escapees from mental institutions should be restricted to New York only, unless the authorities of the institution specifically desire dissemination outside New York. All File 5 original messages on persons wanted must begin the body of the message with "WANTED," followed by the name of the crime or other item justifying the arrest.

FILE 6: Do not use for persons wanted for a crime. Use only in cases of persons missing over 24 hours, except no waiting period is required in case of young children, females 18 years of age and under, mentally incompetent persons or persons known to have been operating a motor vehicle. All File 6 messages must include the time or approximate time the subject left home and must indicate that either the sending authorities or the family or parents will promptly assume the duty of returning children, youths and mentally incompetent persons when located. If the missing person was known to be using a motor vehicle, the license plate number should be included in the message.

FILE 7: Use specifically for burglary. Do not include any larceny without burglary. File 7 original messages must state the type of building burglarized, methods of entry, and complete description of property taken and persons wanted.

FILE 8: Use for all robbery. Messages must adequately describe property taken and persons wanted.

FILE 9: Use for all messages relating to property which has been lost or is missing, except motor vehicle license plates (which are classified in File 16). Stolen property cannot be the subject of a File 9 message, nor any property which has been the subject of a crime. Original messages must adequately describe the property involved.

FILE 10: Use for all messages dealing with stolen property or property which has been the subject of any larceny. This includes aircraft and boats (but not motor vehicles, trailers, motorcycles or vehicle license plates, as these are File 1 and File 16, respectively). Property involved must be adequately described. Long lists of unidentifiable property have little value and should not be sent.

FILE 11: Use only for assault cases. (Motor vehicle hit-and-run cases are not included in File 11 but are classified in File 4).

FILE 12: All messages concerning homicides must be classified in File 12, including all criminal negligence homicides, whether vehicle or other.

FILE 13: Messages are to be classified in File 13 when they do not relate to a specific crime or arrest request in other file classifications and are of interest to police generally or in a special area. They may be sent direct to one or more stations or as all points bulletin as the facts indicate. File 13 messages would include reports of confidence games, notice that specific persons have been apprehended who may be wanted by other departments and their modus operandi (specifying distinctive or unusual features thereof). File 13's would also include notice that specific property has been recovered (including adequate description) and general police warnings. In all instances where a person is arrested for a serious crime, his name, aliases, description and fingerprint analysis or classification should be sent as an all points bulletin under File 13 for the information of all departments on the basic system.

FILE 14: This classification is only used by the New York State Police.

FILE 15: Use on messages requesting information from special files, arrest or criminal records, firearms records, dog licenses, ear tags, birth, marriage and death records, aircraft license data, lost, missing or overdue aircraft and other types of information.

FILE 16: Use only for messages dealing with motor vehicle or motorcycle license plates, whether lost or stolen. List plate numbers at beginning of 5th message line. The plate number must always be the first item on the fifth line of any File 16 message.

FILE 20: This classification is only used by the New York State Police.

FILE 24: Use on all messages concerning notice of new laws, legal opinions, legal bulletins and inquiries concerning laws or legal opinions. It is largely used by the New York State Police but may be used by any agency.

FILE 25: Use for all messages not dealing with crime and which do not fall within any file classification previously set out. It would include messages concerning notification of relatives of persons who have been killed. No messages may be sent under a File 25 classification in criminal cases.

FILE 26: Any report of trouble on the basic system or with a teletypewriter installation should be File Classification 26.

FILE 27: This classification is used solely for official fallout data.

FILE 28: This is used for road condition and weather reports.

FILE 44: Used for test messages.

L. DATA AVAILABLE ON PERSONS OR PROPERTY

The COPS computer is located at Communications Headquarters, New York State Police, Albany. On receipt of properly coded messages, it stores in its memory banks for later search all File 1 and File 16 message data on stolen motor vehicles, trailers, motorcycles and lost or stolen license plates. It also stores data as to vehicles used in commission of a crime and as to lost or stolen vehicle parts (by identification or serial number). Data on vehicles are stored by both license plate number and vehicle identification number ("VIN").

In addition, Communications Headquarters, State Police, Albany, maintains manual record files on stolen property and guns and on lost property. These will be automatically checked on receipt of messages concerning recovered property or guns.

The National Crime Information Center (NCIC) at Washington, DC, stores in its computers information on stolen vehicles and license plates, stolen or missing property and guns and on persons wanted for felonies or missing. Data on property is stored in the NCIC computers for individual items valued at $500 or more, or on loot from a single "job" worth $2,000.00 or more.

The New York State Identification and Intelligence System (NYSIIS) maintains files on persons wanted or missing covering New York. NYSIIS may be checked directly for wanted or missing persons data, by teletype message, or otherwise, such as direct telephone inquiry.

M. COMPARISON OF NCIC, NYSIIS, COPS DATA

The NCIC computer in Washington, DC, stores data received from the continental United States, including, of course, data from New York. Its "wanted" data cover the whole country. The same is true of its stolen car, stolen property or other banks of data. NYSIIS files cover only "wanted" or "missing" from New York state.

The COPS computer at Communications Headquarters, State Police, Albany, also stores only New York data. This includes New York vehicles or plates stolen anywhere and any vehicles or plates stolen in New York.

N. ENTERING DATA AND MAKING INQUIRIES

The COPS computer file on lost or stolen license plates and vehicle identification numbers and license plates is made up of data from File 1 and File 16 messages which automatically go into the computer when the proper function code is stated in Line 1 of the message. If the message's data meet the criteria required for entry into the NCIC computer in Washington, DC, the message is also automatically switched to the NCIC computer by the COPS computer.

Wanted data on persons should be forwarded to NYSIIS in accordance with the instructions pertaining thereto, as well as by appropriately coded message to NCIC, Washington, DC.

In checking on whether a "want" is outstanding for an individual, an inquiry should be sent to the NCIC Computer in Washington, DC. If a negative reply is received, inquiry will then be made automatically, by the State Police, by *"hot line"* telephone to NYSIIS at Albany, and the inquiring agency will be automatically informed of the result of the NYSIIS inquiry.

The COPS computer and the basic system are directly connected with the NCIC computers in Washington, DC. This *"interface"* makes all the information stored in the NCIC computers automatically available to those making inquiries on the basic system. Inquiries to NCIC and COPS can be made from any teletype machine on the basic system. If a *"no record"* reply is received by an inquirer, from the COPS computer in Albany, on a license plate or "*VIN*" inquiry, the inquiry is automatically routed to the NCIC computers in Washington. A reply will be sent from NCIC within approximately two minutes.

O. MESSAGE RECORD SHEET

Each teletypewriter control point must list and periodically check status of all teletype messages originating in its area which are subject to cancellation. A form similar to the one shown should be used by other stations. Messages should not be entered on the form until they are ready for filing on the fourth day after their receipt.

1. Each teletype installation is expected to use the form to list in numerical order all messages originating at the installation. Messages which are subject to future cancellation should be checked at least once each month, to keep all files clear of inactive messages.
2. In Column 2, *"origin,"* designate for each message the agency originating the message.
3. Sample form:

HASKINS POLICE DEPARTMENT
TELETYPE MESSAGE NUMBER AND
CANCELLATION RECORD

MSG. #	*ORIGIN*	*FILE*	*DATE*	*SUMMARY*	*CANCEL MSG. #*
1	Haskins	4	4-15-08	Hit-Run A/A	
2	"	5	4-15-08	John Jones,Petit Larc.36	
3	"	11	4-16-08	Assault Case	
4	Lake Como	6	4-16-08	Leo Moran, Missing	

P. CANCELLATIONS AND CORRECTIONS

A cancellation is advice that a prior message is no longer valid and that no further action is to be taken in respect to the prior message. A correction amends a previous message. Stations are responsible for promptly sending all necessary full or part cancellations and all corrections. Failure to cancel or correct a message or part of a message may result in serious harm when police action is taken on the basis of a message which should have previously been cancelled or corrected and was not. The responsibility for any such occurrence will be placed squarely on the offending department and its responsible personnel.

TELEMETRY AND COMMUNICATIONS

TABLE OF CONTENTS

		Page
Unit 1.	Emergency Medical Services Communication System	1
	Phases of an Emergency Medical Services Communication System	1
	System Components	3
	Radio Communications: Voice and Telemetry	4
Unit 2:	Communications Regulations and Procedures	7
	Federal Communications Commission	7
	Protocols and Communication Procedures	7
	Dispatch Procedures	7
	Relaying Information to the Physician	11
	Techniques	12
Glossary		14

TELEMETRY AND COMMUNICATIONS

Unit 1. Emergency Medical Services Communication System

An emergency medical services (EMS) communication system helps coordinate all groups and persons involved in emergency response and care. Such a communication system should be able to coordinate emergency medical services and resources during major emergencies and disasters, as well as during individual emergencies.

Phases of an Emergency Medical Services Communication System

Access and notification. How to notify the system when an emergency has occurred is an important aspect of EMS communications. Although telephones are the most common means of access available to the public, their usefulness is limited by their number and location and by the public's confusion as to whom to call for emergency assistance. The Yellow Pages of the telephone directory may offer a wide choice of emergency ambulance services; and, furthermore, operators may be unprepared to accept and refer a true emergency call.

The telephone is most useful in an emergency when the 911 universal access number is available. A bystander then can dial 911 from a home telephone or a callbox without needing correct change to notify the dispatch agency. The call goes to a communications coordination center (CCC) for police, fire, and medical emergencies. The emergency services operator in the center then notifies the appropriate emergency service.

Some communities also have free telephones or callboxes available on the highways for emergency use. When these highway phones or callboxes are properly connected for prompt access to an emergency services center, they make it easier for citizens to obtain emergency services.

The notification phase of emergency medical communications can be improved through public education. The public should know when emergency care is needed, whom to call to obtain appropriate aid, what to say in order to obtain advice, and what to expect in the way of a response.

Dispatch. Once the system has been notified, there must be a process through which appropriate emergency vehicles are selected and directed to the scene of the illness or injury. Vehicles can be dispatched by telephone (hard-line communication), radio, or a combination telephone/radio connection (phone patch).

It is easier and more economical to coordinate emergency services if the CCC dispatches police, fire, and emergency medical vehicles. Such centers can be organized to cover county or other regional areas, depending on local policy and municipal preferences. The CCC is especially helpful in coordinating emergency services during major emergencies and disasters.

Communication between dispatcher and emergency personnel. The Emergency Medical Technician-Paramedic (EMT-P) must have use of a radio at all times: en route to the emergency scene, at the scene, during transport to the hospital, and while returning to base after completing a call. The capability for rapid interconnection to medical advice should be at the fingertips of the dispatcher.

Dispatcher-to-paramedic communication is important for several reasons. It enables the dispatcher to give the EMT-P additional information while en route. It lets the dispatcher know where the emergency vehicle is and about how long it will be busy. It also allows redirection of the vehicle either when en route to the original destination or when traveling to the base station after completing a call. Further, it allows the EMT-P to request police or fire department assistance, additional ambulances, or additional emergency medical personnel.

Three-way communication among the paramedic physician and emergency department. Physicians, although usually hospital based, may be linked to the ambulance by a communication system in their cars, homes, or offices so that they can order advanced life-support procedures at the scene and during transport. In some States, specially trained nurses, operating under standing orders from physicians, can provide this consultation link with EMT-P's.

Communication with emergency department personnel allows the EMT-P to report the patient's condition and expected arrival time. This procedure gives the emergency department time to assemble necessary equipment and prepare for specific problems. In addition, such communication allows redirection of the EMS team to another facility if the original one does not have adequate treatment capabilities or bed space for a particular case.

Paramedics often use two-way radios to communicate with the physician, nurse, and emergency department. By means of the communication patching capabilities at the base station, the ambulance en route can communicate by mobile radio via phone patch or cross-frequency radio patch to someone at the accident scene. In addition, the ambulance en route or at the scene can communicate by mobile radio via patch to a physician at home or in a vehicle equipped with a telephone or citizens band (CB) radio.

Portable radio transmitter/receivers can be used for communications between the emergency scene and the hospital physician, usually via the ambulance relay. In this way, the EMT-P can receive instructions at the scene without having to return to the vehicle to use the mobile transmitter/receiver.

Communication among area hospitals. In a mass casualty situation, communication among area hospitals may be necessary to request blood or special supplies. In this phase, communication among hospitals may be by radio, telephone, or radio-telephone combination.

Communication links with support agencies. Communication with such support agencies as the fire and police departments and civil defense office or with crisis intervention teams can be accomplished through CCC's or through separate dispatch centers.

Although it is possible for dispatch centers to communicate by telephone, such connections may be disrupted or overloaded during a disaster. Therefore, dedicated telephone lines (lines used exclusively between two points) and/or a backup radio network should be available.

Coordination of other radio networks to be used in contingency planning. Private communication systems that normally are available during disasters include the. following:

- The Amateur Radio Public Service Corps (ARPSC) (Contact the ARPSC at the American Radio Relay League, Inc., Newington, Conn. 06111, for information on specific area groups.)

- The Radio Amateur Civil Emergency Service (RACES) (Contact local civil defense officials for information on community resources.)
- Business and municipal radio service systems (e.g., taxi-dispatching and trucking services)
- CB highway safety groups, such as REACT and NEAR (Some have been specially organized to respond to emergency situations through Channel 9, a designated emergency channel.

System Components

The hardware (components) used for medical communications varies considerably from system to system. A description of some of the coon hardware components of a communication network follows.

Base station transmitters and receivers. The base station is used for dispatch and coordination and, ideally, should be in contact with all other elements of the system. Directional antennas should be placed in the proper position to serve the desired area for radio coverage and at the same time not interfere with bordering service areas. The highest point is not necessarily the best location. Wire connections from base radio units to the dispatch center may be the most desirable method for reducing the number of airwave (radio) transmissions. This method allows greater use of radio channels and precludes interference to neighboring services. Transmission levels are limited by the Federal Communications Commission (FCC). The minimum usable levels for signal reception are limited by manmade noise such as automobile ignitions. A good antenna system can compensate partially for these limitations.

Base stations with multiple channels to provide automatic rotation to an open channel are available.

Mobile transmitter/receivers. Mobile transmitter/receivers are mounted in the emergency vehicles. They come in different power ranges. The antenna system, the power range of the transmitter/receiver, the kinds of buildings in the area, and terrain features determine the distance over which the units can transmit a signal. The reliability and radio transmission range can be insured substantially if the network of base stations and telephone interconnections is properly engineered.

Portable transmitter/receivers (two-way portable radios). Portable transmitter/receivers are handheld so that they can be carried outside the emergency vehicle by the EMT-P. Medical control physicians also carry portable transmitter/receivers for use when they cannot be reached immediately via the hospital-circuit radio.

Portable units usually have a power limitation of 5 watts. The signal of a handheld transmitter can be boosted to equal the range of a mobile unit by retransmission through the vehicle or base station for network connection. Portable transmitter/receivers can transmit and receive multiple frequencies.

Repeaters. Essentially repeaters are miniature base stations used to extend the transmitting and receiving range of a telemetry or voice communications system. Repeaters receive a signal on one frequency and retransmit it on a second frequency.

Repeaters may be fixed or mobile (carried in the emergency vehicle). Many systems employ both fixed and mobile repeaters. Repeaters are useful for extending the transmission range in hilly and mountainous areas, as well as for extending the range of portable transmitter/receivers. In both cases, the primary hardware (the patient-side radio) transmits the signal via the repeater in the vehicle; the signal then is retransmitted to the base station.

<u>Remote console.</u> The remote console is a control console connected to the base station by telephone lines. It allows use of the base station from another location such as a hospital emergency department.

The remote console both receives voice and telemetry signals from the field and transmits verbal messages back through the base station equipment. Remote consoles usually contain an amplifier and a speaker for incoming voice reception, a decoder for translating telemetry signals into an oscilloscope trace or readout, and a microphone for voice transmission.

<u>Encoders and decoders.</u> The dispatch center, ambulances, and hospitals in a communications system all share a small number of radio frequencies. Radio receivers on the same channel would be activated by every message if signals were not directed by the transmitting individual to the desired recipient. The encoder and decoder are the means by which incoming messages are directed to the desired recipient.

The encoder resembles a telephone dial. When a number is dialed, the encoder transmits a pulsed tone; the number of pulses equals the number dialed. All receivers operating on that frequency receive the pulsed tone. However, each receiver responds to only one pulsed code, which is its own three- or four-number address code. When this code reaches the receiver, the decoder opens the receiver's audio circuit. The encoder-decoder system does not prevent other users from listening in, but it does keep them from receiving unwanted messages.

<u>Telephone.</u> In addition to radio communications, many systems employ hard-line (telephone) backup to link fixed components of the system, such as hospitals, and fire and police services. Telephones can also be patched into radio transmission through the base, station ox through manual control at the CCC. This can allow communication between paramedics using radios in the field and physicians using their telephones at home. Although some telephone lines are already provided with amplifiers to insure a strong, undistorted signal, line clearing may be required at individual locations.

<u>Radio Communications: Voice and Telemetry</u>

<u>Radio frequencies.</u> Radio frequencies are designated in cycles per second. One cycle per second is defined as a hertz. The following abbreviations commonly are used:

hertz (Hz)	=	1 cycle per second
kilohertz (kHz)	=	1,000 cycles per second
megahertz (MHz)	=	1,000,000 cycles per second
gigahertz (GHz)	=	1,000,000,000 cycles per second

Radio waves are part of the electromagnetic frequency spectrum, which is assigned for different purposes. Different frequency bands have different properties. In general, higher frequency bands have a shorter transmission range but also have less signal distortion (interference and noise).

Emergency medical communications use both the very-high-frequency (VHF) band and the ultrahigh-frequency (UHF) band. The VHF band extends from about 30 to 175 MHz and is divided into a low band (30 to 50 MHz) and a high band (150 to 175 MHz). The low-band frequencies have ranges of up to 2,000 miles. However, these ranges are unpredictable because changes in atmospheric conditions sometimes produce "skip" interference that results in patchy losses in communication. The high-band frequencies are almost free of skip interference but have a shorter range. Specific frequencies in the VHF high band have been allocated by the FCC for emergency medical purposes.

The UHF band extends from 300 to 3,000 MHz. Most medical communications are in the 450- to 470-MHz range, which is free of skip interference and has little noise (signal distortion). The UHF band has better building penetration than VHF. The UHF band, however, has a shorter range than the VHF band, and UHF waves are absorbed more by environmental objects like trees and bushes.

Both VHF and UHF communication use frequency-modulated (FM) equipment rather than amplitude-modulated (AM) equipment. (Citizens band radios, in contrast, are AM.) There is less noise and interference with PM than with AN equipment.

The FCC assigns frequencies and has set aside frequencies on both bands for emergency, radio communications. A special set of 10 channels (paired frequencies) for EMS communication allows substantial channel space and great flexibility of use for voice and telemetry.

Biotelemetry. The term "biotelemetry" refers to a technique for measuring vital signs and transmitting them to a distant terminal. When the term "telemetry" is used in emergency medicine, it usually refers to transmission of an electrocardiogram (EKC) signal from the patient to a distant receiving station. In the EMS system, EKG telemetry is multiplexed on a normal voice channel using a subcarrier of 1,400 Hz, which may result in minor degradation of the voice transmission over the same channel. The hospital must be able to communicate with the paramedic while biotelemetry is in progress.

The EKG signal consists of low frequencies (100 Hz and less). Radio modulation techniques (in particular, FM) exhibit decreased responsiveness below 300 Hz. To avoid distortion, the EKG signals, are coded into a higher frequency using a reference audio tone of 1,400 Hz. The 1,400-Hz tone then is, modulated by the EKG signal for radio transmission. When the transmission reaches the distant terminals, it is amplified and demodulated to produce a signal voltage exactly like the original EKG signal.

Distortion of the EKG signal by extra spikes and waves is called "noise." This interference can result from the following conditions:

- Loose EKG electrodes
- Muscle tremors of the patient
- Sources of 60-cycle alternating current such as transformers, power lines, and electrical equipment

- Weakening of transmitter power due either to weak batteries or to transmission beyond base station range

Use of frequencies in a system. Assigned frequencies are used in different systems. In a simplex system, portable units can transmit in only one mode: (voice or telemetry) or receive only voice at any one time; such systems require only a single radio frequency. When a network uses two frequencies simultaneously, it is referred to as duplex. Another alternative is to combine, or multiplex, two or more signals so that they can be transmitted on one frequency at the same time.

Unit 2. Communications Regulations and Procedures

Federal Communications Commission

The FCC is a national regulatory and controlling agency. It assigns frequencies and licenses individuals and communications systems. In addition, the FCC establishes and enforces communications regulations.

To enforce its regulations, the FCC monitors frequencies and performs road checks. It also spot checks base stations and their records.

The FCC has offices throughout the country. All communication plans must be coordinated with these field offices. The EMT-P's should be familiar with FCC regulations.

Protocols and Communication Procedures

Standard operating, procedures (SOP's) are necessary to insure appropriate and efficient use of the medical communications system. Standard procedures eliminate unnecessary communication that could overload communication channels. By providing a structure, for essential communications, SOP's make it possible for the physician to quickly receive information about a patient's condition and rapidly transmit orders for the patient's care.

The possibility of misunderstood messages is reduced with SOP's. When these procedures involve coded messages, all persons using the communication system must understand the code and use it properly. These individuals include paramedics, dispatchers, physicians, emergency department staff, and others directly involved in radio communications.

Dispatch Procedures

The dispatcher gathers, information about the emergency, directs the appropriate vehicle to the scene, and advises the caller how to manage the emergency until help arrives. In addition, the dispatcher monitors and coordinates field communications. While performing these duties, the dispatcher must con form to FCC guidelines.

Information gathering. The dispatcher usually collects information by asking a short series of questions. When a call for an ambulance is received, the dispatcher records the necessary information as rapidly as possible. If tape recording equipment is available, a tape should be made of each call to serve as a backup record.

The dispatcher should obtain the following information:

- Phone number of the caller. This allows the dispatcher to contact the caller for more information (e.g., if the rescue team is unable to find the address and needs better directions). Asking for the caller's phone number also reduces nuisance calls because prank callers usually are reluctant to give their phone numbers. In addition, the phone number can help the dispatcher determine the caller's location if the caller (e.g., a traveler calling from the highway) is unfamiliar with the area.

- Name of the patient (if known). This information will help the rescue team to identify the patient.

- Exact location of the patient, including street name and number. The dispatcher must obtain the proper geographic designation (e.g., whether the street is East Maple or West Maple) and the community name, since nearby towns may have streets with the same names. If the call comes from a rural area, the dispatcher should establish landmarks, such as the nearest crossroad or business, or a water tower, antenna, or other easily identifiable landmark that will help the rescue team to orient itself.

- Nature of the patient's problem.

- Specific information about the patient's condition. (Is the patient conscious, breathing, bleeding badly, or in severe pain?)

- Whether the emergency is a highway accident. If it is the dispatcher should obtain the following additional information:

  -- Kinds of vehicles involved (cars, trucks, motorcycles, buses). If trucks are involved, the dispatcher should ask what they are carrying to determine the possibility of noxious fumes.

  -- Number of persons involved and extent of injuries. Even if the caller can only guess at this information, it can give the dispatcher an idea of the size of problem

  -- Known hazards, including traffic dangers, downed electrical wires, fire, submerged vehicles, and so forth. Information about these hazards allows the dispatcher to contact other agencies that will need to become involved, such as the utility department to deal with downed wires.

A special, preprinted form can help the dispatcher obtain all the necessary information and can provide a record of the call. Figure 14.2 provides a sample of such a form.

Dispatch. After the dispatchers receive the necessary information, they should ask callers to wait on the line. Dispatchers then must make several decisions.

- What is the nature of the problem? Is it life threatening?
- Are paramedics needed?
- Are support services needed (police, fire, heavy rescue)?
- Which crew(s) and vehicle(s) should respond? This decision will depend on the nature and
- location of the call and on which units are available. Thus, the dispatcher must know, the status of every area vehicle and crew in order to decide which to dispatch.

In order to make these decisions about medical emergencies, the dispatcher needs training in emergency medical care. The Division of Emergency Medical Services of the U.S. Department of Health, Education, and Welfare recommends that EMS dispatchers receive the same EMT training as the medical crews that they dispatch. The Department of Transportation has developed a special curriculum for dispatchers.

Records. Either the EMT-P or dispatcher or both should record key times for each call. This information should include the times that the call was received, the vehicle began the run, the crew arrived at the emergency scene, the crew left the scene, the patient reached the hospital, and the vehicle and crew were back in service.

Date ______________________ Log No. __________________

TIMES

Call received ____am./p.m.
Car out ____

Arrived at scene ____
Left scene ____
Arrived at hospital ____
Back in service ____
Patient's name ____
Address ____
City/town ____

PATIENT STATUS

Conscious ______________________________
Breathing ______________________________
Bleeding _______________________________
Other _________________________________

If vehicular accident:

Number and kinds of vehicles involved:

______ Cars ______ Trucks ______ Buses ______ Other

Number of persons injured ____

Extent of injuries ____

Are persons trapped? ____

Hazards:
______ Traffic ______ Wires down ______ Fire ______ Hazardous car
______ Unstable vehicle ______ Debris ______ Submerged vehicle

Caller: Name ____________________________ Phone No ______________________

Vehicle dispatched ________________________

Crew ______________________________ Other units called ___________________

Figure 14 .2. Sample dispatch record form.

Relaying Information to the Physician

Radio communications between the EMT-P's and their physician directors should be brief and accurate. To insure that information is transmitted in a consistent manner and that nothing significant is omitted, the paramedic should follow a standard procedure for relaying patient information. Such information should include:

- Patient's age and sex
- Vital signs
- Chief complaint
- Brief history of present illness
- Physical findings

  - State of consciousness
  - General appearance
  - Other pertinent observations

The following is an example of a concise, informative transmission for a patient in congestive heart failure:

> We have a 53-year-old man with a pulse of 130 and regular, blood pressure 190/120, and respirations per minute. He is complaining of severe shortness of breath that wakened him from sleep and is worse when he is lying down. He has a history of high blood pressure and takes Diuril at home. He is alert but in considerable distress. He has rales and wheezes in both lung fields. We are sending you an EKG.

The above transmission takes less than 30 seconds but efficiently provides the physician with the information needed to rapidly dignose the problem and order appropriate treatment.

In contrast, the following dialogue can be considered:

EMT-P:	We have a patient with a pulse of 130, blood pressure of 190/120, and respirations of 30. We are sending you a strip.
Doctor:	Fine, but what's his problem?
EMT-P:	He's short of breath.
Doctor:	How long has this been going on?
EMT-P:	Just a minute. (Pause) He says it woke him up from sleep about an hour ago.
Doctor:	Does he have any underlying medical problems?
EMT-P:	He takes medicine for hypertension.
Doctor:	Is he in any distress?
EMT-P:	Yes, he's having a hard time breathing.
Doctor:	What do his lungs sound like?
EMT-P:	Just a minute. (Pause) He has rales and wheezes all over.

This type of communication obviously is less efficient. It wastes time and annoys and frustrates everyone. Information should be gathered at the scene and organized clearly in the EMT-P's mind before the physician is contacted. The reporting procedure can be written on a card posted in the vehicle or on the transmitter, so the paramedic can refer to it when reporting in.

Techniques

Radio communications equipment varies from manufacturer to manufacturer. Therefore, the directions in this section are general, rather than specific. These directions must be supplemented with more specific instructions for the equipment in use.

Use of a mobile transmitter/receiver. The EMT-P should:

- Turn unit on
- Adjust squelch
- Listen to be sure airways are free of other communications
- Hold microphone far enough from the mouth to avoid exhaled air noise
- Push the push-to-talk button, and pause before speaking
- When calling another unit, use its call letters first, and the sender's second
- Follow these guidelines when using the radio

  -- Use an understandable rate of speech
  -- Do not talk too loudly -- Do not hesitate
  -- Articulate clearly
  -- Speak with good voice quality
  -- Avoid dialect or slang
  -- Do not show emotion
  -- Avoid vocalized pauses (such as "urn," "uh," "hmm") -- Use proper English
  -- Avoid excessive transmission

- Use the call sign to let others know the transmission is completed

Use of a portable transmitter/receiver. Use of a portable transmitter/receiver is similar to use of a mobile transmitter/receiver. Since the antenna on the portable unit is not fixed in place, however, it must be kept vertical while in use so that the signal can be properly transmitted to the vehicle. From the vehicle, the signal can be transmitted to the base station.

Use of a digital encoder. The EMT-P should:

- Turn unit on
- Adjust squelch
- Listen to be sure airways are free of other communication
- Select address code to be dialed
- Dial selected numbers
- Hold microphone far enough from the mouth to avoid exhaled air noise
- Push the push-to-talk button, and pause before speaking
- Call dialed unit
- Use the call sign to let others know the transmission is completed

Transmission of patient assessment information and telemetry. The EMT-P should:

- Turn unit on
- Adjust squelch
- Listen to be sure airways are free of other communication
- Hold microphone far enough from the mouth to avoid exhaled air noise
- Push the push-to-talk button and pause before speaking

- Call physician either directly or through a relay system
- Connect or attach electrodes to telemetry transmitter
- Follow local procedure for relaying patient assessment information
- Activate telemetry transmitter for the minimum amount of time required by the receiving physician (approximately 15 seconds)
- Verify physician's reception and quality of transmission

14

GLOSSARY

dispatch: To transmit calls to emergency medical, services and to direct emergency vehicles, equipment, and personnel to the scene of a medical emergency.

duplex: A radio communications system employing more than one frequency.

Federal Communications Commission (FCC): The Federal regulatory agency that assigns radio frequencies and licenses individuals and communications systems.

frequency: The number of periodic waves per unit of time; radio waves are expressed in cycles per second.

frequency modulation: A method of converting an analog signal, such as an electrocardiogram, into a tone of varying pitch that can be transmitted over the radio.

gigahertz (GHz): A unit of frequency measurement equaling 1 billion Hz; indicates frequencies of 1 billion cycles per second.

hertz (Hz): A unit of frequency measurement; 1 Hz equals 1 cycle per second.

kilohertz (kHz): A unit equaling 1,000 Hz; it indicates frequencies of 1,000 cycles per second.

megahertz (MHz): A unit equaling 1 million Hz; indicates frequencies of 1 million cycles per second.

multiplex: In a radio communications system, a method by which simultaneous transmission and reception of voice and electrocardiogram signals can be achieved over a single frequency.

noise: Extra spikes, waves, and complexes in the EKG signal caused by various conditions such as muscle tremor, 60-cycle alternating-current interference, improperly attached electrodes, and out-of-range transmission.

patch: Connection of telephone line and radio communication systems making it possible for police, fire department, and medical personnel to communicate directly with each other by dialing into a special phone.

repeater: A miniature transmitter that picks up a radio signal and rebroadcasts it, thus extending the range of a radio communications system.

response time: The length of time required for the emergency medical services team to arrive at the scene of an emergency after receiving a call for help.

simplex: A communications system that can transmit only in one mode at a time, or receive voice transmissions only.

telemetry: The use of telecommunications for automatically indicating a recorded measurement at a location different from the measuring instrument, such as an electrocardiogram sent from an ambulance and received at a hospital.

UHF band: The ultrahigh-frequency band; refers to the portion of the radio frequency spectrum between 300 and 3,000 MHz.

VHF band: The very-high-frequency band; refers to the portion of the radio frequency spectrum between 30 and 150 MHz.

www.ingramcontent.com/pod-product-compliance
Lightning Source LLC
Chambersburg PA
CBHW082039300426
44117CB00015B/2542
* 9 7 8 1 7 9 9 3 3 5 9 4 8 *